Wisdom Literature

SCM CORE TEXT

Wisdom Literature

Alastair Hunter

scm press

© Alastair Hunter 2006

The Author has asserted his right under the Copyright, Designs
and Patents Act, 1988, to be identified as the Author of this Work

British Library Cataloguing in Publication data

A catalogue record for this book is available
from the British Library

0 334 04015 9/978 0 334 04015 6

First published in 2006 by SCM Press
9–17 St Alban's Place,
London N1 0NX

www.scm-canterburypress.co.uk

SCM Press is a division of
SCM-Canterbury Press Ltd

Typeset by Regent Typesetting
Printed and bound in Great Britain by
William Clowes Ltd, Beccles, Suffolk

Contents

Introduction

It is hard to avoid the charge of intellectual arrogance when one embarks on a study entitled *Wisdom*. It is perhaps the least felicitous of the genre designations coined by the guild of Old Testament scholars – would that something more modest, like *pedagogy*, had been the jargon of choice. But the opportunity to name the terms in which we work is given only to the pioneers; those, like the present author, who come late on the scene, have limited scope to re-invent the technical language. Without pre-empting the longer discussion of definition which will be found in the opening chapter of this book, let me say – for the record – just three things at this point. First of all, the use of 'wisdom' as the inclusive term for what this book is about does have solid justification in the Old Testament itself, both in respect of the frequency with which the Hebrew word for wisdom is used, and in respect of the dramatic presence of a personified female Wisdom at significant turns. Second, by using wisdom as our defining term, we successfully point the reader in the direction of an intellectual tradition which is not out of keeping with the best traditions of scholarly intellectual investigation. The books we shall consider, and the human story-telling skills which accompany them, depend for their success on the same humanist values that inform all academic work, whether it be the rational traditions of the classical age or the Enlightenment values of modern universities. And third, without wishing to argue my own case too strongly, it is my hope that you, dear reader, will find me, if not wise, at least not incorrigibly foolish.

The range of books which is usually deemed to represent wisdom can be sorted into various categories. At the core are the three undisputed representatives within the Old Testament proper: Job, Proverbs and Ecclesiastes. While there is much that differentiates them from each other, they undoubtedly share both stylistic conventions and methodological similarities. They tend to focus on the discussion of issues from a human, if not humanistic perspective, and they pay on the whole little attention to matters which are of specifically Israelite concern. There is no history of the tribes or the kings, little reference to the worship and festivals, and no mention of the prophets.[1] The one area which might be of common concern is observance of the law; but even that is uncertain, since the rabbinic technical term 'Torah' might simply mean 'teaching' when it is found in these wisdom books. The word itself is found just once in Job (22.22) and twelve times in Proverbs; of these just over half (6.20, 23; 7.2; 28.4, 7, 9; 29.18) *might* be taken to refer to Torah in terms of the first five books of the Bible. The phrase most often used to characterize these books is 'international wisdom', which is understandable in that it expresses the sense of material which could easily be at home in a fairly broad society, but misleading in that it conjures the perhaps inappropriate image of a wide community of scholars exchanging ideas and texts across international boundaries. I discuss the problems associated with this assumption in Chapters 2 and 3.

It is natural, on the basis of this core group of texts, to extend the scope of our survey. This can be done in two ways: by taking into account writings relevant to Judaism but not included in the Old Testament canon, and by paying some attention to other ways in which the broadly humanistic spirit of wisdom was given expression within the canon. In the former category the most frequently cited is *Ecclesiasticus*, known also as *Sirach* or *Ben Sira*. The stylistic similarities with Proverbs are quite evident, and the pedagogical intention of the book is quite clear both from the author's own statements and from the testimony of his grandson who translated the book into Greek, and who left us an intriguing prologue. But in another way Sirach is quite distinctive: it is closely interested in the Torah, the rituals and functionaries of the religious institutions of Jerusalem, and the great figures of the past whom it celebrates in the famous 'Hymn of Praise to the Ancestors' (chapters 44–50). Furthermore, it is an intensely nationalistic work: there is no way that it could be transformed into a representative of 'international wisdom' without substantial rewriting. That said, it remains a quintessentially wisdom book, though one which has been appropriated deliberately in the service of the religious institutions of the second-century Jerusalem community.

Two other works might have warranted inclusion in the present volume. One bears the title *The Wisdom of Solomon* – a designation which at first sight might seem to brook no argument. But a closer examination reveals this to have much more of the nature of an apocalyptic work. It

---

1 One verse in Proverbs (29.18) reads, in the NRSV, 'Where there is no prophecy, the people cast off restraint, but happy are those who keep the law.' The word translated 'prophecy' here really means 'vision'. The associated verb occurs elsewhere in Proverbs and Job (including the physically close Proverbs 29.20); in all these instances NRSV translates it as 'seeing'. Thus this verse could just as well be translated: 'Where there is no vision, the people cast off restraint, but happy are those who observe what they are taught.'

does have a section (chapters 7–9) which describes the attractions of wisdom, but in the main its interests lie elsewhere, in the realm of prophetic judgement. While I shall make passing reference to this book, I have decided that it is not directly relevant to the themes I wish to explore. The other candidate is the epistle of James in the New Testament, a work of whose qualities Luther was famously dismissive ('an epistle of straw'). Along with this book we might take into account some of the style of the Synoptic Gospels – the use of parables for teaching purposes, the inclusion of numerous epigrammatic sayings attributed to Jesus, and the formal structure of such passages as the Beatitudes ('Blessed are . . .'). On the whole it has seemed to me wiser to restrict my survey to the pre-Christian texts, partly for reasons of economy, and partly because an entirely new theological perspective would be introduced which would require a different approach.

Finally, I should offer some explanation for the inclusion, in the final chapter, of material which might appear to be of a different character to that in the remainder of the book. Through many years of working with and teaching this material I have become convinced of the direct relevance of those creative human impulses which deploy the techniques of story-telling to explore meaning and decipher mysteries. Like the more pedagogical wisdom writers, they depend not upon revelation or special knowledge, but rather use that instinctive universal wit which characterizes human discourse and has produced such a wide, but profoundly interconnected, range of folk material. This too is wisdom, and this too is found – though somewhat transformed – in the biblical texts. I think that it is good to acknowledge this and to offer, in however rudimentary a form, an introduction to what is a fascinating field of study.

Throughout I have tried to highlight key information, to provide pointers for further exploration of topics at the end of each chapter, and to indicate a selection of the many books that have informed my own study and which should be regarded as the hidden but essential substructure of this work. Like the wise men and women of old, we belong to a community of scholarship that would be well advised to recall the words of an ancient scholar: 'There is nothing new under the sun.'

Acknowledgements

A book like this, which deals with a diversity of material and wanders down a complex network of exegetical country lanes, can only be the product of many influences and much opportunity for reflection. Many centuries ago Jesus Ben Sira, the author of the book of Ecclesiasticus, wrote that 'The wisdom of the wise depends on the opportunity of leisure; only the one who has little business can become wise'. I would like to acknowledge that, with all the imperfections and administrative burdens of the modern university, there still remains sufficient leisure to gain wisdom, and enough freedom from business to write something on the subject. My first debt, therefore, is to the system which has afforded me the necessary space to work, together with a plea that future generations be given the same privilege.

My second debt is to several generations of students who have helped to shape what is now presented. They have undoubtedly contributed to this book in an organic way, shaping my own responses and exposing many of the weaknesses which were too obviously manifest. The remaining flaws will have to await the cynosure of future readers! On a pragmatic level, the material that is covered here has been tested and refined by both individuals and groups as to its fitness for purpose, and I am as satisfied as I can be that it represents a workable resource for those who wish to explore wisdom in the Old Testament beyond the introductory level.

I am grateful to SCM Press, and in particular to Barbara Laing, for commissioning this book in the first place, and for the help I have received in bringing it to fruition. The gap between manuscript and published work is larger than mere authors sometimes realize; I appreciate the way that those responsible have bridged the gap.

Finally, I want to acknowledge a debt to the past, summed up in the words of Proverbs 1.8: 'Hear, my child, your father's instruction, and do not reject your mother's teaching.' I dedicate this book to the memory of my parents, whose wisdom becomes more evident the older I become.

PART 1

What is Wisdom?

1

Defining Wisdom as a Genre

Opening skirmishes

The term 'wisdom' is at first sight a strange one to use as the definition of a genre of writing. Unlike *law* or *poetry* or even *prophets*, all of which can be understood in a wider literary context, there is no real parallel in secular literary theory to this term. There are bodies of writing from ancient Egypt, Babylonia and Assyria that have much in common with what is found, for example, in the Book of Proverbs; and as we shall see in Part 3, certain very familiar genres from the study of folk-tales can be fruitfully applied to the biblical material. But the word itself, which has become well established in the scholarly study of the Bible, requires at least some explanation before we embark upon the main business of this volume. In particular, it is necessary to clear the ground somewhat lest we import into our discussion inappropriate contemporary meanings of the term. For this reason, the whole of this first chapter is devoted to a review of what the word 'wisdom' might mean in biblical terms and why it has come to be used as a defining term for a certain group of biblical texts. The advantage this gives us is more than just clarity of definition, for at the end of the journey to that undoubtedly laudable aim we shall have covered a lot of ground in terms of what the Bible itself does with the concepts and words we need to consider.

In modern usage we think someone is wise if they are widely knowledge-able and show signs of being able to apply that knowledge in a sensi-tive and imaginative manner – able, for example, to read situations and extend their existing experience to devise new solutions. We have in mind a certain depth of understanding and insight, and an ability to 'read' the world, which is a rather special quality. It sometimes, but by no means always, accompanies extensive education. We can express the relation-ship as follows:

- being wise is not dependent upon education; *however*
- those who are instinctively wise benefit from education; *and*
- some who are not at first wise become so through the educational pro-cess; *but*
- many survive quite extensive periods of study without ever acquiring wisdom.

We take wisdom to refer to the somewhat abstract quality that characterizes such people, but we would not expect to be able to set down in any
detail what constitutes wisdom in this sense. And we would certainly not
regard a piece of writing as being in itself wisdom, though we might say
that a certain book contains much wisdom. People who are wise manifest their wisdom in all sorts of ways, but the quality itself resists direct
observation. Rather like the wind, we know it by what it does, rather
than by what it is.

Clearly this kind of approach is problematic as a genre description.
How can a *text* be 'wise' in the sense defined above? Do we assume that
the 'wisdom' involved is that of the authors, or the putative authors?
But that too presents a problem – in most cases we have no idea who the
author might have been, so we cannot use this definition. We might, perhaps, employ the term to suggest that what we thus classify is the kind of
material that we would expect wise people to write. But that also is circular and question-begging – and assumes that we as *readers* are competent
to make such judgements. When we come to consider the use of the term
in biblical studies, therefore, we have to reverse most of our instinctive
ideas. Our concern is for *books* which are classified as 'wisdom', and we
have every expectation that we should be able to describe and catalogue
these works, establishing reasonably objective criteria by means of which
we can decide whether or not a book, a chapter or a particular passage
merits this soubriquet of 'wisdom'.

What other scholars have suggested

That the definition of wisdom understood as a genre is problematic was
recognized more than thirty years ago by Gerhard von Rad in his classic
study, *Wisdom in Israel* (1970, ET 1972). Scholarship of the late nineteenth and early twentieth century regularly classified wisdom as a late,
post-exilic literature of rationalism and scepticism strongly influenced by
Greek philosophical systems, with Proverbs, Job and Ecclesiastes as its
principal representatives. But the discoveries of extensive bodies of similar literature in Egypt and Mesopotamia brought about a radical change
of perspective, which von Rad used to reposition wisdom as a very ancient
and basic tradition found in all developed societies, devoted in essence
to the preservation and communication of experiential knowledge. The
means by which this was carried out was the proverb or maxim, which
he defined as follows:

> The maxim – if we disregard, for the moment, its individual types –
> can function in the most varied contexts. As a trivial proverb it can
> belong to the world of the simple. It can, however, like a precious stone
> among trinkets, outshine a poem of the highest quality. The demand

which it must always satisfy is that of brevity, of compactness and yet of intelligibility, with, if possible, a clear graphic quality; in short, that of being easily remembered. (p. 5)

The problem is that, although von Rad is confident that 'Ancient Israel, too, participated in the business of cultivating her experiential knowledge', the forms in which it was expressed are diverse, resisting simple categorization. The books and the category which is supposed to describe them – *wisdom* – do not directly imply any simple unity of form: 'If, in fact, one removes this blanket term, then one comes face to face with literary documents of the most diverse type' (p. 7). In the end, von Rad seems to settle for a rather broad defining statement: 'That wisdom has to do with *human* understanding, that it is a particular form of *human* knowledge and behaviour, is not disputed' (p. 8, emphases added). He then goes on: 'We are thus perhaps doing a service in approaching the subject first of all . . . in enquiring more closely after Israel's search for knowledge, that is, in what particular way and by what means Israel sought to prove herself.' So, in short, wisdom stands for a *human* process of understanding and a quest; and the scholar's task, it seems, is to recapitulate that quest.

James Crenshaw, one of the leading proponents of the scholarly study of wisdom in the twentieth century, wrote an account of the form critical approach to wisdom in 1974,[1] and in 1981 published the first edition (revised in 1998) of his *Old Testament Wisdom: An Introduction*.[2] In the former he contrasted the idea of wisdom as 'non-revelatory speech' – which leads to a rather broad range of texts, since such writing can plausibly be found in many places outside the conventional wisdom group – with that of the types displayed by the core group of Job, Qoheleth, Proverbs, Sirach and Wisdom of Solomon. Unfortunately, even this restricted group does not lead to a definitive set of formal features, since 'no particular form is limited to one period of the wisdom movement or to any type of wise man'.[3] The problem we face is that the texts we start with are selected not on the basis of a set of formal features, but because they separate themselves in a rather natural way as the non-poetic section of the Writings (the third, miscellaneous section of the Hebrew Bible). For the purposes of genre, what they seem to share is not style or form but attitude and intention, neither of which translates readily (if at all) into recognizable literary patterns. In his later study Crenshaw hardly advances

---

1 Reprinted in James L. Crenshaw, *Urgent Advice and Probing Questions* (Macon, GA, Mercer University Press, 1995), pp. 45–77.

2 James L. Crenshaw, *Old Testament Wisdom: An Introduction* (second edition; Louisville, KY, Westminster John Knox Press, 1998).

3 Crenshaw, *Urgent Advice*, p. 47.

from this somewhat unsatisfactory – or at least, unresolved – account. Thus he begins (*Old Testament Wisdom*, p. 3) with this: 'The goal of all wisdom was the formation of character.' Unfortunately this tells us nothing about what it looked like, and is scarcely less fatally flawed than the notion of 'non-revelatory speech'. Nothing in what follows (pp. 4–16) takes us any closer to a definition, since he proceeds rather to provide religious and literary comparisons between the core biblical group and other texts, and does not return to the question of what (if anything) justifies our assumption that wisdom is a genre in its own right.

R. N. Whybray, in a very useful survey article in *The Expository Times* (89, 1977–78; pp. 359–62),[4] suggests that wisdom literature represents the product of reflection, by those of innate intellectual ability, on a body of common tradition. This literature has a didactic purpose: it serves as the basic teaching and learning material for those in each generation whose calling is to be wise. And – significantly – he further notes that this traditional material must surely encompass the popular oral wisdom passed down through less sophisticated means. We shall return to this in the final chapters when we consider directly the place of folk-tale genres in the study of the Old Testament. But in the end Whybray suggests that we should attend to the origins of 'wisdom' as a technical term in the writings of scholars such as S. R. Driver who, in 1909, 'defined it as the work of writers who "applied themselves . . . to the observation of human character as such, seeking to analyse conduct, studying action in its consequences, and establishing morality, upon the basis of principles common to humanity at large".' We begin to perceive a theme: the emphasis placed by each source so far on the human dimension of wisdom.

Donn Morgan's 1981 book, *Wisdom in the Old Testament Traditions*, attempts a kind of historical approach which shows the development of wisdom over the centuries from the pre-monarchical era to the post-exilic period. I do not intend at this point to evaluate that approach; we will return to it shortly. For the moment, I want to focus on Morgan's comments on the problem of definition, which are to be found in pp. 20–26. He offers an overview (similar to my own in this section) of the attempts of others at a definition, and concludes that a set of six hypotheses rather than a short definition might mark the way forward. The three which are most pertinent to the attempt to produce a genre definition are:

1 'The wisdom tradition [which is assumed to have existed] is responsible for the wisdom literature found in the Old Testament (Proverbs,

---

4 R. N. Whybray wrote extensively on wisdom subjects; many of his essays have been collected in a very useful volume edited by Katharine J. Dell and Margaret Barker, *Wisdom: The Collected Articles of Norman Whybray* (SOTS Monographs; Aldershot, Ashgate, 2005).

Job, Ecclesiastes, a few Psalms). Therefore literary forms and the social and theological perspectives which have their provenance and occur primarily in this literature should form the foundation for any discussion of the nature, scope, and particular perspectives of the wisdom tradition.'

2 'The wisdom tradition is responsible, directly or indirectly, for the wisdom influence found in non-wisdom literature of the Old Testament.'

3 'The wisdom literature has at least one sociological base, that is, a means by which its literature and world-view is communicated.'

The other three points he makes are more directly related to Morgan's own thesis, and we need not consider them now. I will make just this observation, that there is an obvious circularity built into (1) and (2) in that it is assumed in advance what the corpus of the wisdom literature is, and this is then taken as the norm for defining its nature. There may be no avoiding this circularity; but it needs to be recognized. His other point – the existence of a sociological base – is interesting, though once again it is not clear whether such a base can be discerned independently of the materials which it produced. The idea that, from the earliest kingdoms onwards, Israel – and subsequently Judah – had a well-developed school system is a good example of the dangers of such reading; we shall return to this particular hypothesis in a subsequent chapter.

I turn finally to Katharine Dell's *'Get Wisdom, Get Insight'. An Introduction to Israel's Wisdom Literature*, published in 2000, where she discusses these issues (pp. 1–13). Dell offers a fairly pragmatic definition, using Proverbs as a starting point (circularity again?): 'If a book seems to contain to a large extent the same kinds of form and content and possible context that we have found in Proverbs, we might well want to classify that book as "wisdom literature".' She then goes on, however, to allow development and change in order to accommodate (for example) Ecclesiastes; but this, however appropriate, begs the question of the normative role of Proverbs. Her assessment of earlier definitions which emphasize the human, non-revelatory, intellectual and pragmatic nature of wisdom is that, however apt these may be, it is impossible in the Jewish context to wholly elide the theological perspective.

When we come to offer our own working definition we shall take note of – while not necessarily agreeing with – these various scholarly proposals. But first it is fair to admit that there is a presumption that the three classic 'wisdom' books (Job, Proverbs and Ecclesiastes) are the likely focus of our study, whatever other books or individual passages may also be included.

The Hebrew evidence

While it is clear that we cannot resolve the matter by recourse to the English dictionary, we still have a major source of defining material which we should examine in our quest for understanding. The term in Hebrew – *hokhmah* – which is usually translated by the English expression 'wisdom' is found throughout the books that are usually classed under this heading. It would seem logical, therefore, to begin our quest by discovering how it functions in the biblical texts.

> We should note that in modern Hebrew usage the word closest to the English idea of intellectual wisdom is *binah*, which is usually translated 'understanding' in the Bible, and occurs regularly in parallel with *hokhmah*. Thus there is an in-built uncertainty to our discussion, which is increased by the fact that there is a whole range of terms used in parallel with 'wisdom' – a quite extensive vocabulary of the intellect. Ultimately the reason for preferring *hokhmah* is that it takes on a clearly heightened significance in a number of Hebrew and Jewish texts – not least in the form of a personified female figure – which distinguishes it from *binah* and other related words.
>
> A note on pronunciation:
>
> *hokhmah* sounds like 'chochmah' – where both of the *ch* sounds are roughly the same as the 'ch' in the Scots word 'loch'
>
> *binah* is pronounced 'beenah'
>
> The stress in both cases is on the second syllable.

It would be tedious to have to look through the long list of all the passages in the Hebrew Bible that make us of the noun 'wisdom', the adjective 'wise' and the verb 'to be/become wise'. Nevertheless, such a survey – as long as it is careful to look at the contexts in which they occur – might provide us with a series of signposts with which to identify a path through the 'wisdom' semantic field and, hopefully, construct some kind of definition of our task. As a compromise, I have carried out such an exercise on behalf of the reader; the results are summarized in the following description of the categories into which biblical uses may be divided. Selected passages which illustrate each use are provided; those with time on their hands or of an untrusting nature may look up the rest, given in parentheses at each definition.

Technical skills (A)

One of the first things to understand about *hokhmah* is that it refers at root to pragmatic skills and talents. It is, of course, not appropriate to create a kind of portmanteau expression into which, at the end of our analysis we pack every meaning we have found on the way – something that James Barr rightly, and long ago, criticized in his classic study, *The Semantics of Biblical Language*. But it may well be that some of what we discover will contribute to the 'style' of *hokhmah* as a technical term, and hence may help to explain why it is also useful as a genre description. Sadly, most of the passages which use *hokhmah* in this way refer to men. Women no doubt possessed many skills in Ancient Israel, but only a very few of them are mentioned: specifically, only two – spinning in Exodus 35.25–6 ('All the *skilful* women spun with their hands, and brought what they had spun in blue and purple and crimson yarns and fine linen; all the women whose hearts moved them to use their *skill* spun the goats' hair') and mourning in Jeremiah 9.17–18 ('Consider, and call for the mourning-women to come; send for the *skilled* women to come; let them quickly raise a dirge over us, so that our eyes may run down with tears').

The skills attributed to men who are 'wise' include the design and tailoring of the garments to be worn by Aaron and his priests (Ex. 28.2–4), those who can work with precious metals and gemstones, and who can produce fine carving (Ex. 31.3–6; cf. 35.31–6, where it is interesting to see that though the women spin the coloured fabrics, it is men who embroider and weave), and the builders (Ex. 35.10–19). This last passage serves as a kind of catalogue of every skill that will be required to build the tabernacle (the portable sanctuary which was supposed to have been carried in the wilderness), to furnish it, and to clothe the priests. (For further examples of similar skills described within the provenance of *hokhmah*, see Ex. 36.1–8; 1 Kings 7.14; 1 Chron. 22.15, 28.21; 2 Chron. 7, 13–14; Isa. 40.20; Jer. 10.9; Eccles. 10.10). Two other isolated examples remain: the skill of sailors (Ezek. 27.8, 9 'The inhabitants of Sidon and Arvad were your rowers; *skilled men* of Zemer were within you [he is speaking of the city of Tyre], they were your pilots. The elders of Gebal and its *artisans* were within you, caulking your seams'), and the craft of the magician. In Isaiah 3.3, in the midst of a catalogue of all those who will be removed from Jerusalem when disaster strikes we find the 'captain of fifty and dignitary, counsellor and *skilful* magician and expert enchanter'. Apart from anything else, the implication that magicians were a good thing is interesting.

In 1961 James Barr, at the time based in New College in the University of Edinburgh, published a book entitled *The Semantics of Biblical Language* which undertook a detailed analysis and critique of a then fashionable process of theological etymology. This entailed a kind of organic view of language: Greek was believed to be essentially of a different character from Hebrew (more abstract rather than concrete, philosophical rather than practical). It also made considerable use of theological word-books which would treat key expressions as sources or compendia of significant meaning, with the effect that interpreters were tempted to find all the meanings of a word in each of its occurrences. A classic example of the latter kind of exegesis is to be found in a popular book by Professor William Barclay, then of the University of Glasgow, entitled *Jesus As They Saw Him*. The principal representative of the former was Thorlief Boman's *Hebrew Thought Compared with Greek* (published in German, 1954; ET 1960). Barr was relentless in his criticism of this sort of essentialism, arguing that words had context as well as history, and that languages could not be given personalities. Any language is surely capable of both abstract and concrete expression, of practical and philosophical reflection.

To take an English example, the word 'nice' does not now mean what it originally did (which was 'precise' or 'particular'). Teachers of a certain kind used to take pleasure in telling pupils that the 'real' meaning of the word was what it – historically speaking – once meant, where in fact the only place where that older meaning survives is in the expression, 'that's a nice point' (meaning: a precise, or pedantically accurate, point).

My treatment of *hokhmah* here could be at risk of this fallacy; I trust that the reader will understand this review of its uses as a kind of fairground of meanings, rather than a single undifferentiated semantic whole. To be precise (or nice?), the fact that Solomon was 'wise' does not mean that he could build sanctuaries or carve precious stones!

Administrative skills (B)

The essence of this defining group is a focus on royal functionaries – people who served kings in an advisory capacity. As such, it is not surprising to find that some of these references are to officials in Egypt and Babylonia (including that familiar Egyptian 'prime minister', Joseph: Gen. 41.33, 39–40, cf. Ps. 105.22, and Daniel and his friends playing a similar role in Babylon according to Dan. 1.20). Thus we have Pharaoh's impotent wise men (Gen. 41.9; Ex. 7.11), and similar advisers at the court of Ahasuerus in Esther 1.13; 6.13. The prophet Isaiah is scathing about such people, excoriating them in a striking diatribe (Isa. 19.11–12):

The princes of Zoan are utterly foolish;
  the *wise* counsellors of Pharaoh give stupid counsel.
How can you say to Pharaoh,
  'I am one of the *sages*, a descendant of ancient kings'?
Where now are your *sages*?
  Let them tell you and make known
  what the Lord of hosts has planned against Egypt.

(Compare similar oracles in Jer. 10.7; 49.7; 50.35–8 and 51.57 and Obad. 8.)

There is evidence that a similar category of advisers was known in Israel and Judah, though it is somewhat unclear how official they were and at what period we might recognize their existence. Perhaps the best evidence comes from Jeremiah 18.18, in an often-quoted passage. The speakers are Jeremiah's opponents: 'Then they said, "Come, let us make plots against Jeremiah – for instruction shall not perish from the priest, nor counsel from the *wise*, nor the word from the prophet."' Many scholars accept this as proof that a clear division of professional functions existed in court circles at least in Judah of the late seventh century. Jeremiah 8.8, 9 and 9.23 provide corroborative support for this thesis. Isaiah 44.25 and, less clearly, 29.14 seem to refer to a similar professional category as that in Jeremiah, while Deuteronomy – though ostensibly dealing with the origins of the nation in the wilderness – might well be an indirect witness to practices in the period when it most likely composed, the late seventh century.[5] Thus 16.18–19, while possibly idealized, seems to deal with governmental systems in place throughout the land:

You shall appoint judges and officials throughout your tribes, in all your towns that the LORD your God is giving you, and they shall render just decisions for the people. You must not distort justice; you must not show partiality; and you must not accept bribes, for a bribe blinds the eyes of the *wise* and subverts the cause of those who are in the right.

See also Deuteronomy 1.13, 15.

Finally, we should note that women are twice recorded as being 'wise' in a sense very close to that discussed above, but with the distinct impression that they are in some way outside the norms of regular society. They

5 The dating of Deuteronomy is highly controversial. Without entering into an extensive review of the theories, ranging from the claim that it originated as an ancient document brought to Judah by survivors of the fall of Israel in 714 BC, to – at the other extreme – the proposal that it was part of an intensive scripture-producing endeavour in the Persian period (fifth century BC). I am persuaded that its links with the Books of Kings and its traces through many other parts of the Pentateuch place it not much earlier (in its finished form, at any rate) than the sixth century.

have something in common with the medium consulted by Saul at Endor, though she was indisputably beyond the pale (1 Sam. 28.3–25). The Bible is distinctly ambivalent about what might be regarded as magical observances. Female practitioners are unequivocally condemned – see, for example, the injunction in Exodus 22.18, 'You shall not permit a female sorcerer to live', which formed the pretext for murderous misogyny during the European witch hunts. But, as we have already seen, magicians would seem to have had a legitimate role in ancient Near Eastern courts, including Jerusalem (Isa. 3.3). Judges 5.29, in the poem celebrating the rule of the only female Judge, Deborah, makes reference to the '*wise* ladies' of Sisera's mother's entourage, and women described as wise are twice featured in the murky events of the latter days of David's reign (2 Sam. 14.2, 20; 20.16, 22).

It will come as no surprise to most readers that the Bible offers very limited and grudging space to women among its skilled craft-workers, its courtly advisers and its ruling classes. There is one female judge, Deborah, one queen, Athalya, who comes to a bad end, and a few 'prophetesses' who mostly tag along with their male equivalents. Perhaps this is related to Israel's famous hatred of female deities and its desire to exclude altogether from Yahweh's presence any idea of a consort or a divine mother.

However, there is, within the wisdom literature in particular, a curious counter-trend. Based, perhaps, on the accident that the word *hokhmah* has feminine grammatical gender, many passages of a more reflective kind make use of this to create a metaphoric system in which women and wisdom are intimately related. Whether this goes so far as to reintroduce an actual female divinity is another question. We shall return to it in due course; in the meantime, those who regret the dominant male ownership of wisdom so far should not despair.

King Solomon's gift (C)

In our review of the political dimensions of wisdom we saw that certain functions seemed to be shared across the more advanced ancient Near Eastern states. As a refinement of that classification, I turn now to wisdom as a specifically royal attribute. And here we find a particular association with the East (echoed much later in Matthew's legend of the Magi who came to pay their respects to the infant Jesus). Solomon is of course the *fons et origo* of this convention in the Bible, in terms both of the biographical material in 1 Kings and the continuing use of his name as the 'author' of all sorts of later books. The association of Solomon with wisdom begins with David's dying charge to his son (1 Kings 2.6, 9): 'Act therefore according to your *wisdom* . . . for you are a *wise* man . . .' It is important to register that this is not merely conventional, for David himself is nowhere associated with this quality.

Two stories in particular epitomize Solomon's wisdom: the tale of the two prostitutes in 1 Kings 3.16–28, the solution of whose problem by the king culminates in a public recognition of his wisdom (v. 28 'All Israel heard of the judgement that the king had rendered; and they stood in awe of the king, because they perceived that the *wisdom* of God was in him, to execute justice.'), and the visit of the legendary Queen of Sheba (1 Kings 10.1–13, cf. 2 Chron. 9.1–9), who 'came to test him with hard questions . . . Solomon answered all her questions; there was nothing hidden from the king that he could not explain to her' (10.1, 3). In general, we find that it is important to the Deuteronomistic authors of Kings to emphasize the extent to which Solomon's wisdom was acclaimed not just by his own people but by other nations (Sheba, Hiram of Tyre – 1 Kings 5.7, 12, cf. 2 Chron. 2.12; and 'the whole earth' – 10.23–4, cf. 2 Chron. 9.22–3). The source and extent of this particular Solomonic gift are elaborated upon in 4.29–34 (see below) where it is made clear that it came from God, surpassed all the wisdom of the East, was celebrated among the nations, and issued in a breadth of knowledge about the natural world together with linguistic and literary skills. Finally, it is mentioned in his epitaph (1 Kings 11.41). The only places where it is explicitly generalized are in Proverbs 20.26 ('A *wise* king winnows the wicked') and, arguably, 24.23 where the phrase 'These also are sayings of the *wise*' introduces a new section. Given the biblical convention that Proverbs was composed by Solomon, these 'wise men' might be intended to have royal connections. On the other hand, they might simply be the class of advisers described above (see pp. 10–11).

1 Kings 4.29–34

God gave Solomon very great wisdom, discernment, and breadth of understanding as vast as the sand on the seashore, so that Solomon's wisdom surpassed the wisdom of all the people of the east, and all the wisdom of Egypt. He was wiser than anyone else, wiser than Ethan the Ezrahite, and Heman, Calcol, and Darda, children of Mahol; his fame spread throughout all the surrounding nations. He composed three thousand proverbs, and his songs numbered a thousand and five. He would speak of trees, from the cedar that is in the Lebanon to the hyssop that grows in the wall; he would speak of animals, and of birds, and reptiles, and fish. People came from all the nations to hear the wisdom of Solomon; they came from all the kings of the earth who had heard of his wisdom.

The story of the two prostitutes (1 Kings 3.16–28) is a classic testing tale by means of which the hero (Solomon) reveals his superior intelligence. The women lived together, and each had a baby. One child died in the night, so its mother switched them so that in the morning the dead baby was with the wrong woman. She knew what had happened, but how to prove it? Faced with this conundrum, Solomon proposes a drastic solution: calling for a sword, he proposes to divide the living baby and give half to each woman. The true mother immediately begs the king to give the living baby to the other woman, which (of course) demonstrates to Solomon who is the true mother. Result! Brecht used a similar device in Act Five of his play, *The Caucasian Chalk Circle*. I will not reveal it, lest the play be spoiled for those who have not seen it.

Finally, there are a couple of references in the prophets to the wisdom of foreign kings: the king of Assyria in Isaiah 10.13 and the extended, and seemingly genuine praise of the king of Tyre in Ezekiel 28.3–7, 12–17; cf. Zechariah 9.2 – where the description (albeit of a vanished world) is heightened indeed: 'You were the signet of perfection, full of *wisdom* and perfect in beauty' (v. 12). Of course, the point is that the king has exceeded the bounds of morality by proclaiming himself to be divine; but the wisdom he possessed was genuine – the pity is that it was put to a corrupt end. Perhaps this adds further weight to Hyram of Tyre's praise of Solomon's wisdom.

Native wit (D)

Some instances of wisdom are regularly translated using terms like 'shrewd' or 'shrewdness', craft(iness), cunning. These largely feature with reference to political, economic or personal life, and include references to those who are 'wise in their own eyes'. The most egregious examples of political shrewdness are, first, Pharaoh's 'cunning plan' to deal with the immigration problem caused by the expanding numbers of Joseph's descendants (Ex. 1.10), and second, the advice given to Amnon by his 'crafty friend' Jonadab on how best to plan Amnon's rape of his half-sister Tamar (2 Sam. 13.1). We should include with these two named individuals the warning in Jeremiah 4.22 about those who are 'skilled in doing evil'.

The second major group of texts is that which despises those who are 'wise in their own eyes' (Isa. 5.21; 47.10; Job 5.13; 15.8; 37.24; Prov. 3.7; 26.5, 12, 16; 28.11). They are not culpable in the same sense as Pharaoh and Jonadab, but are nonetheless a reminder of the strict limits of wisdom where it is a purely human, street-wise quality. Compare here also the mockery of those who imagine they can purchase wisdom (Prov. 17.16), and the reminder in 21.30 that at the end of the day 'No wisdom, no understanding, no counsel, can avail against the Lord.'

Finally, there are a couple of passages in Proverbs (1.6; 21.22) which seem to indicate a kind of savvyness on the part of the sages in general, and an odd and somewhat obscure verse (Psalm 58.5) which appears to have to do with skilled snake charmers!

Lifelong learning (E)

This and the final category comprise the majority of references, indicating that they are the aspects of greatest interest to the biblical writers. What we are dealing with here is, essentially, the idea of wisdom as common sense: the knowledge and understanding gained through life experience and attention to one's teachers and mentors. Biblical writers do not consider this to be an automatic possession, and are not slow to hold up as a grim warning those who never lose their youthful naivety or who persist in self-destructive foolishness. But it is not a particularly religious quality – it can be learned through discipline, obedience and attention, and is in Israel particularly linked to the learning context of the family, where both mothers and fathers have a teaching role.

By far the majority of such uses of wisdom are in the three classic wisdom books of Job, Proverbs and Ecclesiastes which together account for 120 of the grand total of 133 – a statistic that contains within itself a powerful argument for the existence of a specific genre. It would be to tax the reader's patience beyond endurance if all of these were to be examined. I shall therefore be content to illustrate this aspect of the term through selected examples.

The primary context for many of these essentially human readings of what wisdom is about is that of *instruction literature*, a genre found also in the Egyptian tradition. Characterized by the use of the imperative, it imagines a teaching situation where the instructor – often a father or a father figure, and in Proverbs sometimes a mother – offers the student the benefit of years of both learning and experience. Typical of these is Proverbs 4.1–5 (the source of the title of Dell's book):

> Listen, children, to a father's instruction,
>   and be attentive, that you may gain insight;
> for I give you good precepts:
>   do not forsake my teaching.
> When I was a son with my father,
>   tender, and my mother's favourite,

he taught me, and said to me,
'Let your heart hold fast my words;
    keep my commandments, and live.
Get wisdom; get insight: do not forget, nor turn away
    from the words of my mouth'.

The inclusion of the mother in v. 3 is significant, and is reinforced by 6.20, 'My child, keep your father's commandment, and do not forsake your mother's teaching (*torah*).' While wisdom is not explicit here, the fact that she has responsibility for the *torah* (even in its more general sense of teaching or guidance) is powerful. Proverbs 10.1 (compare 15.20) implies a similar joint parental ownership of the duty to instruct: 'A wise child makes a glad father, but a foolish child is a mother's grief', and the famous description of the ideal wife in 31.10–31 notes that she 'opens her mouth with wisdom, and the teaching of kindness is on her tongue' (v. 26). For further examples of the voice of the parent/teacher, see Proverbs 2.1–10; 5.1; 8.32–3; 22.17 and 23.15, 19, and Elihu's pose in Job 33.33—34.2.

Many of the references deal with wisdom as a matter-of-fact, though desirable, goal aspired to by all mature and sensible people. Qoheleth's[6] lifelong search, for example, while despairing of the ultimate difference that wisdom can make, is nonetheless an excellent portrayal of the teacher's calling. See, in particular, Ecclesiastes 2, and compare with the reflections of a later sage, Ben Sira, on his lifelong quest to find wisdom (Ecclesiasticus 51.13–22).[7] Proverbs 1.2–6, which forms the prologue to the book, is essentially a programmatic version of the individual quest outlined in these passages.

Not surprisingly, the delineation of wisdom often employs contrasts. That between the wise and the foolish is of course the most common (Prov. 10.8, 13–14, 23, 31 and many others). Proverbs 10.13–14 is a fairly typical example:

On the lips of one who has understanding wisdom is found,
    but a rod is for the back of one who lacks sense.
The wise lay up knowledge,
    but the babbling of a fool brings ruin near.

A less common, but striking contrast is with those who mock or scoff;

---

6 Qoheleth is the Hebrew word for the author of the book known in English as Ecclesiastes. I shall use that designation more often than not for the book as well as its author.

7 The author of Ecclesiasticus is known either as Sirach or as Ben Sira. My usual practice is to use the former for the title of the book and the latter for the name of its author.

one might surmise a social context in which the rude and uneducated mock and pillory the 'intellectuals' of their day rather as 'swots' at school find themselves the butt of their peers' wit (though it is unlikely that the sages of Israel would deem 'wit' to be an appropriate term!). Proverbs 9.7–8, in a deft character sketch, addresses this theme (see also Prov. 13.1; 14.6; 15.12; 21.11; 29.8):

> Whoever corrects a scoffer wins abuse;
>> whoever rebukes the wicked gets hurt.
> A scoffer who is rebuked will only hate you;
>> the wise, when rebuked, will love you.

Lastly, there is the contrast between material wealth and the value which wisdom adds. Proverbs 3.13–15 expresses it succinctly (see also Job 28.15–16; Ps. 19.7–10; Prov. 8.10, 19; 16.16):

> Happy are those who find wisdom,
>> and those who get understanding,
> for her income is better than silver,
>> and her revenue better than gold.
> She is more precious than jewels,
>> and nothing you desire can compare with her.

An ethical and religious quality (F)

The nature of wisdom as an explicitly religious quality is expressed in a number of ways, mostly though not exclusively in Job, Proverbs and Qoheleth, but in rather general terms. This is not a trivial remark, despite the truism that the Bible is a book about God. For there is a distinctly international feel to the wisdom literature; it is in many ways separated from any particular national or cultic roots – a feature also of its exemplars in other societies. While there is no question of atheism, and the relevant god is firmly present, albeit in the background, the writers seem to have had little interest in portraying their own society or its beliefs and practices. We can summarize these religious aspects under four headings.

1 Wisdom and the fear of the Lord

The claim that there is an intimate connection between wisdom and a proper fear (that is, awe or respect) before God is very important. While it is relatively rarely mentioned, its presence in two key sections of wisdom literature, and its persistence into the later material (for example, it is discussed at some length in Sirach 1.11–30) give it a special significance. In Job it forms the climax of chapter 28, where the author dwells on the problem of wisdom's inaccessibility, coming to the conclusion that 'Truly, the fear of the Lord, that is wisdom; and to depart from evil is understanding'. In Proverbs 1—9, which is almost certainly a self-contained unit added at the end of the development of the book, this sentiment brackets the whole. It is announced at the start, in 1.7, ('The fear of the Lord is the beginning of knowledge; fools despise wisdom and instruction') and again in the final chapter, 9.10 ('The fear of the Lord is the beginning of wisdom, and the knowledge of the Holy One is insight'). In a passage which forms part of the material described as 'Wise Sayings of Solomon', probably the earliest portion of Proverbs, it appears in a more down-to-earth form: 'The fear of the Lord is instruction in wisdom, and humility goes before honour' (15.33), which may perhaps represent a commonplace which is enhanced as a religious truth by the later writer of Proverbs 1—9. Elsewhere it is found also in Isaiah 33.6 and Psalm 111.10, and there is a negative form of this idea in Proverbs 30.3: 'I have not learned wisdom, nor have I knowledge of the holy ones.'

2 Wisdom given by God

The idea that wisdom might be a gift from God is found occasionally, but rarely in the core wisdom texts. Given that we have already reviewed an extensive range of 'secular' uses of the term, it is perhaps not surprising that little is made of what might be seen as a short-cut to intelligence. The one reference of this kind in Proverbs 2.6 turns out, on closer examination, to be another way of presenting the belief that it is through 'fear' that knowledge and wisdom are acquired. The statement that 'the Lord gives wisdom' in no way undermines the need for human commitment and participation. Here is the wider context in Proverbs 2.1–6:

> My child, if you accept my words
>   and treasure up my commandments within you,
> making your ear attentive to wisdom
>   and inclining your heart to understanding;
> if you indeed cry out for insight,
>   and raise your voice for understanding;
> if you seek it like silver,
>   and search for it as for hidden treasures –
> then you will understand the fear of the Lord
>   and find the knowledge of God.
> For the Lord gives wisdom;
>   from his mouth come knowledge and understanding.

The most obvious setting for wisdom as a direct gift is the well-known prayer of Solomon at his accession where he famously asks for wisdom rather than power or wealth – and is granted all three as a reward (1 Kings 3.9–12; 2 Chron. 1.10–12). Wisdom also appears to be given directly to Daniel and his companions (Dan. 1.17), while the spirit of wisdom rests on the (messianic?) heir of Jesse (Isa. 11.2). Both of these have something of the same air as the Solomon story: the granting of a necessary skill to kings or those required to deal with kings. The spirit of wisdom is also given to Joshua (Deut. 34.9), another man required to exercise leadership. Zophar in Job 11.6 rather anticipates chapter 28 when he insists that only God can teach wisdom, a thought echoed by Elihu (35.11) and the Psalmist (51.6).

3 *Wisdom as an attribute possessed by God*

God uses wisdom to found the earth, according to Proverbs 3.19, and similar ideas are recorded in Job 38.36–7, Psalm 104.24 and Jeremiah 10.12 (= 51.15), and are enhanced by the vivid pen picture in Proverbs 8.22–31 where wisdom is in God's presence throughout the act of creation. In Job 9.4 and 12.13 his wisdom enables God to demolish what he has created!

Isaiah 31.2 declares, simply, that God is wise; extending this we find the more forceful statement that because wisdom belongs to God it is almost impossible for humankind to have access to it. Though this claim may seem religiously unexceptionable, it is surprisingly rare, forming the main thesis of Job 28, and addressed in passing twice in Qoheleth (7.23–5 and 8.16–17).

4 *'The goddess'*

One of the most intriguing possibilities which emerges from the fact of *hokhmah* having feminine gender in grammatical terms is that 'she' can be personified. Proverbs 1—9 makes highly effective use of this, and we shall examine it in detail in a later chapter. One particular possibility, among the many available, is to position Wisdom (the person) as a quasi-divine or supernatural being. In Proverbs we find her portrayed as a prophet, speaking out in the city gate (1.20; 8.1, cf. 24.7), as a mysterious and possibly supernatural 'sister' (7.4), as God's first-born companion (8.22–31), and as the priestess (?) of a temple which she has herself built (9.1, cf. 14.1). At this stage, these can only be set out as hints of something to be explored in more depth, and they should be read alongside a remarkable passage in the post-biblical literature, Sirach 24, which comes as close as anything to presenting wisdom as a goddess.

The review of the use of *hakham* in the Bible which we have just concluded reveals some interesting features, not least the way that different types of definition occur in very different proportions. I have separated the books of the Old Testament into three categories: Historical and Prophetic Books (HPB); Wisdom (Job, Proverbs Ecclesiastes) (WB); and others, effectively the non-wisdom books in the Writings, the third section of Tanakh (OB). The aspects of wisdom identified fall into two classes: more pragmatic uses of the word, those under headings A–D; and more ethical/religious, those under headings E–F. What is clear is that the former are overwhelmingly found in non-wisdom books, and the latter in wisdom books.

The figures turn out as follows:

	Percentage		Number of Instances	
	A–D	E–F	A–D	E–F
HPB	81%	9%	83	16
OB	5%	7%	5	13
WB	15%	84%	15	148

The distribution pattern is rather striking, and does suggest that there are good grounds for singling out the group containing Job, Proverbs and Ecclesiastes for special attention in respect of the use of wisdom as a more abstract phenomenon.

'Wisdom': definitions

The range of meanings

While the various headings given above are reasonably self-explanatory, the *range* is perhaps more surprising. Moreover, the evidence gathered in the information box above, while we should not place too much stress on raw data, does indicate that the genre description 'Wisdom Literature' given to Job, Proverbs and Ecclesiastes might well have some basis in semantic actuality.

When we look in more detail at the categories we have identified, one thing is clear: *wisdom* has a range of applications in Hebrew rather different from its common use in English. We would not normally think of skilled craft workers and artisans as *wise* – at least in terms of their profession. Plumbers and electricians may well be like gold, especially when a domestic crisis confronts us; but nothing illustrates this difference in meaning more clearly than the fact that if we think a plumber is wise, that is a judgement distinct from his or her skill as a plumber.

This is an important distinction, which deserves to be borne in mind as we traverse the list of six categories which have been identified as a broad description of the use of *wisdom* as a semantic field in biblical Hebrew. For while there is clearly a shift from *practical* definitions in (A) through (D) to more *ethical* and *theological* uses in (E) and (F), the functional character of the concept remains important. Wisdom is a means to an end more than it is a psychological or intellectual quality – it is a skill which we can acquire, as the tag in Proverbs 4.7 reminds us:

> The beginning of wisdom is this: Get wisdom,
>   and whatever else you get, get insight.

Throughout the first nine chapters of Proverbs there is a recurrent theme to the effect that wisdom is something we can learn, a quality we can acquire, by means of which our natural naivety will be overcome. The fool is not *born* stupid; he (or she – but in Proverbs fools are mostly male!) is stupid as a result of rejecting the opportunity to become wise. For the writers of the 'wisdom school' – of which more in Chapter 2 – the acquisition of wisdom depends upon discipline: application to study, obedience to a qualified teacher, and attention to the ethical principles of Israelite religion. This last point is represented to some extent by the repeated epigram in (F1), 'The fear of the LORD is the beginning of wisdom'; but even so, it remains largely a human endeavour. It is noteworthy that the only aspect of (F) in which there is a majority of biblical references outside the wisdom books is (F2): the idea that wisdom is a gift from God. This is clearly *not* something that formed a major part of the practical task of acquiring wisdom.

Wisdom, in short, is available to those who will make the effort. To become wise is the responsibility of every mature adult, and nothing but contempt is reserved for those who remain willfully ignorant.

Towards a definition: formal features

If wisdom is an identifiable genre (or range of genres) it would be helpful to have some objective criteria with which to make the identification in particular cases. The first, and most obvious, is the presence of the word *hokhmah* and its related forms. Proverbs and Ecclesiastes between them account for 136 of the Bible's total of 277 occurrences, virtually all drawn from categories (E) and (F). To this total we might reasonably add the references in 1 Kings and 2 Chronicles which deal with Solomon's legendary gifts, an additional 23 instances. No fewer than 159 out of 277, or 57 per cent, focus on the two core texts and their historical background. Thus our first objective criterion is the presence of a particular semantic unit used in certain clearly defined ways.

Still restricting our attention to Proverbs and Ecclesiastes, a second objective marker is the presence of the didactic imperative form familiar from instruction literature in Egypt and Mesopotamia as well as Israel.[8] Examples abound in Proverbs, and are evident, though less frequent, in Ecclesiastes (for example, 5.1–6; 8.2–3). This is sometimes combined with the voice of the teacher, as we have seen in Proverbs ('Listen, children, to a father's instruction') or Ecclesiastes ('The words of the Teacher').

Third, we should recognize the wise saying in the form of a couplet, often using the kind of parallelism familiar from Hebrew poetry, but conveying a truth (or truism) of a secular kind – perhaps the single most ubiquitous formal marker in both of these books. Proverbs 10 and Ecclesiastes 10 are classic examples of this pattern. A subset of this is the numerical saying, as in Proverbs 6.16–17; 30.15–31; the only echo of this in Ecclesiastes is 11.8 'Divide your means seven ways, or even eight.'

Two further features should be mentioned, though neither is, in purely formal terms, exclusive to wisdom. I refer to the *first person deliberation on life experience* and the use of *reflective poems*. The former is characteristic in that it constitutes a kind of self-conscious analysis or appraisal of the writer's life and times in a didactic mode. Examples are Proverbs 24.3–9 and Ecclesiastes 1.12—2.26. Reflective poems can be used to probe the nature of wisdom herself (thus, for example, Prov. 1.20–31; 8.22–31), to muse on the mystery of creation (Eccles. 1.2–11; 3.1–8), to comment on life and its challenges (Prov. 7.6–27; Eccles. 12.1–8) or – famously – to celebrate the value of a powerful, capable woman (Prov. 31.10–31).

While it is clear that both Proverbs and Ecclesiastes belong to a genre defined on the basis of these five features, they are nevertheless quite distinct books with a very different tone, the one appearing as a broadly traditional text (though, as we shall see, with some intriguing and provoking things to say about wisdom and women) and the other famously as a cynical, sceptical or world-weary composition. On the other hand, other books not yet considered might be included. Certainly Sirach meets all of these criteria, including numerical sayings (23.16; 25.1–2, 7–8; 26.5–6; 50.25–6), and should be considered unequivocally to be part of the wisdom genre. The Wisdom of Solomon, despite its title, is hard to classify under this heading (see, for example, Dell's discussion pp. 128–39), though it does contain a justly celebrated paean to Wisdom (7.22—8.1) set within a wider retrospective on Solomon's relationship to wisdom (6.1—9.18), which is in turn followed by a section which portrays Wisdom as the one who guided and protected the Israelites from Adam to Moses (10.1—11.14). This last passage shares a perspective with Sirach

---

8 A more extensive technical account of the characteristic features of wisdom is to be found in Crenshaw, *Urgent Advice and Probing Questions,* pp. 45–77.

24 where Wisdom takes on a role similar to that of God in the Torah narratives. We shall return to these in our discussion of Sirach.

Towards a definition: the writers' perspectives

The glaring omission from the list of books identified by means of formal linguistic features is the book of Job, yet there is effective unanimity among scholars that it belongs in this category. Dell (pp. 39–42) resolves this problem in part by noting a few examples of formal writing – some proverbial sayings – often presented as rhetorical questions (for example, 8.11–12) – numerical sayings (5.19–21; 13.20–22; 33.14–15), and a poem on the quest for wisdom which is similar to the reflective poems in Proverbs and Ecclesiastes. But there remain considerable differences of content which cannot be subsumed under formal categories. What I propose is that the intuitive urge to include Job can best be explained by looking at another kind of characteristic: the underlying perspectives which emerge from a consideration in broader terms of what these books are concerned with.

These can be summed up as (1) a universal perspective on life, (2) a humanistic view of the problems addressed, (3) evidence of curiosity about the natural and everyday world and (4) an intellectual approach to solving them. While some of these can be found in other places, it can be argued that, as a group, they combine to effectively characterize the kind of material we have been talking about. The first is largely obvious: even in Sirach, where the writer has an undoubted interest in his own religious traditions, he never forgets the universal dimension. Even in chapter 24, where there is an intense series of references to Jewish religious experience, the whole issues in a flooding of wisdom into the four corners of the world, represented by the four rivers of Eden with the addition of the Nile and the Jordan (24.25–7). The other three books make very little reference to anything specific to Israel – for though Yahweh's name is used, and Yahweh is a member of the dramatis personae in Job, he is not otherwise identified with anything specifically Jewish – and were it not for the conventional attribution of authorship to Solomon, we could relocate most of what they contain without much effort. Indeed, Job and his curiously named debating partners are located in the unknown land of Uz.

The humanistic perspective comes out in the way that the language of revelation is ignored. Phrases like the prophetic 'Thus says the Lord' are absent, knowledge is passed down the generations without benefit of the supernatural, and advice is pragmatic and practical, perhaps best summed up in the bathos of 'Go to the ant, you lazybones' – a phrase which also serves to illustrate the characteristic interest of wisdom writers in the natural and everyday world. The most dramatic example of this is of course in the final chapters of Job, 36.24—41.34, but compare also the allegory in Ecclesiastes 12.1–8, the list of practical illustrations in Proverbs 26, the description of various trades in Sirach 38.24–34, and the description of Solomon's talents in 1 Kings 4.29–34, especially v. 33.

But most important of all is the intellectual approach to the problems and challenges of life. It may be that this is a more modern term than is strictly appropriate; but it is hard to think of a better one to explain both the relentless interrogation of wisdom by Qoheleth and the long process of debate between Job and his three interlocutors. Most of Proverbs is delivered at the level of fairly predictable standard advice, but there is a sharper intellect at work in chapters 1—9, as we shall discover in due course.

To sum up: there is a good case to be made for including Job, if we allow the importance of these perspectival dimensions. However, it cannot be denied that a number of other genres are involved which are *not* typical of other wisdom literature, such as the scene in the divine court, the element of folk-tale which opens and closes the book, the use of lament and the process of quasi-legal debate that goes on between Job and his neighbours on the one hand, and between Job and God on the other.

Folk-tales and popular tradition

Through years of teaching the subject of wisdom literature, I have always included a discussion of the folk-tale tradition in the Old Testament. There is a logic to this, which depends upon seeing human curiosity and fascination with the inexplicable as central to the whole wisdom approach. Some have proposed (as we shall see in the next chapter) a kind of historical development from folk wisdom at the beginning to religious didactic teaching at the end, from stories told 'round the camp fire', as it were, to teaching offered in synagogue and school. Every society has a body of folk-tales, myths and legends which – even in the most sophisticated – serve to preserve the most basic of the community's instincts about the nature of the world. The persistence with which certain groups cling to 'Adam and Eve', for example, is tribute to the strength of such stories. Everyone knows (or thinks they know) that Adam ate an apple which brought evil into the world. Gilgamesh has a story about how immortality escaped the grasp of humans – they couldn't keep awake and a snake stole the prize! These are attempts to speak truth through narrative, and their power lies not in their historical or scientific accuracy (they possess neither), but in their effectiveness in evoking both the life questions that confront us and the sorts of answers that we like to test. For these reasons, I believe that it is constructive and appropriate to include within our introduction to wisdom a study of the ways in which the folk tradition has impinged upon and is recorded within the biblical materials.

Some points to think about

This chapter has tried to show that there is some consistency to the generally accepted view that Job, Proverbs, Ecclesiastes and Sirach constitute a natural group. Are you in a position to evaluate whether or not this has been achieved?

The book of James, in the New Testament, is sometimes said to have close affinities with the Wisdom tradition, as indeed are some of Jesus's teachings – the Sermon on the Mount, for example. What do you think of this claim?

There was a warning box early on about the dangers of the 'etymological fallacy'. Has the discussion of the meaning of 'wisdom' above avoided that danger?

Wisdom, if it is indeed a recognizable literary phenomenon, need not be confined to these particular books. Writers are free to embellish their texts in any way they choose, even if scholars would prefer them to be consistent! Examine the following passages to see whether any, some, or all of them might deserve to be described as 'wisdom literature': Genesis 11.1–9; Deuteronomy 5.7–21; Judges 14.10–18; Isaiah 5.1–7; Amos 3.2–8; Job 23.1–17; Psalm 32.8–9.

Further reading

Blenkinsopp, Joseph (1995) *Wisdom and Law in the Old Testament: The Ordering of Life in Israel and Early Judaism* (revised edition), Oxford, Oxford University Press

Charlesworth, James H. and Michael A. Daise (eds.) (2003) *Light in a Spotless Mirror: Reflections on Wisdom Traditions in Judaism and Early Christianity*, Harrisburg, PA, Trinity Press International

Crenshaw, James L. (1995) *Urgent Advice and Probing Questions: Collected Writings on Old Testament Wisdom*, Macon, GA, Mercer University Press.

Crenshaw, James L. (1998) *Old Testament Wisdom: An Introduction* (revised and enlarged edition), Louisville, KY, Westminster John Knox Press

Dell, Katharine (2000) *'Get Wisdom, Get Insight': An Introduction to Israel's Wisdom Literature*, London, Darton, Longman & Todd

Dell, Katharine and Margaret Barker (eds.) (2005) *Wisdom: The Collected Articles of Norman Whybray*, Aldershot, Ashgate

Morgan, Donn F. (1981) *Wisdom in the Old Testament Traditions*, Oxford, Basil Blackwell

Rad, Gerhard von (1972) *Wisdom in Israel* (ET James D. Martin), London, SCM Press

Westermann, Claus (1995) *Roots of Wisdom*, Edinburgh, T. & T. Clark

---

2

Wisdom in Context in Ancient Israel

Introduction

It is natural to wonder whether some social reality might lie behind the kind of texts we have identified as 'wisdom' in Chapter 1. If Israel and Judah were reasonably advanced societies, with functioning legal, religious and social institutions, then the existence *in principle* of various sorts of official is not in doubt. The king (*melekh*), the priest (*kohen*), the 'scribe'[1] (*sopher*), the prophet (*nabi'*), the elder (*zaqen*) and the judge (*shofet*) are all attested in the texts, though with varying degrees of confidence that they in fact represent specific functionaries.[2] Much has been written on this subject, and the conclusions are quite diverse. At one time, for example, it was thought that by the time of Solomon (early tenth century BC) there was a significant royal court which encouraged scribal activity, and that this issued in such works as an early version of the Pentateuch and a History of the Succession of Solomon[3] (now found in 2 Sam. 9—20 and 1 Kings 1—2). The international dimension was held to be manifestly present in the texts themselves, and was a result of Solomon's extensive diplomatic relationships with Egypt and Tyre. Others have expressed scepticism about such a scenario, and have appealed to archaeological evidence which seems to show a much poorer economy at that time than could have supported a scribal school. We face, it must be admitted, more questions than answers in this area.

---

1 This term is somewhat problematic, as Stuart Weeks, *Early Israelite Wisdom* (Oxford, Oxford University Press, 1994), pp. 117–24 makes clear. Not least of the problems is that the root may well have more to do with counting than writing!

2 A useful review of the biblical evidence is provide by Lester L. Grabbe, *Priests, Prophets, Diviners, Sages: A Socio-Historical Study of Religious Specialists in Ancient Israel* (Valley Forge, PA, Trinity Press International, 1995). Despite the title, he does also discuss the function of the king.

3 See, for example, R. N. Whybray, *The Succession Narrative* (SCM Press, 1968).

Were there scholars who had a specific responsibility for 'wisdom' texts?

Who read them?

What purpose did they serve?

Were ancient Israelites or Judaeans literate in any meaningful way (that is, beyond the ranks of professional functionaries)?

Wisdom material seems to display both knowledge of and similarities with a range of texts from the ancient Near East. Does this mean that texts circulated across political borders, or that individuals from Israel worked as ambassadors or emissaries in places like Egypt, Babylon and Assyria?

Indeed, were such influences primarily written, or could they result from a more generalized oral culture?

Writing materials were costly, and writing for other than court or cultic purposes was rare; most writers required state sponsorship, which in turn presupposes a civil society with a rather sophisticated organization, and resources to devote to scribal activities. Was this true of Israel or Judah, and at what times?

Is there any archaeological evidence that can help to clarify these matters?

Since much of the evidence has been drawn from the Bible itself, it is clearly important to appraise its value and significance carefully, and to try to avoid building too much on the basis of purely textual evidence. It is important to know (at least approximately) when the texts that contain some evidence were written, and to judge whether they in turn have accurate information about the past, or whether they should rather be used as evidence for the time when they were written. For example, the Books of Kings were not completed before the mid-sixth century BC,[4] but they tell of events from Solomon's reign onwards. How should we interpret any information they might seem to give us about reading, writing and scribal activity three or four centuries earlier?

In this section we shall look at three approaches to this problem. The first represents a fairly traditional use of the Bible as a primary source of historical information (Heaton, Morgan and Westermann). Such

---

4 Since 2 Kings ends with an account of the last kings of Judah, and of the conditions experienced by the exiled king Jehoiachin 37 years into his exile, dating the Books of Kings to the mid-sixth century seems uncontroversial.

approaches commonly suppose (or claim to have proved) the existence from early times of schools, and often propose a hypothetical reconstruction of possible stages of development. The second – radically different – begins from or takes very seriously the archaeological and comparative cultural evidence (Jamieson-Drake, Lemaire, Niditch and Weeks) to build up what is often, though not always, a rather less confident picture of rudimentary education in early Israel. Finally, there are more critical attempts to evaluate the biblical evidence in order to arrive at plausible explanations which do not do violence to the cultural and archaeological evidence (Blenkinsopp and Crenshaw).[5]

From popular proverbs to scriptural sagacity

The basis of the first approach lies in the assumption that in societies in general, and Israel in particular, there is a progression from simple forms of wisdom – folk-tales, proverbs, riddles and traditional adages – through various stages to the highly sophisticated intellectual products of courts and religious scholars. The cultural context within which such a development might be imagined begins with a fairly primitive, non-literate society of limited scope – perhaps some kind of clan or nomadic set up – advancing through the kind of basic literacy associated with trade and local administration, until the emergence of advanced cultures linked to extensive ruling classes with surplus wealth – including those of a religious kind. At some of its more primitive stages (the hypothesis goes) there are associations with women – perhaps witches, magic in general, and the 'mysterious other'. In biblical terms this seems to be spelled out in the form of a fascination with the East – the Magi in the Gospel of Matthew constitute an interesting later example. Once societies become sufficiently advanced or sophisticated, the process of transmission becomes the business of 'schools' which both educate the next generation of *tradents* (the skilled literate class) and create, or modify, the tradition itself. This collection of hypotheses, though difficult to prove, is intuitively attractive, gaining its plausibility from observations of both pre-literate societies and popular proverbs and the like in everyday use, and the structures of advanced societies. The idea of a simple chronological development is, however, undermined by the reality that every human society continues to preserve and circulate popular wisdom alongside the most sophisticated forms of philosophical and logical learning, nor has any society fully abandoned a subculture of magic, witches, wizards and necromancy. Nevertheless, it has frequently been advocated in various forms, and deserves to be considered.

---

5 Details of the works referred to in this paragraph are provided at the end of the chapter.

Heaton's 1994 Bampton Lectures, *The School Tradition of the Old Testament*, take as their starting point the existence of schools in Ancient Israel, and 'experiment with the hypothesis that the literature which has been at the centre of the discussion [of wisdom] was the product of Israel's schools' (pp. 4–5). The book then proceeds to examine the biblical material in the light of this assumption, providing extensive examples of comparative material from Egypt and Mesopotamia and devoting chapters to wisdom as education, the school tradition among the prophets, story writing, and doubt and scepticism. His analysis tacitly assumes both an extensive educational system and a literate audience more or less continuously from the time of Solomon:

> There can be no doubt about the pre-exilic origin of the centre of learning and teaching which maintained the non-sacerdotal school tradition, although in recent years scholars have become more critical of the view that it was founded by Solomon himself. It is, indeed, arguable that the idea of a far-reaching 'Solomonic enlightenment' is based on late and unreliable sources, but there is enough archaeological evidence of the king's enterprise to support the conclusion that he needed a great many administrators and started a school for their training. By the eighth century, at least, this royal establishment had developed into a fully-fledged teaching institution after the Egyptian model.[6]

Heaton further proposes a kind of 'seminary' tradition from the time of Ezra which presumably promulgated the new Torah-based covenant whose origins are recorded in Nehemiah 8.1–12. The problem with both of these hypotheses is that, however plausible and attractive they may seem, the direct evidence for their existence is problematic. I shall not pursue the seminary approach here; but we must look more closely at the question of schools.

Donn Morgan's work, on the other hand, provides a broad framework of four stages for the development of the wisdom tradition. While he does not directly discuss the question of schools, his attempt to locate the wisdom tradition of the early monarchy leads him to conclude that,

> regarding the social class and setting of such a tradition, there appears to be some evidence that the administrators of the monarchy were at least part of its constituency. While the questions of wisdom schools cannot be answered definitively, it is difficult to attribute the traditions in Gen. 2–3 and 1 Kings 3–11 [which he associates with wisdom] to

---

6 E. W. Heaton, *The School Tradition of the Old Testament* (Oxford, Clarendon Press, 1994), p. 196.

administrators with no responsibility for the transmission of wisdom teaching.[7]

The kernel of his approach, however, lies in a chronological progression from the simplest and most down-to-earth folk wisdom to the highly professionalized world of the early rabbis.[8] I have simplified the analysis to a four-stage development.

Popular (pre-monarchic) wisdom

So-called popular wisdom is represented in the Old Testament mainly through certain literary forms[9] which are assumed to be rather elementary in structure. Other aspects of possibly early strands are what may be taken to be a somewhat naïve association with the east, and the character of the wise woman/witch/medium. The 'wisdom of the east' is represented in various ways: by comparison ('Solomon's wisdom surpassed the wisdom of all the people of the east, and all the wisdom of Egypt' 1 Kings 4.30–31), by example (the Queen of Sheba, in 1 Kings 10.1–10, has a particular interest in Solomon's wisdom) and by implication (a number of portions of the Book of Proverbs quote almost directly from Babylonian sources). Women are associated with wisdom at various levels (as we shall see when we look in detail at Proverbs 1—9). Thus the references to 'wise women' in 2 Samuel 14.2 and 20.16, Judges 5.29, and the fear of witches (illustrated by the law in Ex. 22.18) which may hint at a very basic form of cultural discrimination in which women are both feared and admired for their supposed secret or esoteric knowledge. Saul's ill-fated consultation with the 'witch' or 'medium' of Endor (1 Sam. 28) is a good example of this ambivalence – the woman's skills are necessary, but their use only confirms Saul's worst fears.

---

7 Donn F. Morgan, *Wisdom in the Old Testament Traditions* (Oxford, Basil Blackwell, 1981), p. 58.

8 Something of the same approach is adopted by Claus Westermann, *Roots of Wisdom* (Edinburgh, T. & T. Clark, 1995). Following a discussion of Proverbs 10—31 compared with Proverbs 1—9, Job and Qoheleth, he observes: 'The combined witness of these sources confirms that a later wisdom expressing itself through didactic poetry and other forms is to be distinguished from an earlier wisdom that is characterized by proverbial sayings.'

9 For a much more detailed discussion of the forms of wisdom literature, see James L Crenshaw, 'Wisdom' in *Urgent Advice and probing Questions*, 1995, pp. 45—77.

On technical terms

The application of descriptive terms familiar from English literature to Old Testament writing is problematic.

We possess a wide range of words that can be used to identify quite specific forms: simile, metaphor, allegory, parable, proverb, adage, maxim, riddle, pun, and *double entendre* are representative and familiar to most experienced readers.

Hebrew has hardly any words which can be unambiguously matched to these terms. We shall see (pp. 75–9) how varied are the uses of *mashal* ('proverb'). The word for 'riddle' (*hidah*) is only applied to one specific example, though there are a number of generalized references. Another term – *melitsah* – which is found in Proverbs 1.6, is only found twice in the Old Testament and so it is difficult to determine what its reference might be. The verb from the same root usually means 'to mock'. There is nothing that singles out specifically the idea of a fable.

Identification of these forms in the Bible is therefore a matter of judgement based on the formal features of the passage in question, and it must never be assumed that the writers themselves were aware of the kinds of distinctions we might wish to draw.

Our main concern, however, will be with those literary forms that might come under the heading of popular wisdom: *proverbs* (in the English sense[10]), *parables*, *riddles*, and *fables*. There is a certain irony in the fact that these are all recorded in texts which display a high degree of literary sophistication; their connection with a supposed early stratum of oral tradition is, therefore, quite speculative.

1 *Proverbs* properly speaking are relatively rare, but one reported in 1 Samuel 24.13 is interesting for its appeal to antiquity: 'As the ancient proverb says, "Out of the wicked comes forth wickedness"'; moreover it combines just the level of banality with inaccuracy that characterizes the genre in general (compare such English gems as 'Many hands make light work' and its antithesis, 'Too many cooks spoil the broth'). The famous example from Ezekiel 18.2, 'What do you mean by repeating this proverb concerning the land of Israel, "The parents have eaten sour grapes, and the children's teeth are set on edge"?' has a direct parallel in Jeremiah 31.29, and may represent the reworking of a traditional adage in the context of a shared exilic theological position. Finally, we must note the special position of the Book of Proverbs. Because of its extensive

---

10 As we shall see later, the Book of Proverbs contains very few instances of what we commonly think of as 'proverbial wisdom'. The title in Hebrew in fact has the meaning of 'The Book of Comparisons'.

use of couplets mostly displaying parallelism, it is effectively impossible to identify anything which might belong to this basic proverbial genre; a more detailed examination of the meaning of the title 'proverb' (Hebrew *mashal*) will be presented in Chapter 3.

> McKane[11] lists eleven examples (10.5; 13.4, 7, 8; 16.26; 20.4; 24.27; 26.13, 15, 27; 27.7), none of which can be separated from its literary context. The most likely candidate is perhaps 26.27:
>
> 'Whoever digs a pit will fall into it'
>
> but it is paralleled with:
>
> 'and a stone will come back on the one who starts it rolling'.
>
> Either, both, or neither might have originated as an 'ancient proverb'; there is, it seems to me, no way of knowing.

2 *Parables* are a staple of Gospel literature. They are inevitably identified with Jesus, who is probably the only proponent of the form known to most readers. The etymology of the word is not dissimilar to that of the Hebrew *mashal* – at root a bringing of terms together for the purposes of comparison. However the word has acquired, through its New Testament associations, a more specialized meaning, well summed up in Liddell and Scott's Greek-English Lexicon:

parabolê 3. a parable, i.e. a fictitious narrative by which some religious or moral lesson is conveyed.

The essence is that a story, however brief, is told and by means of this the point is made. There are obvious parallels with a related technical term, *allegory*, the difference being that an allegory achieves its end by means of detailed points of contact between each element of the story and the interpretation to which it points. The boundaries are, of course, blurred – does the parable of the sower, for example, make a single religious point, or does it provide a template for analysing a whole spectrum of personalities in their responses to God? Certainly the explanation offered in Matthew 13.18–23 seems to treat it more like an allegory.

There are a few examples in the Old Testament, perhaps the most famous being Nathan's story about the poor man's lamb (2 Sam. 12.1–4) used to bring David to a proper sense of his guilt in the matter of

---

11 William McKane, *Proverbs: A New Approach* (London, SCM Press, 1970), p. 32.

Bathsheba and Uriah the Hittite. The other clear instance is the piece entitled 'The Song of the Vineyard' (Isaiah 5.1–2) the elegant brevity of which is somewhat masked by the relatively lengthy explanation it receives in vv. 3–7.

> Let me sing for my beloved
>   my love-song concerning his vineyard:
> My beloved had a vineyard
>   on a very fertile hill.
> He dug it and cleared it of stones,
>   and planted it with choice vines;
> he built a watch-tower in the midst of it,
>   and hewed out a wine-vat in it;
> he expected it to yield grapes
>   but it yielded wild grapes.

The prophet Ezekiel, who often makes use of very strange imagery, provides one further possible example in the account of the boiling pot in Ezekiel 24.3–5, which is again followed by a long exposition (vv. 6–13). This piece is introduced by a verb from the same root as *mashal*, presumably meaning 'to draw a comparison'; this illustrates the problem of trying to identify literary forms in Hebrew, in that the language itself has very few pertinent terms. Almost the only one we have – *mashal* – is required to cover traditional proverbs, parables, allegories, and the kind of stylized comparisons which are typical of the book of Proverbs.

3 *Riddles* have a special term to designate them – *hidot* – but are in fact very rarely found. The only explicit example is that posed to the Philistines by Samson in Judges 14.14: 'Out of the eater came something to eat. Out of the strong came something sweet.' The answer is the swarm of bees in a lion's carcass; we might think it somewhat unfair, since it does not hold its solution within itself, depending on the accident of the bee-infested body. Otherwise the word itself is used in Numbers 12.8, 1 Kings 10.1 (= 2 Chronicles 9.1), Ezekiel 17.1, Habakkuk 2.6, Psalms 49.4 and 78.2, and Proverbs 1.6.

Funny, or what?

1. (2 Kings 14.9)

A thornbush on Lebanon sent to a cedar on Lebanon, saying, 'Give your daughter to my son for a wife'; but a wild animal of Lebanon passed by and trampled down the thornbush.

2. (Judges 9.8–15)

The trees once went out to anoint a king over themselves. So they said to the olive tree, 'Reign over us.' The olive tree answered them, 'Shall I stop producing my rich oil by which gods and mortals are honoured, and go to sway over the trees?' Then the trees said to the fig tree, 'You come and reign over us.' But the fig tree answered them, 'Shall I stop producing my sweetness and my delicious fruit, and go to sway over the trees?' Then the trees said to the vine, 'You come and reign over us.' But the vine said to them, 'Shall I stop producing my wine that cheers gods and mortals, and go to sway over the trees?' So all the trees said to the bramble, 'You come and reign over us.' And the bramble said to the trees, 'If in good faith you are anointing me king over you, then come and take refuge in my shade; but if not, let fire come out of the bramble and devour the cedars of Lebanon.'

4 *Fables* are usually taken to be exemplary moral stories which make use of animals or plants to play the parts which a more literal presentation would give to human actors. There are a number of potential fables in the Old Testament, such as Judges 9.8–15, 2 Kings 14.9, Ezekiel 17.3–10 and Ezekiel 19.2–9. In the traditions of Aesop there was often a humorous slant to such stories. This could be said of the example in Judges, and is certainly true of the pithy account in 2 Kings (see box, above). However, the two from Ezekiel have a much more intense, dark atmosphere, and are perhaps better read as rhetorically developed oracles based on the model of the fable.

Royal and bureaucratic wisdom

The second stage, according to the theory we are exploring, sees popular wisdom becoming institutionalized with the development of a royal bureaucracy in Israel.[12] While there is little doubt that a class of learned advisers ('wise men') existed in Egypt and Babylon, given the very extensive finds of written materials from both regions, the absence of any significant body of written material from Israel and Judah means that the case for a class of wise men in Israel depends upon the Bible's account of Solomon's 'empire'. Solomon himself remains enigmatic – he is presented as the only-begetter of all Old Testament wisdom; but this is clearly a conventional ascription, and there is little likelihood that he actually penned (for example) Proverbs or Ecclesiastes.

---

12 See the evidence we considered in Chapter 1, pp. 10–12.

Solomon is of course the epitome of royal wisdom, though not the only example. His skills in this area were truly legendary (1 Kings 4.31–4):

> He was wiser than anyone else, wiser than Ethan the Ezrahite, and Heman, Calcol, and Darda, children of Mahol; his fame spread throughout all the surrounding nations. He composed three thousand proverbs, and his songs numbered a thousand and five. He would speak of trees, from the cedar that is in the Lebanon to the hyssop that grows in the wall; he would speak of animals, and birds, and reptiles, and fish. People came from all the nations to hear the wisdom of Solomon; they came from all the kings of the earth who had heard of his wisdom.

The use of strange, presumably kingly names in this passage is echoed in the names of Agur son of Jakeh and King Lemuel (who learned his wisdom from his mother!) in Proverbs 30.1 and 31.1, and the visit of the Queen of Sheba (another woman with a passion for knowledge) in 1 Kings 10.1–10. There is undoubtedly a naïve or 'primitive' quality to this account which is perhaps best illustrated by the way that the legendary queen is so easily dismayed by Solomon's display of conspicuous consumption (10.4–5):

> When the queen of Sheba had observed the wisdom of Solomon, the house that he had built, the food of his table, the seating of his officials, and the attendance of his servants, their clothing, his valets, and his burnt-offerings that he offered at the house of the Lord, there was no more spirit in her.

This passage also seems to imply the existence of a range of officials occupying the kind of positions which would naturally accompany a bureaucracy, to which we should add secretaries or scribes (2 Sam. 8.16f; 20.24–6; 1 Kings 4.2f; 2 Kings 12.10; 18.18; 22.3; 25.19; Jer. 8.8–9; 36.10–12, 20–27; 37.15) and translators or linguists (2 Kings 18.26; Neh. 8.8). We must be cautious, however, in attempting to line up these references with the much more clearly defined official positions in the Egyptian, Assyrian and Babylonian courts; the English renderings of a few rather non-specific Hebrew terms can lend a spurious air of authority, and the fact that these terms often occur in passages whose primary purpose is to criticize or cajole or cast aspersions means that they may well be unreliable as guides to formal structures.[13]

In common with many advocates of the school hypothesis, Morgan finds the beginnings of formal scribal practice, wisdom writing, and edu-

---

13 See again Weeks, pp. 117–24.

cational processes in the so-called 'Solomonic enlightenment', a concept which originated with the work of the great German scholar Gerhard von Rad. In his *Old Testament Theology*[14] (Volume I, pp. 48–56) he set out an elaborate picture of the rather sudden emergence of a sophisticated, literate and powerful monarchy under Solomon which gave rise to three major works – 'the history of David's rise to power . . . the history of the succession after David . . . and the Jahwist's history' (p. 49). The era 'was a time when people had started gathering and classifying information about natural science' which, together with the historical works already cited, 'rounds off a picture of an age of intense enlightenment and of general spiritual initiative.' He goes on:

> Nor is that all. This newly awakened appreciation of the human, this focusing of attention upon man, this interest in the psychological and the cultivation of rhetoric, give us every right to speak of a Solomonic humanism. (p. 55)

This account was enormously influential, and remains so despite many subsequent qualifications and criticisms. Its dependence on analogy with the European Enlightenment is, in retrospect, obvious, as is its reliance on the more or less unquestioned historicity of the biblical narratives which deal with the lives of David and Solomon. Few today would be quite so optimistic that Samuel and Kings can be taken as straightforward history; nevertheless, the legend of Solomon's Enlightenment survives as a kind of disembodied datum which underpins the popular idea of a longstanding intellectual tradition in Israel and Judah.

Wisdom in the Prophets

Morgan's chronological approach depends upon a timeline which places the pre-exilic prophetic books generally later than the histories which define the Solomonic period (see above on the 'Solomonic Enlightenment'). It is undoubtedly the case that many of the prophetic books contain passages which might reasonably be defined as wisdom, which in turn might suggest the persistence of the effects of the 'enlightenment'. The difficulty facing this thesis is that the dates of composition of the historical and prophetic books do not fall into a similar straight line. Parts of some of the prophets are likely to be earlier

---

14 Gerhard von Rad, *Old Testament Theology* (two volumes) (Edinburgh, Oliver & Boyd, 1962).

in date than most of the historical and many of the Pentateuchal texts, making it difficult to sort out a clear chronology.

As an exercise, indicate what feature or features of each of the following passages might suggest that we should class them as wisdom fragments:

Amos 3.3–6; Hosea 4.11; 5.12; 8.7; Isaiah 28.23–9; Jeremiah 17.5–11; Micah 7.1–7

Wisdom and religion

It is assumed that the writings produced by the educated class during the monarchy were in the service of the state. Proverbs (as a book) would have formed part of the school curriculum, the learned histories supported the claims, in particular, of the Davidic dynasty in Jerusalem, and wisdom contributions to the psalms (for example, 37, 39, 49, 73) would presumably have affirmed the sophistication of the royal cult as it was practised in the Jerusalem Temple. After the exile, and certainly by the time of Ezra and Nehemiah, Judah emerged as a religious state in which leadership fell to the priests and the focus of worship was the covenant between Israel and Yahweh expressed in Torah. Accordingly the focus of the writings and the people responsible for them was directed to specifically religious knowledge; in particular, the knowledge of God which is to be found through the covenant.

Several scholars have proposed that the Levites had a particular responsibility for guarding the scrolls of the law and interpreting them for the people. According to Deuteronomy 31.9–13, 24–6 there was a ceremony every seventh year – during *sukkoth* (the festival of booths, in September) – at which the law was to be read out to the assembled people 'so that they may hear and learn to fear the LORD your God and to observe diligently all the words of this law' (v. 12). (It is appropriate to recall at this point that one of the key slogans for wisdom is 'the fear of the LORD is the beginning of wisdom'.) The Levites also appear with a similar responsibility in 2 Chronicles 17.7–9 and 34.13, and in Nehemiah 8.7–8. The fact that none of these responsibilities is attributed to the Levites in the earlier historical books of Samuel and Kings might suggest that this is a genuinely late development. Indeed, Blenkinsopp[15] suggests that the development of the legal traditions associated with Deuteronomy may

---

15 Joseph Blenkinsopp, *Wisdom and Law in the Old Testament* (Oxford, Oxford University Press, 1995), pp. 84–119.

be attributable to this group; Morgan[16] also considers the significance of Deuteronomy as a product of the scribes, but is less willing to endorse the identification of the Levites as the particular group responsible.

The focus of wisdom from this period onwards is strongly directed towards a right relationship with God. This is what underpins the teaching of Proverbs, and in Deuteronomy 4.5–6 and Psalm 119.97–8[17] we find an explicit connection between wisdom and the observance of the law. Ezra, the priest who supervised the so-called Great Synagogue (Neh. 8) which bound the people of Jerusalem into a Torah covenant, is described in Ezra 7.10 as having 'set his heart to study the law of the LORD, and to do it, and to teach the statutes and ordinances in Israel'. This new profession, of the learned scholar who seeks wisdom in order to advance the claims of Torah, finds its apogee in Jesus ben Sira, author of the book of Ecclesiasticus (also known as Sirach) which was composed in the early second century BC. Thus Sirach 32.14ff:

> One who seeks God will accept his discipline,
>   and those who rise early to seek him will find favour.
> One who seeks the law will be filled with it,
>   but the hypocrite will stumble at it.
> Those who fear the Lord will form true judgements

and, more explicitly, 38.34b–39.3:

> How different the one who devotes himself
>   to the study of the law of the Most High!
> He seeks out the wisdom of all the ancients,
>   and is concerned with prophecies;
> he preserves the sayings of the famous
>   and penetrates the subtleties of parables;
> he seeks out the hidden meanings of proverbs
>   and is at home with the obscurities of parables.

As we shall see when we look at this book in more detail, the whole of chapter 24 is a magnificent hymn to wisdom which binds her as closely as possible to the Torah which defines the being and meaning of the Jewish people.

---

16 Morgan, *Wisdom in the Old Testament Traditions*, pp. 94–105.

17 Deut. 4.5–6: 'See, just as the LORD my God has charged me, I now teach you statutes and ordinances for you to observe in the land that you are about to enter and occupy. You must observe them diligently, for this will show your wisdom and discernment to all the peoples, who . . . will say, "Surely this nation is a wise and discerning people!".' Psalm 119.97–8: 'Oh, how I love your law! It is my meditation all day long. Your commandment makes me wiser than my enemies, for it is always with me.'

Scribes, Pharisees, and rabbis

As the importance of the written Torah increased, and the idea of studying a book became central to the religious identity of the Jews, so the pro-
fessionalization of wisdom advanced. At some point, probably not too
long after the period of Ezra and Nehemiah, a class of scholar-teachers
emerged (the writers of Ecclesiastes and Sirach are good examples) who
made the study of wisdom their calling and the teaching of young men
their profession. The books they studied – apart from the Jewish scriptures – may well have included familiar classics of the Hellenistic world.[18]
There is certainly evidence that Ben Sira in the second century BC knew
something of Greek philosophy, and the great Alexandrian Jewish phil-
osopher, Philo (a contemporary of Jesus) directly addressed the challenge
of interpreting the Jewish faith in Greek philosophical terms.

We shall not deal with this topic further at the moment, since it will
be given fuller treatment below. Suffice to say that the pattern of learned
teacher (sage) and pupil (disciple) becomes the paradigm for Pharisaic,
and then Rabbinic Judaism, and is a key element in the relationship
between Jesus and his intimate circle as presented in the Gospels.

Wisdom in Israel: archaeological evidence

The direct appeal to archaeology is always emotionally attractive, in that
it gives the impression of a body of firm, objective evidence with which
to confront both the genuine enquirer and the sceptic. Unfortunately the
experience of 150 years of archaeological work in Israel, Palestine and
Mesopotamia shows that though buildings, pots, grave goods and carv-
ings may be satisfyingly concrete, they rarely reveal their human secrets
unambiguously. And if this is true for these solid objects, it is corres-
pondingly much more difficult to recover the social, religious and political customs of antiquity. The best evidence is often to be found in texts
excavated from a known stratum – the library of Ashurbanipal,[19] for
example, or the mythic texts of Ugarit[20] – but these are often copies of

---

18 It may be necessary to explain that from the time of Alexander (330 BC)
onwards the world of the eastern Mediterranean was steeped in Greek literature
and culture, and educated people in that region would almost certainly have
been familiar with the Greek language. This general cultural phenomenon is
known as Hellenism.

19 Ashurbanipal (c. 668–627 BC) was the ruler of Assyria at the height of its
military and cultural fame. His military successes are now largely forgotten,
but the library he established in Nineveh survived in part. It was not the first of
its kind but it was one of the largest and one of the few to survive to the present
day.

20 The ancient city of Ugarit was rediscovered at the site of Ras Shamra in

more ancient works, and (where they represent the triumphs of kings or emperors) are to be taken with a pinch of salt. Most rulers at most times have greatly exaggerated their triumphs and understated their losses!

In the territories of ancient Israel and Judah there is a paucity of written materials,[21] with the result that it is almost impossible to reconstruct the life of the people directly. There are, of course, numbers of fragmentary inscriptions on ostraka (tiles or potsherds), tablets, pots, and walls, and claims have been made, most persuasively by Lemaire,[22] that these provide physical proof of the existence of educational establishments at various locations in Israel and Judah. The problem with Lemaire's case, as Weeks points out in some detail,[23] is that it depends both on often doubtful interpretations of the epigraphic evidence and on an assumption that the existence of (say) a single inscription proves the presence of a 'school'. Weeks shows in some detail how unsafe are Lemaire's conclusions that these fragments are school exercises, even where they contain alphabets:

> There is probably no single interpretation to be put on all the abecedaries which have been recovered, and the automatic association of abecedaries with the learning of writing, let alone schools, is to be regarded with profound suspicion. (p. 151)

He makes the interesting point, first advanced by Albright, that the 22-character alphabet was in fact reasonably easy to learn, so that there is no reason to discount the possibility of a low-level functioning literacy which was quite widespread. However, this does not imply the existence of schools, nor does it compel the conclusion that more than a handful of people would have had access to, or been able to read, the kind of compositions which we regard as belonging to wisdom. His overall conclusion is instructive:

> Were it reasonably clear that schools actually existed, then we might at least entertain the possibility that wisdom literature was used in them, or even composed for use in them. However, there is neither

---

Syria in the 1920s. A large collection of clay tablets was found, many of which contained mythical, ritual and poetic pieces. Their language was quickly discovered to be a semitic one related to Hebrew; the texts themselves were written in the fourteenth century BC.

21 The Dead Sea Scrolls are from a much later time (250 BC–AD 100), and are unique in their extent and state of preservation.

22 A. Lemaire, *Les Ecoles et la Formation de la Bible dans l'ancien Israël* (OBO 39; Fribourg, Editions Universitaires; Göttingen, Vandenhoeck and Ruprecht, 1981).

23 Weeks, *Early Israelite Wisdom*, pp. 137–51.

strong evidence for schools nor any convincing reason to suppose that they would have existed. Our ignorance of educational methods in Israel remains profound, and claims for the use of wisdom literature in schools are entirely speculative. (p. 156)

The analysis so far has related in the main to written evidence. One of the most interesting of recent attempts to resolve the dilemma of schools in Israel took a rather different approach, seeking to evaluate the indirect physical evidence. I refer to Jamieson-Drake's 1991 monograph,[24] the purpose of which was to identify evidence for serious scribal activity within the archaeological evidence available from Israel and Judah during the biblical period. By 'scribes' are meant 'professional administrators'; that is, we are looking for evidence that literary skills have a formal function within a structured society. This is an important clarification, because the mere statement that there were literary skills available is a truism, and does not tell us anything about the existence of the resources to produce and store public documents and to employ these in a significant way in the religious and political arenas.

Two questions are often posed:

Did schools exist for the training of professional scribes for state adminstration?

Were there institutions for the promotion of general literacy?

We have already seen that epigraphic evidence is indecisive and that the Bible is at best an indirect witness. Arguments from analogy have often been employed – Israel is compared with other ancient Near Eastern societies about which we know much more. The trouble is that the comparisons are usually made with large imperial regimes such as those of Egypt, Babylon and Assyria while Israel and Judah were arguably more like Moab, Edom and the like: small states with poorly developed infrastructures. We cannot simply transfer the known institutions of Egypt to the Israelite context as though we were comparing like with like.

Jamieson-Drake proposes a model which might provide us with testable evidence. It has three parts: (A) what we would expect to find in a literate society; (B) what (properly speaking) constitutes a 'school'; and (C) what archaeological correlates we might look for. In detail:

A1   Centralized administrative control (economic, social or political) in which writing is used to monitor economic and social transactions.

---

24 D. W. Jamieson-Drake, *Scribes and Schools in Monarchic Judah: A Socio-Archaeological Approach* (JSOTSup 109; Sheffield, Sheffield Academic Press, 1991).

A2 Control by urban elites over agricultural producers – social stratification.

A3 The existence of full-time administrators and other non-agricultural specialists.

B1 In a school, literacy is taught.

B2 Teaching is at a fixed location outside the home.

B3 Fees are paid to a professional educator.

B4 Schools are used to train professional administrators.

C1 We look for monumental architecture of appropriate *scale* and *style*.

C2 We need to determine settlement patterns and provide estimates of site sizes.

C3 We would require to analyse the distribution of luxury items (since these provide evidence for the presence of surplus value to support a literate community.

    1 quantity suggests wealth and social stratification.

    2 provenience suggests trading relationships.

    3 surface analysis indicates direction of exchange and relative importance of sites on a trade route.

    4 locally produced luxury items provide direct evidence for other full-time artisans.

Space does not permit us to go into the detail of the survey here; what Jamieson-Drake did was to review all the available archeological evidence for the period from the twelfth century to the sixth century BC (that is, from the pre-monarchic period represented by the Judges to the return to Jerusalem in the post-exilic era). He found that there was little evidence to suggest a society capable of extensive literary production prior to the eighth century, and that it is only with the rise of Jerusalem as the single influential urban centre after the fall of Samaria that we begin to see the conditions for a professional literary class.

There is a high increase in luxury items in the eighth and seventh centuries, though virtually no evidence for systematic or sustained foreign trade. There are few signs of skilled artisanship; such as there is has its main focus on the Jerusalem complex in the seventh century. It is significant that there is also evidence at this time of the centralization of control in Jerusalem (jars labelled 'belonging to the king'). What we can tentatively conclude is that, while there is no evidence prior to the eighth century which would point to the conditions for a professional scribal class and the education of administrators, it seems likely that something of the sort emerged subsequently. It must be stressed, however, that this is a *likely* conclusion, not a *proven* result.

It will be clear that enthusiastic claims for the extensive literary culture of the period of David and Solomon (eleventh and tenth centuries) must be significantly scaled back, if not completely eliminated, if the work of Jamieson-Drake and Weeks is valid. The former notes that there is a real problem vis-à-vis Jerusalem, where centuries of continuous occupation make it impossible to access much of the evidence. It may well be that, from the time that Jerusalem became the dominant centre, there is more material culture of the relevant kind than we can at present list. While this might strengthen the case for literacy and scribal activity in the seventh century, it hardly affects the rest of the argument. Archaeology, in short, does not support the outline presented in the previous section. Susan Niditch[25] explores the implications of these findings in some detail, describing a society in which, without denying the existence of a class of people able to write, we should think in terms of a largely and effectively illiterate population (see the extended quotation in the box, below). The size of the literate class at various times would be indicated by Jamieson-Drake's evidence; in practice, however, the reality is of a mainly and practically speaking oral culture up to the fourth century BC.

Back to the Bible – with a health warning

Having reviewed both the strong case for schools in ancient Israel and the limited, if not negative, relevance of archaeology and epigraphy to the problem, we can return finally and cautiously to the biblical evidence. A number of biblical passages have been put forward by scholars as evidence for the existence of 'schools' in Israel. You are now invited to revisit the biblical evidence for yourself, but with a more sceptical eye, in order to evaluate how it can contribute to our knowledge of schools and the intellectual traditions of Israel. The list of passages given below contains those which have from time to time been put forward as evidence of literacy in Israel; two health warnings are essential. (1) The date of composition of a text may be very different from the period it purports to describe. In such cases judgement is necessary as to which period the evidence under examination is relevant to; this in turn necessitates a view of the accuracy, or otherwise, of oral tradition. More will be said about orality at the end of this book; in the meantime, Susan Niditch is a good guide. (2) The nature of the text itself must be considered. If it is straightforward narrative, or part of the biography or autobiography of a sage, we might be justified in taking a fairly literal view of the material. But if we are in the middle of a prophetic harangue or an archaizing 'historical' passage, we need to be sceptical about the degree of literality with which the information can be regarded.

---

25 Susan Niditch, *Oral World and Written Word. Orality and Literacy in Ancient Israel* (London, SPCK, 1997), especially pp. 39–77.

The Bible offers ample evidence of an Israelite literate mentality: writing on deeds and decrees; letters; references to genealogical and other written lists or surveys; rubrics that cite royal and other annals; some references to the composing of literature in writing or to the writing down of oral compositions; the importance of the concept of a written Torah; specific references to details of a written Torah and quotations that can be found in the Pentateuch as it now stands.

While some of these indications of literate mentality are in preexilic texts, the majority are in late passages . . . And yet even in the passages at the literate end of the continuum are nuances of orality, a reminder of the oral context that frames the use of reading, even in the postexilic period. In the Hebrew Bible, the written and signed deed serves as symbolic action; written edicts are read aloud by heralds; it is assumed that written materials will be reoralized . . . Thus even at the literate end of the spectrum, the oral mentality is present and active, informing the way writing is used.

Niditch, *Oral World and Written Word*, pp. 97–8

Something to think about

In the table that follows, most passages have been provided with estimated dates. Where there is only one, it refers to the estimated date of composition of the document itself. Where there is another date (in square brackets), that second reference is to the period to which the text ostensibly refers. Job and Proverbs are undatable. Most of these dates are what scholars are pleased to call 'educated guesses'. Non-scholars are honest enough to leave out the word educated from that phrase! You are invited to write a brief description of what you think is significant about each passage as a source of evidence for writing and literacy in Israel and Judah.

1	Deuteronomy 24.3	650–550 [1250]
2	Joshua 18.9	650–550 [1150]
3	Judges 8.13–19	750–550 [1100]
4	2 Samuel 8.17	750–550 [950]
5	Isaiah 8.16	750–700
6	Isaiah 10.19	760–700
7	Isaiah 28.9–13	600–500
8	Isaiah 29.11–12	600–500
9	Jeremiah 8.8	600–500
10	Jeremiah 32.9–12	600–500

11	Habbakuk 2.2	450–400
12	Job 31.35–37	?
13	Proverbs 3.3	?
14	Proverbs 4.1–9	?
15	Proverbs 8.32–36	?
16	Proverbs 17.16	?
17	Proverbs 22.17–21	?
18	Ecclesiastes 12.9–10	250–200
19	Sirach 51.23–30	200–150

'Answers' are not provided. Weeks[26] discusses some of them, as does Crenshaw.[27] Standard commentaries may also be of assistance, but you are encouraged to try to reach your own conclusions.

Further reading

Blenkinsopp, Joseph (1995) *Wisdom and Law in the Old Testament*, Oxford, Oxford University Press

Grabbe, Lester L. (1995) *Priests, Prophets, Diviners, Sages: A Socio-Historical Study of Religious Specialists in Ancient Israel*, Valley Forge, PA, Trinity Press International

Heaton, E. W. (1994) *The School Tradition of the Old Testament*, Oxford, Clarendon Press

Jamieson-Drake, D. W. (1991) *Scribes and Schools in Monarchic Judah: A Socio-Archaeological Approach* (JSOTSup 109), Sheffield, Sheffield Academic Press

Lemaire, A. (1981) *Les Ecoles et la Formation de la Bible dans l'ancien Israël* (OBO 39), Fribourg, Editions Universitaires; Göttingen, Vandenhoeck and Ruprecht

Morgan, Donn F. (1981) *Wisdom in the Old Testament Traditions*, Oxford, Basil Blackwell

Niditch, Susan (1997) *Oral World and Written Word. Orality and Literacy in Ancient Israel*, London, SPCK

Weeks, Stuart (1994) *Early Israelite Wisdom*, Oxford, Oxford University Press.

Westermann, Claus (1995) *Roots of Wisdom*, Edinburgh, T. & T. Clark

---

26 *Early Israelite Wisdom*, pp. 132–6.
27 *Urgent Advice and Probing Questions*, pp. 236–9.

3

Wisdom in the Ancient Near East

Methodological points

Everyone who studies the wisdom literature agrees that the phenomenon it deals with had a distinctly international character, and that the genres it represents are spread across the ancient Near East. Most also claim that there is significant direct influence on at least some of the biblical materials. The most often cited is the supposed dependence of Proverbs 22.17—23.10 on the Egyptian *Instruction of Amenemope*. Another widely distributed text, probably of Syrian origin, the *Sayings of Ahikar*, is also cited as the source of several individual sayings. There are two separate questions at stake: whether there is any real interdependence, and if so, how did it come about? Since we have effectively ruled out the once normative picture of a vast Solomonic bureaucracy staffed by courtiers, scribes, secretaries and ambassadors eagerly scanning the latest publication from Thebes or the newest scroll from Nineveh, the practicalities of any supposed influence need to be examined closely. As to the fact of influence, it is important to distinguish between general platitudes ('spare the rod and spoil the child' is a good example), which might well arise spontaneously in any society, and genuinely diagnostic citations. This is precisely where the lines of influence are blurred. At the one extreme there are those who see every echo as the result of a professional translation from Egyptian or Akkadian or Aramaic into Hebrew; at the other, there are sceptics who prefer to reserve judgement pending a parallel text of Amenemope in Egyptian and Hebrew incontrovertibly signed by an Israelite royal scribe.

Somewhere between these extremes might lie a more modest but not unhelpful compromise. Susan Niditch[1] puts it neatly when she remarks that 'Israelite literacy in form and function is not to be confused with modern literacy and . . . ancient Israelite literacy has to be understood in the context of an oral-traditional culture. Literacy and orality are part of an ongoing continuum even in the latest biblical period.' While she applies this insight primarily to the question of intertextuality within the Old Testament, it is equally relevant to the quest for mechanisms that

---

1 *Oral World and Written Word*, p. 99.

might explain apparent influences from the outside world on Israelite wisdom. Stuart Weeks[2] provides an extended discussion of the probability and likely nature of cross-fertilization of cultures. He points out that a number of assumptions traditionally made by Old Testament scholars have been called in question: the genre of Egyptian wisdom is more likely to be '*belles-lettres*' than classroom texts; the circles that produced them would have been a scribal class which was responsible for all types of Egyptian literature; some of the classic texts were already ancient when they were reproduced in Egypt – their use was 'comparable to the reading of Shakespeare or Chaucer in a modern English school' (p. 19). All these factors make the question of influence more complex than many commentaries might suggest. Thus Weeks (p. 8):

> . . . with the probable exception of *Ahikar*, we know nothing of the wisdom literature which may have been produced in the nations closer to Israel, and which may have served as a conduit for Egyptian and Mesopotamian material. Furthermore, material could have been transmitted orally, and this route, naturally, would have left no trace. The problem is compounded, finally, by the possibility of coincidence: similar thoughts and sayings may have originated quite independently in different times and places.

For convenience we use terms like 'literature', 'text', 'document' and 'book' when referring to the written traditions under consideration. Many of these, especially from Mesopotamia, are inscriptions on clay or limestone tablets; the Egyptian examples are, of course, written on papyrus. Nevertheless, the conventional modern words are good enough as long as we understand them to refer to *what is written* rather than *the manner of its writing*.

We shall proceed on the assumption that some writers in Israel were familiar with some material from other cultures, and that there is the possibility of direct textual borrowing. However, this is more likely at the latest stages – almost certain in the time of Ben Sira, probable in Persian and Hellenistic times, and possible in the seventh century BC. What is more likely, however, is that types of saying circulated orally and were mimicked by Israelite writers who also quite naturally developed their own specific examples. The pattern of instruction, where an authority figure speaks, could easily have circulated without any need for physical texts, and the sayings genre using parallelism is hardly in need of any

---

2 *Early Israelite Wisdom*, pp. 6–19.

overt external influence. That said, it remains useful to review the extant documents from Egypt and Mesopotamia, bearing in mind that they represent only the accidental survivors of a much larger corpus.

Selected examples of international wisdom

What now follows is a selection of materials which demonstrate the widespread phenomenon of wisdom writing.[3] It is primarily intended for information – for browsing and reference. However, some attempt is made to illustrate the kind of influences, whether direct or indirect, which we have discussed in the previous section. Where possible both texts are provided, though it should be pointed out that these are comparisons in English translation of texts originally in two different languages. What appears similar, therefore, may do so because of the mediation of the translator.

The principal reference works are James Pritchard's classic *Ancient Near Eastern Texts Relating to the OT*[4] (abbreviated as ANET) and William Hallo's more recent *The Context of Scripture*[5] (abbreviated as Hallo). These are both substantial volumes provided with indices which assist the search for possible scriptural parallels – though it is important to use these with care, since the judgment that a parallel exists is often quite subjective. No dates have been provided for the extracts presented, since they are often quite broad (for example, 'Egyptian Middle Kingdom' refers to a span of about 350 years) and we are emphatically not proposing direct quotation as the normal form of influence.

> The texts usually associated with the wisdom tradition in the Ancient Near East come predominantly from Egypt and from Mesopotamia. Within the latter we can recognize subdivisions into Sumerian and Akkadian documents. The other major sources of comparative materials (Hittite, Ugaritic and Aramaic) have produced less in the way of wisdom literature, though we shall consider a few of them.
>
> The Egyptian materials come mainly from the Middle Kingdom, dated

---

3 Similar accounts will be found in Dell, *'Get Wisdom, Get Insight'*, pp. 98–111, Crenshaw, *Old Testament Wisdom*, pp. 205–26, Heaton, *The School Tradition of the Old Testament*, pp. 45–64, and McKane, *Proverbs*, pp. 51–208.

4 James B. Pritchard, *Ancient Near Eastern Texts Relating to the Old Testament* (third edition with Supplement; Princeton, NJ, Princeton University Press, 1969).

5 William W. Hallo and K. Lawson Younger (eds.), *The Context of Scripture*, three volumes (Leiden, Brill, 2003).

very roughly to 2150–1750 BC, with one important text associated with the Ramesside period (1320–1150). There is, of course, often a gap between the date of the papyrus in question and the likely date of composition.

Sumerian culture flourished for a millennium from 3000 to 2000 BC, based on city states around the Tigris and the Euphrates. Some of the writing from that period has similarities with Egyptian material from the Middle Kingdom, and it is reasonable to suppose trading and cultural links. In so far as Sumerian texts are pertinent, it will be through their having been copied and translated by later cultures in the region.

Akkadian was the language of Assyria and Babylon, flourishing until the early first millennium when it was replaced with Aramaic. Documents of some relevance to Israelite wisdom from this source belong largely to the mid- to late-second millennium.

Aramaic came into its own from about 700 BC. Like Akkadian and Hebrew it is a semitic language; it became the lingua franca of the region from the eastern Mediterranean to Babylonia with the dominance first of the Babylonians from 625 BC and then the Persians, who adopted the language of Babylon for their empire. For our purposes only one text, Ahikar, is relevant.

Hittite is an Indo-European language spoken by a people who ruled Anatolia (modern Turkey) from 1740 to 1200 BC. It has similarities with Greek, and the ancient town of Troy was probably in their territory.

Egyptian examples

1 *The Dispute Between a Man and His* Ba[6]

This composition was once taken to be that of a man contemplating suicide – this is how it is represented in ANET, pp. 405–7. However 'a preferable assumption would be that of a monologue reflecting the internal struggle of a despairing man'.[7] It has affinities both with the themes and debates in Job and with some of the perspectives of Qoheleth. The following excerpts reflect the latter:

> They who build in blocks of granite, and constructed halls (?) in nice pyramids of fine work; the builders become gods, yet their offering stones are destroyed, like the weary ones, who are dead on the riverbank without a survivor. The flood takes its toll, and the sun likewise. The fishes of the water's banks talk to them.

---

6 Hallo, III, pp. 321–5. The *ba* is Egyptian for 'soul'.
7 Nili Shupak in Hallo, III, p. 321.

Listen to me! Behold, it is good for people to listen. Follow the happy
day and forget worry!   (lines 60–9)

To whom shall I speak today?
There are no righteous ones,
The land is left to wrongdoers.   (lines 122–3)

The sentiment of the first of these quotations is similar to one which is
prevalent in Qoheleth. Thus 2.24, 'There is nothing better for mortals
than to eat and drink, and find enjoyment in their toil.' (Compare also
3.12, 22; 8.15; 9.7–9; 11.7–8.) The second has a parallel in 3.16 and
5.8:

> Moreover, I saw under the sun that in the place of justice, wickedness
> was there, and in the place of righteousness, wickedness was there as
> well.

> If you see in a province the oppression of the poor and the violation of
> justice and right, do not be amazed at the matter.

These parallels are not verbally close; all that they really suggest is that
the kind of issues explored by books like Qoheleth and Job were familiar
subjects of reflection, and had been for many centuries before the biblical
writers engaged with them.

An interesting aspect of this Egyptian example is the poetic structure
that it displays. It consists of three dialogues between the *ba* and the man
(similar to the central structure of Job), four poems, and a final speech
of the *ba* which receives no response from the man (we are reminded
of Job's relative silence in the face of Yahweh's intervention). The four
poems contain respectively eight, sixteen, six and three stanzas. Each is
characterized by an opening refrain followed by two explanatory lines;
the refrains are. 'Behold, my name is detested', 'To whom shall I speak
today?', 'Death is before me today' and 'Truly, he who is there'. There are
interesting parallels in two poems in Amos which are often associated
with the wisdom tradition – Amos 3.3–8 and 4.6–11; compare also the
extended numerical saying in 1.3—2.11.

2 *The Instruction of the Vizier Ptah-Hotep*[8]

The opening of this text refers to King Izezi whom the translator dates
to the fifth dynasty, around 2450 BC. The surviving papyri are considerably later, and it is possible that the attribution is pseudonymous. There

---

8 ANET, pp. 412–14. Hallo does not appear to include this text.

is some evidence that this practice was adopted in later times to lend authenticity – something we are of course familiar with from the biblical materials. Whether or not this is the case, the antiquity of the surviving text means that there is little likelihood of direct influence. Once again we can note parallels which simply reinforce the similarity of this thought world over the best part of two millennia.

> Oldness has come; old age has descended. Feebleness has arrived; dotage is coming anew. The heart sleeps wearily every day. The eyes are weak, the ears are deaf, the strength is disappearing because of weariness of heart, and the mouth is silent and cannot speak. The heart is forgetful and cannot recall yesterday. The bone suffers old age. God is become evil. All taste is gone. What old age does to humankind is evil in every respect. The nose is stopped up and cannot breathe. Simply to stand up or sit down is difficult.   (lines 5–25)

Comparison with Qoheleth 12.1–8 is irresistible. The most obvious difference is that the Israelite sage uses more subtle metaphors to soften his message: 'the strong men are bent, and the women who grind cease working because they are few, and those who look through the windows see dimly'. Other passages in Ptah-Hotep find echoes in Proverbs. For example, 'To hear is of advantage for a son who hearkens . . . How good it is when a son accepts what his father says! Thereby maturity comes to him' (lines 534, 543–4) and 'As for the fool who does not hearken, he cannot do anything. He regards knowledge as ignorance and profit as loss. He does everything blame-worthy, so that one finds fault with him every day. He lives on that through which he should die, and guilt is his food' (lines 575–83) may be compared with Proverbs 4.1–2: 'Listen, children, to a father's instruction, and be attentive, that you may gain insight; for I give you good precepts: do not forsake my teaching' and Proverbs 1.22, 29–31:

> How long, O simple ones, will you love being simple?
> How long will scoffers delight in their scoffing
>   and fools hate knowledge?
> Because they hated knowledge
>   and did not choose the fear of the Lord,
> would have none of my counsel,
>   and despised all my reproof,
> therefore they shall eat the fruit of their way
>   and be sated with their own devices.

Again, these show a similarity of approach and ethos, but in no way support any case for direct influence.

3 Merikare[9]

The genre is that of a royal testament in the form of a treatise on kingship, 'a literary genre that was to flourish many centuries later in the Hellenistic world and subsequently in the Islamic East as well as in medieval Europe'.[10] There is an interesting example of a similar form in 1 Kings 2.1–9 where David on his deathbed gives advice to Solomon, and perhaps in Proverbs 31.1–9 where King Lemuel records his mother's teaching. Finally, following Qoheleth's own attribution of authorship to Solomon, or at least to a king in Jerusalem, we can understand that book also as a royal testament, even if its message is not the advice that would traditionally have been passed on to the heir to the throne!

In terms of specific content, there is one intriguing passage which bears comparison with the creation myth in Genesis 1, which has some connections with wisdom forms and concerns.

> Well directed is mankind, god's cattle,
> He made the sky and earth for their sake,
> He subdued the water monster,
> He made breath for their noses to live.
> They are his images, who came from his body.
> He shines in the sky for their sake;
> he made for them plants and cattle,
> fowl and fish to feed them.   (lines 131–3)

The fact that scholars have suggested that some of the influences on Genesis 1 might be Egyptian is perhaps relevant here. If knowledge of Egyptian creation myths was in general circulation, details like the 'image of god' idea which is present in the above text could have been part of that general information.

4 The Instruction of Any[11]

This is not a royal document; rather it comes from the sphere of the educated middle class. Though the beginning is apparently missing, it was probably couched in the form of instruction from a father to a son. This is made more likely by the unusual epilogue in which Any the scribe and his son Khonshotep, also a scribe, engage in a dialogue about the difficulty of learning. The principal interest for us lies in a passage which is strongly reminiscent of Proverbs 7, where there is an extended allegory

---

9 Hallo, I, pp. 61–6.
10 Miriam Lichtheim in Hallo, I, p. 61.
11 Hallo, I, pp. 110–15.

of the dangers posed by a foreign woman. Apart from that, there is a passage on over-indulgence in alcohol which has parallels in Proverbs 20.1 and 23.29–35. It would be idle to suppose that there ever existed a society which did not come up with platitudes about the dangers of drink entirely under its own steam! Finally, a short section is reminiscent of Qoheleth's advice on going to the Temple. Two examples follow.

> Beware of a woman who is a stranger,
> One not known in her town;
> Don't stare at her when she goes by,
> Do not know her carnally.
> A deep water whose course is unknown,
> Such is a woman away from her husband.
> 'I am pretty,' she tells you daily,
> When she has no witnesses;
> She is ready to ensnare you,
> A great deadly crime when it is heard.   (lines 3.13ff)

The Proverbs passage does not in so many words say that the woman is foreign, but the fact that she has made vows which require to be fulfilled through sexual congress (vv. 14–15) and the reference to Egyptian linen on her couch (v. 16) hint at this. She is obviously out to attract (vv. 10–11), and the outcome is inevitably bitter (vv. 21–23). The setting of the Proverbs narrative is night-time (v. 9), and there is a sense of furtiveness provided by the reference to her lying in wait at street corners (v. 12). As before, we cannot claim literary dependence, and the theme of the danger of the woman from another society is the stock in trade of male misogyny; nevertheless, the parallels are striking.

The other passage I want to quote concerns behaviour in the Temple. Once again, though verbal dependence is not the issue, the thematic links are thought-provoking. Incidentally, the similarity of the Egyptian passage to some of the teaching attributed to Jesus is also striking (Matthew 6.5–6). I have set the two passages out in parallel for easier comparison.

Do not raise your voice in the house of god,	Guard your steps when you go to the house of God; to draw near to
He abhors shouting;	listen is better than the sacrifice
Pray by yourself with a loving heart,	offered by fools; for they do not know how to keep from doing evil.
Whose every word is hidden.	Never be rash with your mouth,
He will grant your needs,	nor let your heart be quick to utter
He will hear your words,	a word before God, for God is in
He will accept your offerings.	heaven and you upon earth;
Libate for your mother and father,	therefore let your words be few.
	(Qoheleth 5.1–2)

Who are resting in the valley;
When the gods witness your
   action,
They will say: 'Accepted.'
                (Any, lines 4.2–5)

5 *The Instruction of Amenemope*[12]

This composition is probably the most familiar to those who work with
Proverbs, since it was the one which attracted early attention, and has
been proposed as the *textual* source for Proverbs 22.17—23.11. I have
already noted that this thesis is no longer anything like as secure as when
it was first put forward in 1924; nevertheless, it still finds favour, and
tends to be presented as a given in commentaries on Proverbs.[13] Even
Weeks, while cautious about the way that Israelite wisdom might have
interacted with sources from Egypt, tends to endorse the broad principle
of dependence.[14] Crenshaw[15] regards the matter as pretty much settled,
as does the editor of Amenemope in Hallo: 'It can hardly be doubted
that the author of Proverbs was acquainted with the Egyptian work and
borrowed from it'. However, her assessment is somewhat vitiated by the
view she expresses a few lines earlier, that 'much of Israelite knowledge of
things Egyptian, as reflected in the Bible, resulted from contacts during
[the Ramesside] period', i.e., fourteenth to twelfth centuries BC. Current
thinking on the emergence of Israel as a state would suggest that this is far
too early for any such literary influence to have taken place. Given that
the text of Amenemope, on her own admission, 'abounds in rare words,
elliptic phrases, and allusions whose meaning escapes us', one wonders
what a Judaean scholar, working with a copy of his (or her?) Egyptian
source some centuries down the line from its composition, might have
made of it. Obviously the resolution of such a problem is well beyond the
compass of a book like this. I shall be content to set out a sampling of
what are claimed as parallels to give the reader at least a limited sense of
what is at stake.

(III.9–11) Give your ears, hear   (22.17–18a) Incline your ear and
   the sayings,   hear my words,

---

12 Hallo, I, pp. 115–22.

13 Richard J. Clifford, *Proverbs* (Old Testament Library; Louisville,
KY, Westminster John Knox, 1999), pp. 199–200 is a representative recent
example.

14 See Weeks, *Early Israelite Wisdom*, pp. 66–9.

15 Crenshaw, *Old Testament Wisdom*, pp. 210–13.

Give your heart to understand them; and apply your mind[16] to my teaching;

It profits to put them in your heart. for it will be pleasant if you keep them within you.

(VII.11–14) Do not move the marker on the borders of the field, (22.28) Do not remove the ancient landmark

Nor shift the position of the measuring cord. that your ancestors set up.

Do not be greedy for a cubit of land, (23.10) Do not remove an ancient landmark

Nor encroach on the boundaries of a widow. or encroach on the fields of orphans.

(IX.14–19) Do not strain to seek increase, (23.4–5) Do not wear yourself out to get rich;

What you have, let it suffice you. be wise enough to desist.

If riches come to you by theft,

They will not stay the night with you.

Comes day they are not in your house When you eyes light upon it, it is gone;

Their place is seen, but they're not there;

(X.4–5)They made themselves wings like geese, for suddenly it takes wings to itself, flying like an eagle towards heaven.

And flew away to the sky.

(XIV.5–8) Do not covet a poor man's goods, (23.6–8) Do not eat the bread of the stingy;

Nor hunger for his bread; do not desire their delicacies;

a poor man's goods are a block in the throat, for like a hair in the throat, so are they.

It makes the gullet vomit. 'Eat and drink!' they say to you; but they do not mean it.

You will vomit up the little you have eaten,

and you will waste your pleasant words.

---

16 The Hebrew here is the word for heart.

(XXIII.13–18) Do not eat in the presence of an official	(23.1–3) When you sit down to eat with a ruler,
And then set your mouth before him.	observe carefully what is before you,
If you are sated, pretend to chew,	and put a knife to your throat if you have a big appetite.
Content yourself with your saliva.	Do not desire the ruler's delicacies,
Look at the bowl that is before you,	
And let it serve your needs.	For they are deceptive food.

These five parallels are, in my judgement, the most persuasive of the twenty or so which are commonly proposed.[17] Even so, there are few if any which compel the conclusion that someone had in front of them an actual text of Amenemope. Some belong to the general field of useful metaphors, others may well have circulated orally and been reapplied in a roughly, but not exactly similar setting. Since these constitute the strongest case for direct influence, I believe that they are at best only weak evidence for any formal sharing of texts across the cultures.

One final comparison is often cited: the reference in both Amenemope and Proverbs to 'thirty' chapters or sayings. The former reads (XXVII.6–7) 'Look to these thirty chapters, They inform, they educate' while the latter has (22.20) 'Have I not written for you thirty sayings of admonition and knowledge'. The coincidence – if that is what it is – is striking; surely it is more plausible to argue that here at least the writer of Proverbs displays knowledge of Amenemope. That may be, but the fact that the Egyptian reference is in the summing up while that in Proverbs is in the middle of the relevant section might suggest a more casual link. It is possible that some form of Amenemope was known, mostly through oral transmission, and that the fact that it contained thirty chapters (note that Proverbs refers to *sayings*, not *chapters*) could have prompted a similar, but only loosely dependent comment in Proverbs.

6 *The Satire on the Trades*[18]

This text is too long to quote in full, and difficult to précis. It consists of a series of descriptions of trades and professions all of which are made fun of, by contrast with the profession of scribe, which is highly praised. The carpenter and jeweller get nothing but weariness as a reward, the barber 'strains his arms to fill his belly, like the bee that eats as it works', the

---

17 ANET, p. 424 provides a detailed list.
18 Hallo, I, pp. 122–5.

reed-cutter is pestered by mosquitoes and gnats and the potter 'grubs in the mud more than a pig'. The mason comes in for a particularly scurrilous insult, being described as someone whose 'loincloth is a twisted rope and a string in the rear' – the ancient equivalent of the modern builder's derrière! Carpenters, gardeners, farmers and the weaver (who 'is worse off than a woman'!), the arrow-maker, the courier, the stoker, the cobbler, the washerman, the bird-catcher (who is not even allowed a net; one wonders at the thought of him leaping up and down to catch birds with his bare hands!) and the fisherman are all dismissed in exaggerated terms as people whose lives are nasty, brutish and short. The writer is, as usual, addressing his son – we may surmise that the son was reluctant to attend to his books, and is being warned of the grim alternatives:

> See, there's no profession without a boss,
> Except for the scribe; he is the boss.
> Hence if you know writing,
> It will do better for you
> Than those professions I've set before you,
> Each more wretched than the other.   (c. lines 9.3–8)

The text concludes with more general advice on how the scribe should behave himself, in the course of which the author rather undermines his pride in being his own boss by making it clear that the scribe is distinctly subservient to the officials, the well-born and the members of court who employ him.

There is no direct parallel to this work in the Old Testament itself, but we can compare a striking passage in Sirach 38.24—39.11 which, while not satirical in tone, depicts a similarly unfavourable contrast between the profession of scribe and other trades, and concludes with a glowing account of his own high calling. Ben Sira, however, does not demean the trades; he is careful to record that

> All these rely on their hands,
> and all are skilful in their own work.
> Without them no city can be inhabited,
> and wherever they live they will not go hungry.   (38.31-2)

Mesopotamian examples

1 The Babylonian Theodicy[19]

This composition, written in Akkadian, has certain features in common with Job, both formally and in respect of content. It takes the form of a dialogue, though without any narrative prologue or epilogue. There are just two participants, and no god is directly involved. The opening syllables of each stanza (there appear to be 27, each of 11 lines) taken in order reveal the name and occupation of the author, 'I am Saggil-kinam-ubbib the exorcist, a worshipper of god and king.'[20] These notes will make it clear that, in form at least, there is no close relationship between this text and Job, beyond the device of the dialogue.

Regarding the substance of the debate, we do find some interesting similarities; whether these constitute influence is doubtful, but they do suggest patterns of thinking about the subject which are ubiquitous. The sufferer begins by setting out his situation – orphaned at an early age, and with no one to protect him (I.10–11), to which his friend responds, 'He who looks to his god has a protector, the humble man who reveres his goddess will garner wealth' (II.10–11). The sufferer immediately counters by recording his woes: his 'assets have vanished . . . [his] energies have turned feeble, . . . moaning and woe have clouded [his] features' (III.6–8). Even alcohol offers no consolation. In the light of all this despair, he puts the question: 'Can a happy life be a certainty?' Subsequently, dissatisfied with the traditional proposal that if he attends to justice then he will experience kindness and mercy, the sufferer formulates a complaint which we might recognize from Job and some of the psalms: it is those who do nothing to merit it who experience the greatest blessing.

> The onager, the wild ass, that had its fill . . .
> Did it pay attention to . . . a god's intentions?
> The savage lion that devoured the choicest meat,
> Did it bring its offerings to appease a goddess's anger?
> The parvenu who multiplies his wealth,
> Did he weigh out precious gold to the mother goddess for a family?
> (V.4–9)

The appeal to nature has echoes in Job (especially ch. 39), though used somewhat differently there, where it is part of the argument that human beings cannot understand the ways of God. But the complaint that those who have not earned it prosper, while the righteous not only fail to prosper, but seem to be actively targeted, is familiar.

---

19 Hallo, I, pp. 492–5.

20 Hallo, I, p. 492. In ANET, pp. 438–40 the text is dated to later than 700 BC in respect of extant versions, with composition perhaps a century earlier.

There is no real development in the text. The sufferer continues to make points of a similar kind, while his friend counters with familiar arguments. The undeserving will suffer in due course (VI); we are not equipped to understand the ways of the gods ('The strategy of a god is as remote as innermost heaven, the command of a goddess cannot be drawn out' VIII.5–6 and 'Divine purpose is as remote as the innermost heaven, it is too difficult to understand' XXIV.3–4). But the conclusion seems weak in comparison with the *storm and fury* of Job's violent encounter with naked divinity in the thunderstorm, consisting of the somewhat bathetic

> May the god who has cast me off grant help,
> May the goddess who has forsaken me take pity,
> The shepherd Shamash[21] will pasture people as a god should.

2 Other Mesopotamian 'theodicies'

For some reason we have a number of discussions of the problem of suffering and divide justice including among the surviving Akkadian texts, and none from Egypt which explicitly treat this theme. Why this should be so – unless it is simply a consequence of the accident of survival – is not clear; it is also the case that the kind of instruction literature which is well represented in Egypt is rather scarce in Akkadian. There are collections of proverbs and instruction from Sumer, a millennium earlier, and there is the late Aramaic composition, *The Sayings of Ahikar*, which recent studies now place in Syria and will be considered in the next section. Other examples of Akkadian theodicy included in Hallo are the *Dialogue Between a Man and His God* (I, pp. 485–6) and *The Poem of the Righteous Sufferer* (I, pp. 486–92), and there is one Sumerian example, *Man and His God* (pp. 573–5).

Texts from Asia Minor

1 Some Hittite fables[22]

This interesting text is a bilingual composition in Hurrian translated into Hittite. It consists of a string of stories, many of them animal fables, followed by explanations. There is a considerable element of structure in the text. Each explanation is introduced by the phrase, 'It is not a . . . , but a human', and the passage to the next story in the sequence begins, 'Leave that story'. The animal stories include a deer (twice), a dog and rodent;

---

21 Shamash was the sun god.
22 Hallo, 'Excerpt from the Hurro-Hittite Bilingual Wisdom Text', I, pp. 216–17.

in addition we encounter a cup and a tower which criticise their maker. There are no close parallels in the Old Testament, though Isaiah 45.9 uses a similar device:

> Woe to you who strive with your Maker,
>   earthen vessels with the potter!
> Does the clay say to the one who fashions it, 'What are you making?'
>   or, 'Your work has no handles'?

We noted in Chapter 1 that there are a few fables in the Old Testament; they are, however, quite different in form and tone from those found in this Hittite text.

One of the fables reads very much like a version of the English proverb, 'The grass is always greener on the other side of the fence.' Here is the fable and its interpretation:

There is a deer. He grazes the pastures which lie beside the streams. He always casts his eyes upon the pastures which are on the other side, but he does not reach the pastures of the other side. He does not catch sight of them.

It is not a deer, but a human. A certain man whom his lord had made a district governor – although he was made governor of one district, he always cast his eyes upon a second district. Then the gods taught him a lesson, and he did not arrive at that first district, nor did he even catch sight of the second district.

If this teaches us anything, it is to warn us that proverbial sayings are indeed universal, and that the case for direct influence must always be qualified by the realization that humans come up with the same rather obvious truths quite spontaneously over and over again!

---

2 The Words of Ahikar[23]

The oldest manuscript of this collection is a fifth-century Aramaic text found at Elephantine;[24] and may have been composed in Syria around

---

23 ANET, pp. 427–30. Not included in Hallo.

24 Elephantine, an island in the Nile, was the location of a garrison of Jewish mercenaries in the employment of the Persian rulers of Egypt between around 525 and 400 BC. It produces a fascinating cache of documents, including some which shed light on Jewish religious beliefs and practices of the time. See Bezalel Porten, *Archives from Elephantine: the life of an ancient Jewish military colony* (Berkeley, CA, University of California Press, 1968) and B. Porten, with J. Joel

700 BC. It takes the form of a long collection of sayings set within a dramatic narrative in which the eponymous Ahikar is betrayed by his pupil and nephew Nadin.[25] McKane[26] provides a detailed description of the work, which is sometimes cited as a source of parallels with or originals of sayings in Proverbs. Certainly the existence of the Ahikar in a Jewish colony of the fifth century makes it more likely that it might have been physically available to the writers of Israelite wisdom, assuming they were working that late. A few possible parallels are given below; what is interesting is that even under conditions of maximum probability (i.e., literacy in Jerusalem, a scribal class at work, a text in an accessible language, and documentary evidence that the text in question circulated amongst Jews) there is little to show explicit dependence. When we compare these results with, for example, the irrefutable evidence that the Gospel writers knew each other's work, or the verbal dependence between Chronicles and Samuel/ Kings, it becomes very clear indeed that the hypothesis of international wisdom and schools in which documents from around the region were studied owes much more to the imagination and to European scholarly traditions than it does to any reality in Israel.[27]

(a) Traditional punishment

(Lines 80–83) Withhold not thy son from the rod, else thou wilt not be able to save him from wickedness. If I smite thee, my son, thou wilt not die, but if I leave thee to thine own heart thou wilt not live.

(23.13–14) Do not withhold discipline from your children; if you beat them with a rod, they will not die. If you beat them with the rod, you will save their lives from Sheol. (cf. 13.24; 22.15 and 29.15)

(b) Royal protocol

(The most important of the relevant Proverbs passages are 16.10–15; 20.2, 8, 26–28; 25.2–6; 28.15–16; and 29.12–14; the Ahikar material[28] is drawn from lines 100–8)

Farber et al., *The Elephantine papyri in English: three millennia of cross-cultural continuity and change* (Leiden, Brill, 1996).

25 Weeks, *Early Israelite Wisdom*, p. 189.

26 *Proverbs*, pp. 156–82.

27 In the following examples, I am indebted to Weeks, *Early Israelite Wisdom*, pp. 46–55 for the royal parallels.

28 The translation in ANET is somewhat archaic. I have revised it slightly, for example, by replacing 'thy' with 'your'.

Treat not lightly the word of a king: let it be healing for your flesh.
Soft is the utterance of a king; yet it is sharper and stronger than a
two-edged knife.
Look ahead: a hard look on the face of a king means 'Delay not!'

His wrath is swift as lightning: take heed that he display it not against your utterances and you perish before your time.

(20.2) The dread anger of a king is like the growling of a lion; anyone who provokes him to anger forfeits life itself.

The wrath of a king, if you are commanded, is a burning fire. Obey it at once. Let it not be kindled against you and cover [or *burn*] your hands.

(16.14) A king's wrath is a messenger of death, and whoever is wise will appease it.

Cover up the word of a king with the veil of the heart . . .

Soft is the tongue of a king, but it breaks a dragon's ribs; like a plague which is not seen . . .

(25.15) With patience a ruler may be persuaded, and a soft tongue can break bones.

A king is like the Merciful; his voice also is loud: who is there that can stand before him, except one with whom there is God?

(25.6–7) Do not put yourself forward in the king's presence or stand in the place of the great; for it is better to be told, 'Come up here', than to be put lower in the presence of a noble.

Beautiful is a king to behold like Shamash, and noble is his majesty to them that walk the earth.

(16.15) In the light of a king's face there is life, and his favour is like the clouds that bring the spring rain.

Whatever we may make of these proposed parallels, it is important to recognize that a major aspect of concern to the Israelite tradition is missing in Ahikar; namely the requirement that the king exercise justice, mercy and righteousness in respect of the poor and the oppressed – 16.10–13; 20.8, 26–28; 25.2–5; 29.14. Its counterpart – the dangers of a corrupt king – also appears in Proverbs but not in Ahikar: 28.15–16; 29.12.

(c) Other examples

(Line 111) I have lifted sand, and I have carried salt; but there is naught which is heavier than grief.

(27.3) A stone is heavy, and sand is weighty,
But a fool's provocation is heavier than both.

(Line 141) Reveal not your secrets before your friends, lest your name become despised of them.

(25.9–10) Argue your case with your neighbour directly,
and do not disclose another's secret;
or else someone who hears you will bring shame upon you,
and your ill repute will have no end.

(Line 188) Hunger makes bitterness sweet, and thirst sourness.

(27.7) The sated appetite spurns honey,
but to a ravenous appetite even the bitter is sweet.

Some points to think about

The range both geographically and chronologically of the texts offered for comparison is quite daunting, bearing in mind that from our analysis of the 'school tradition' in Chapter 2, the window of opportunity for cross-fertilization is rather small, certainly not beginning earlier than 700 BC. Do you feel that the evidence has been presented sufficiently clearly for you to understand the issues and to be confident of your own conclusions?

To get a more precise sense of what is at stake, look at 1 Chronicles 17 and compare it with 2 Samuel 7, on which the Chronicler probably depended. Now consider the proposed parallels given above between Amenemope and Proverbs, or Ahikar and Proverbs.

Much of wisdom, certainly as represented by lists of sayings and good advice in Proverbs 10 and following, seems to be little more than common sense. How might this affect our explanation of possible parallels across diverse societies?

Further reading

Crenshaw, James L. (1998) *Old Testament Wisdom: An Introduction* (Revised and Enlarged Edition), Louisville, KY, Westminster John Knox Press, pp. 205–26

Dell, Katharine (2000) *'Get Wisdom, Get Insight': An Introduction to Israel's Wisdom Literature*, London, Darton Longman & Todd, pp. 98–111

Hallo, William W. and K. Lawson Younger (eds.) (2003) *The Context of Scripture* (three volumes), Leiden, Brill

Heaton, E. W. (1994) *The School Tradition of the Old Testament*, Oxford, Clarendon Press, pp. 45–64

McKane, William (1970) *Proverbs: A New Approach* (Old Testament Library), London, SCM Press, pp. 51–208

Pritchard, James B. (1969) *Ancient Near Eastern Texts Relating to the Old Testament* (third edition with Supplement), Princeton, NJ, Princeton University Press

Weeks, Stuart (1994) *Early Israelite Wisdom*, Oxford, Oxford University Press, pp. 6–19, 162–89

PART 2

Wisdom in the Old Testament

4

Structures and Themes in Proverbs

Patterns of Proverbs as a whole

Editorial processes

It is a useful principle, where works of complex origin are concerned, to assume that the controlling mind (the 'author', if you like) is most clearly to be heard in the opening chapters. Matthew's Gospel, for example, presents us with the key ideas of the virgin birth and the son of God right at the beginning; John introduces us to the philosophical concept of the Logos. Genesis begins with the highly structured creation myths, and follows up with the Flood and the Tower of Babel. Isaiah's first chapter covers the major themes of the eighth-century prophet of that name, and Amos opens his book with two chapters that sum up both his message of warning to Israel and the sophisticated, mannered style in which that warning is couched.

This is true also of Proverbs, where we find an opening nine chapters that are strikingly better structured and more thematically coherent than most of the rest of the book. These chapters will form the focus of most of our study of the book of Proverbs; but first we shall look at the book as a whole, in particular the evidence within it of a gradual development from limited collections of sayings to the present 31 chapter volume.[1] This will enable us better to see how the opening section fits with the rest. It is as well to be open at this point, and confess that the hypothesis that Proverbs 1—9 constitutes a carefully constructed prolegomenon to the book as a whole is hard to prove conclusively, and should certainly not be accepted uncritically. Over years of teaching and thinking about this book, it is my considered conclusion that the hypothesis is sufficiently probable to serve as a useful working conclusion. Some of what I go on

---

1 It is rather a shame, given what we said in the last chapter about possible links with Amenemope, that Proverbs was not divided into 30 rather than 31 chapters. Of course, the chapter divisions have nothing to do with how the book was arranged in antiquity; nevertheless, a small adjustment could produce a pleasing symmetry!

to say may seem to endorse this claim, some might depend on its truth: let the reader beware.

Part of the argument derives from the appearance given by the book itself that a process of editing has taken place. Headings and sub-headings are provided at various points, and there are stylistic differences which might possibly be correlated with previously separate pieces. There is a series of hymns and poems in 1—9 which, together with 31.10–31, might form evidence of a controlling mind. If those who see a literary dependence between 22.17—23.11 and Amenemope are right, here is another passage which may once have had a separate existence. Unfortunately, it is almost impossible to distinguish between material which 'grew' – that is, was added to by various hands from time to time, and material which was 'redacted' – that is, combined from existing sources by an editor ('redactor').

The brief discussion of editorial activity which follows may seem at first to be remote from the study of wisdom that we have undertaken. However, it is important to be clear that both form and content have a bearing on the way we read these works. This will be apparent when we look at Job, where I shall argue that the meaning we draw from the book is directly affected by its structure, but it is not unimportant for Proverbs also. Not least, our study will suggest that though the book may appear at first sight to be a rather random collection of common-sense remarks, it takes off into a much more theological mode with the shaping given to it by the last 'editor' (whom I prefer to designate the author of Proverbs).

Four proper names are used to head certain sections of the book of Proverbs, which offer tantalizing possibilities of sources and authors. Sadly, none of them delivers on that initial promise; but as a start, you will find here summarized what can be said.

Solomon

David's son, king of Israel, renowned for his wisdom in the stories which surround him in 1 Kings.

Hezekiah

Son of Ahaz (the king with whom Isaiah crossed metaphorical swords in Isaiah 7). He ruled for 29 years (2 Kings 18.2), and was on the throne when the Assyrians destroyed Israel. Traditions about him are reported in 2 Kings 18.1—20.21. He is credited with having the water supply tunnel built from the Hinnom valley into the city (this is the tunnel which contains a famous inscription carved by its builders). He is well regarded in the tradition, being described as faithful and obedient to the commandments (2 Kings 18.5–6).

Agur son of Jakeh of Massa   Lemuel son of Massa

None of these names is recorded anywhere else in the Old Testament, and the country of Massa (itself an implausible name) is unidentifiable. Note that there is a cluster of strange words in 30.1 – it seems as if the point is to introduce an element of 'the mysterious other'.

Scattered through Proverbs there are seven introductory headings which appear to convey information about both the work of collection and the authorship of many of the sayings it contains. They are:

1 'The proverbs of Solomon son of David, king of Israel.'   1.1 (1.2—9.18)
2 'The proverbs of Solomon.'   10.1 (10.1—22.16)
3 'Incline your ear and hear the words of the wise.'[2]   22.17 (22.17—24.22)
4 'These also are sayings of the wise.'   24.23 (24.23—34)
5 'These are other proverbs of Solomon that the officials of King Hezekiah of Judah copied.'   25.1 (25.2—29.27)
6 'The words of Agur son of Jakeh. An oracle (or Of Massa).'   30.1 (30.1–33)
7 'The words of king Lemuel. An oracle that his mother taught him.'   31.1 (31.2–9)

To these we might add – though it lacks a separate title

8 (Untitled acrostic: 'the ideal woman')   (31.10–31)

We know that both Agur and Lemuel are unknown outside this book, though some traditions have it that they are both alternative names for Solomon. Though this would neatly dispose of a problem, there is no evidence anywhere else for such a claim. Solomon *does* have another name – Jedidiah – which he was given by Nathan (2 Sam. 12.25), but there is nothing mysterious about that. What we *can* say is that another wisdom book – Job – also uses strange, untraceable names, so that it looks as though there is a tradition of attributing wisdom to the unfamiliar (another aspect of the 'wisdom of the east' pattern we identified

---

2 The Greek version simply has the heading, 'The Words of the Wise'.

in Chapter 1). One other point: the reference to Lemuel's mother may be related to the themes of the final author of the book, which are detailed in Chapter Five.

Some of these introductory headings seem to suggest stages which it is tempting to correlate with known history. Solomon, of course, is a conventional figure: no chronological conclusions may be drawn from attributions of authorship to him. Likewise, the generalized references to 'the wise' do not take us very far, except to suggest the existence of a class of sages (whether an informal popular group or a part of the institutions of government we cannot tell). There is one heading, however, which is tantalizing: the 'officials of King Hezekiah'. Hezekiah reigned in Judah from about 715 to 687,[3] nicely within the period which Jamieson-Drake suggests could have seen the beginnings of official scribal activity.[4] The fact that Hezekiah is nowhere else associated with wisdom materials (and so is not named merely in a conventional way) could lead to the conclusion that some (if not the first) scribal activity devoted to the gathering of instruction literature for teaching or other purposes can be roughly dated to the end of the eighth century. Weeks,[5] however, is sceptical, and points out that other traditional forms are also attributed to Hezekiah – for example, the psalm of lament and intercession he is reported in Isaiah 37.9–20 as having written. It seems improbable that a king at this time, even if possessed of basic literacy, would have taken to writing psalms. There is just a suspicion in all of this that certain circles are trying to equate Hezekiah (who is one of the 'good' kings of Judah) with his illustrious ancestors David and Solomon.

We do not know whether the earlier long section (the Proverbs of Solomon in 10.1—22.16) represents something which had a written existence prior to Hezekiah, or whether it is an alternative 'book' collected at the same time. The precise wording of 25.1 ('these are *other* proverbs of Solomon') might suggest the latter. In short, it looks as though there is a decent case to be made for a collection of sayings and instruction having been put together not too long after Hezekiah's reign, perhaps towards the end of the seventh century BC, consisting in the main of chapters 10—29 of what we now call the book of Proverbs. The material attributed to Agur and Lemuel seems likely to have been added somewhat later (perhaps by an enthusiast for mysterious wisdom). If, on the other hand, the Hezekiah reference is a red herring, we can draw no conclusions from

---

3 The reader should be aware that all such dates are inaccurate. Other estimates suggest 725 to 697, or 715 to 697. At least there is agreement about the rough dating at the end of the eighth and the beginning of the seventh centuries.

4 See Chapter 2, pp. 42–4.

5 Weeks, *Early Israelite Wisdom*, pp. 41–6.

it as to date and editorial responsibility. The only other clue (and it comes with significant reservations) is the possibility that Ahikar had a direct influence at some stage, which would tend to push the dating into the sixth century or the post-exilic period.

Proverbs 1–9 and 31.10–31

Two passages have still to be considered: Chapters 1—9 at the beginning of the book, and 31.10–31 at the end. Even a superficial reading suggests that we have here something rather different from the central bulk of Proverbs. More specifically, we can list the evidence which suggests a distinctive role for these passages.

1 Structural evidence

(a) The opening ascription is careful to give Solomon's full title, 'The proverbs of Solomon, son of David, king of Israel' (see the similar ascription at the beginning of Ecclesiastes, 'The words of the Teacher, the son of David, king in Jerusalem').

(b) The first few verses (2–6) define the purpose of the book, and are characterized by a grammatical form using the infinitive at the start of each verse: 'to learn about wisdom . . . to gain instruction . . .'[6] etc., which suggests that these verses are designed to set out the programme of the book.

(c) A thematic motto follows immediately (v. 7, 'The fear of the Lord is the beginning of knowledge') and is repeated in slightly different words in the final chapter of the section (9.10): 'The fear of the Lord is the beginning of wisdom.'

(d) The final poem, in 31.10–31, has the form of an alphabetical acrostic.[7] There are numerous acrostics in the Hebrew Bible, some of the kind evidenced here – the most exaggerated being the notorious Psalm 119 which has 22 stanzas each of 8 verses in which all of the verses in a given stanza begin with the same letter of the alphabet. Others use numbers like 11 or 22 to pattern stretches of material without actually using the alphabet. The Hebrew of chapter 8 suggests just such a schematic process.

---

6 Verse 5 breaks ranks, forming a parenthesis which reads as though it is an aside intended for those in the know.

7 In Hebrew, 22 lines, each beginning with the appropriate letter of the Hebrew alphabet, in order.

An acrostic translated – the author's attempt to turn an acrostic psalm (111) into English, using at the beginning of each line an approximate equivalent to the relevant Hebrew letter. Whatever the virtues of the form in Hebrew, it is evident (at least from this translation) that it is extremely difficult to combine the formal structure with anything of poetic value!

1	('aleph)	Acknowledge the Lord I shall, with all my heart
	(beth)	Before the upright, in the congregation.
2	(gimel)	Great are the works of the Lord,
	(daleth)	Divined by all who take delight in them.
3	(hê)	Honour and majesty define his work,
	(waw)	While his righteousness endures forever.
4	(zayin)	Zealously his wonders we recall:
	(hêt)	Humane and merciful is the Lord,
5	(têt)	To those who fear him giving food;
	(yod)	Year after year we recall his covenant.
6	(kaph)	Keeping the power of his deeds before his people,
	(lamedh)	Lands of other nations he bestows upon them.
7	(mêm)	Mighty are God's deeds, but truthful too and merciful –
	(nun)	Not one of his precepts shall fail;
8	(samekh)	Sure and steadfast for ever –
	('ayin)	Ah, how truly and faithfully they are fulfilled.
9	(pê)	Providing redemption for his people,
	(tsadê)	It's all commanded by his covenant.
	(qoph)	Quintessence of holiness and awe is he!
10	(rêsh)	Right from the start, to fear the Lord is wisdom:
	(sîn)	Sense, good sense is theirs who practise it.
	(taw)	To the end of time we praise him!

Notes:

'aleph and 'ayin: these are guttural letters with no English equivalent. I have used open vowels to represent them.

hêt: sounds like 'ch' in loch.

qoph: pronounced in Hebrew like 'k'.

There is no obvious difference in Hebrew pronunciation between samekh and sîn (both 's') or between têt and taw (both 't').

2 *Thematic evidence*

(a) The theme of the motto – 'the *fear* of *Yahweh* is the *beginning* of *wisdom/knowledge*' – brings together four elements in a way which is almost unique to Proverbs 1—9.[8] The same phrase is found in Psalm 111.10, one of the later psalms, and the theme itself is picked up and elaborated in the second-century Sirach (1.14–20), but within Proverbs it is confined to 1—9, with further echoes in 4.7 and 8.22. It may also be significant that the ideal woman in chapter 31 is described as wise (v. 26 'She opens her mouth with wisdom') and as god-fearing (v. 30 'a woman who fears the Lord is to be praised').

(b) Proverbs 1—9 explores in many different ways the idea of woman as a metaphor for aspects of wisdom and folly. Half of chapter 1, the whole of chapters 7, 8 and 9, and parts of 3, 5 and 6 are devoted to this theme. In the light of this, it is significant that the whole of the acrostic poem in chapter 31 is devoted to the depiction of the ideal woman.

(c) The language used in these chapters deploys similar forms – sayings, antitheses, and imperative instructions – to those which dominate the central portion of the book, but makes more frequent use of the convention of the parent's plea to the child. There is only one section of the rest of the book (23.19–35) which makes use of this in any extended way. Significantly, the last addition prior to the hymn to the ideal woman is a brief passage in which King Lemuel records 'an oracle that his mother taught him'. The juxtaposition strongly suggests deliberation.

There is clearly much here to suggest a carefully contrived preface and afterword to the earlier instruction manual, whether compiled by Hezekiah's officials or later. The two pieces together form what is often described as an *inclusio* – that is, a form of literary 'bracketing' in which diverse material is given a certain shape and closure by the use of similar words, ideas or structure at its beginning and end. Such a contrivance is often evidence of a shaping mind at work – an author – and this is what we propose for Proverbs.

What is a *mashal*?

The Hebrew term *mashal* (plural *meshalim*) is the term translated 'Proverbs' in the title of the book. Before we move on to a closer study of Proverbs 1—9, we must look briefly at the meaning of this expression as used in the book. At first sight Proverbs appears to be a random collection of popular sayings; however, the collection is too large for this to be likely, and closer inspection shows that they are poetic in form, and liter-

---

8 See the earlier analysis of this theme in Chapter 1, 'The Hebrew Evidence' (F1).

ary in character, seeking for effect rather than memorability. Consider, for example, the carefully constructed chiastic parallelism of 25.11–12:

> A word fitly spoken
>   is like apples of gold in a setting of silver.
> Like a gold ring or an ornament of gold
>   is a wise rebuke to a listening ear.

Many of the sayings are scarcely part of everyday experience – for example 23.1–3 gives advice on how to eat in the presence of the king – and there are many signs that the material is primarily designed to display the erudition of the author and his (her?) familiarity with a wide range of subjects and sayings, regardless of their practical application. Other characteristic features are the use of the imperative mode of address and the formal 'father to son' convention.[9] A survey of the way that the root *mashal* is used in the Old Testament reveals a considerable diversity of use, suggesting that – in literary-critical terms – we are dealing with a technical expression more like the English 'figure of speech' than the more specific 'proverb'.[10] What follows is a survey of the range of interpretations given to this root in translation.

Mockery

There are half a dozen or so passages where the word seems to express contempt or mockery; given that the basic sense of the word is 'example', perhaps there is a development in these instances similar to that in English where 'to make an example of someone' is to expose them to criticism or ridicule. In several of these cases the threat of becoming 'an object of horror, a proverb and a byword (Deuteronomy 28.37) is associated with public humiliation 'among all the peoples' or 'among the nations'. Thus also 1 Kings 9.7 (= 2 Chronicles 7.20), Jeremiah 24.9, Job 17.6 and Psalm 44.14. Four instances (Ezek. 14.8; Micah 2.4; Hab. 2.6; Ps. 69.11) lack this explicit reference, and just once – in Isaiah 14.4 – the mockery is directed away from Israel: 'you will take up this taunt against the king of Babylon'.

---

9 We have mentioned this stylistic feature already; for a flavour of how it works, you are recommended to read quickly through Proverbs 1—9.

10 There is, in Hebrew, a completely separate meaning of the root *mashal*: to rule, to be a king/queen. It is best to regard this as a homonym, rather than attempt (as some have) to link 'to rule' with the other basic sense, 'to draw a comparison'.

Drawing a comparison

Indicating a comparison, with one exception (Isa. 46.5) always in a negative context, and most commonly to emphasize human mortality. Thus twice, in Psalms 28.1; 143.7: 'like those who go down to the Pit', in Psalm 49.12, 20: 'like beasts that perish', and in Job 30.19, 'like dust and ashes'. Isaiah 14.10 continues the taunt against Babylon referred to above, and has the shades in Sheol warning the king of Babylon, 'You have become as weak as we are! You have become like us!'

Designating various literary forms

We referred in Chapter 2 (pp. 32–5) to the difficulty of distinguishing specific figures of speech in a language like Classical Hebrew, belonging to a culture whose writers and speakers, however fluently they may have used rhetorical forms, seem not to have explicitly described them. By contrast, both Greek and Roman societies developed a sophisticated meta-language with which to analyse, describe and teach rhetoric. No doubt there were the rudiments of a classification system – there are several passages where different terms are found in sequence, implying (perhaps) different technical usage. The longest chain is in Proverbs 1.6, 'a proverb (*mashal*) and a figure (*melitsah*), the words of the wise (*hakhamim*) and their riddles (*hidah*)'. Psalm 49.3–4 has a somewhat more poetic turn of phrase:

> My mouth shall speak wisdom (*hokhmah*);
>> the meditation (*hagut*) of my heart shall be understanding
>> (*tebunah*)
> I will incline my ear to a proverb (*mashal*);
>> I will solve my riddle (*hidah*) to the music of the harp.

Psalm 78.2 is more succinct: 'I will open my mouth in a parable (*mashal*); I will utter dark sayings (*hidah*) from of old', and Ezekiel pairs the same terms, but uses the verbal form of *mashal* and so is translated as 'propound a riddle, and speak an allegory'. It has to be said that the English terms used here are influenced by the fable-like stories which follow, rather than reflecting any precision in the Hebrew.[11] *Mashal* by itself is associated with Solomon (1 Kings 4.32; Prov. 1.1; 10.1; 25.1) and Qoheleth (12.9) – it is of some interest that neither *hidah* nor *melitsah* finds any specific place in these Solomonic or quasi-Solomonic contexts.

Two other quite different uses seem to suggest that the term under

---

11 For this translation of the verb as 'to form an allegory' see also Ezek. 20.49 and 24.3.

consideration could refer to a longer tract of material. Job 27.1 and 29.1 use it to refer to his whole discourse (see also 13.12), suggesting an intriguing alternative to the usual title of the Book of Proverbs, such as 'The Sayings of King Solomon' (or even 'The Thoughts of Chairman Solomon', in memory of another dictator!). The other somewhat idiosyncratic use is in Numbers, in the story of Balaam (which itself includes a sort of fable in the tale of the talking donkey). Thus 23.7, 18 and 24.3, 15, 20, 21, 23 all refer to what would in other contexts be thought of as prophetic oracles. If we are correct in understanding *mashal* as having its primary locus in the world of wisdom, perhaps this suggests an extension into the soothsaying aspect of the prophetic vocation, hinting at the same connection as we saw in Isaiah 3.2–3 where the prophet laments the loss equally of the judge, the prophet, the diviner, the elder, the counsellor, the skilful magician and the expert enchanter.

Proverb in the English sense

What we have discovered thus far shows that in giving the title Proverbs (in English) to the collection as a whole we significantly misrepresent what it actually consists of. The *proverb*, properly speaking, is in English an essentially cryptic, single statement which avoids the use of comparison (simile and metaphor are largely absent) and often appears to state the obvious ('still waters run deep') while maintaining an openness to diverse application and meaning. Within the Hebrew Bible there are a few examples of this form signalled by the use of *mashal* – though none in the book of Proverbs itself – and some sayings of this type are introduced by other phrases. The complete list, with some New Testament examples, is given in the box below.

> 1 Samuel 10.12 'Is Saul also among the prophets?' (The same proverb is introduced in 1 Sam. 19.24 by the phrase 'therefore they say')
>
> 1 Samuel 24.11 'As the proverb of the ancients says, "Out of the wicked comes forth wickedness".' (There are interesting echoes here of Samson's riddle in Judg. 14.13–14)
>
> Ezekiel 12.22 'What is this proverb that you have about the land of Israel, saying, "The days grow long, and every vision comes to naught"?' (The continuation into v. 23 and beyond uses the proverb as the pretext for a word of judgement which reverses the point made by the proverb.)

Ezekiel 16.44 'Everyone who uses proverbs will use this proverb about you, "Like mother, like daughter".' (The introduction to this saying is intriguing – 'everyone who uses proverbs' – as though this refers not to general popular usage but to some specific class.)

Ezekiel 18.2–3 'The fathers have eaten sour grapes and the children's teeth are set on edge'. (The continuation into v. 3 and beyond uses the proverb as the pretext for a word of judgement which reverses the point made by the proverb. The parallel in Jeremiah 31.29 introduces the proverb with the phrase 'they shall no longer say': cf. the note to 1 Samuel 10.12.)

Genesis 10.9 'Therefore it is said, "Like Nimrod a mighty hunter before the Lord".' (The word *mashal* is not used here.)

1 Kings 20.11 'Tell him, "Let not him that girds on his armour boast himself as he that puts it off".' (The word *mashal* is not used here.)

New Testament examples

Luke 4.23 'Doubtless you will quote to me this proverb (*parabolē*), "Physician, heal yourself".'

2 Peter 2.22 'It has happened to them according to the true proverb (*paroimia*), "The dog turns back to its own vomit", and "The sow is washed only to wallow in the mud".' (*paroimia* is also used to refer to 'riddles' or 'dark sayings' in John 16.25, 29. Elsewhere *parabolē* refers to 'parables'.)

Proverbs 1—9: themes and structures

In a book which aims to present an overview of the subject of wisdom literature as a whole, it is not possible to give anything like a detailed commentary on or analysis of any of the individual books of which it consists. In the case of Proverbs, having said something in general about the structure of the book, I want now to confine the rest of my remarks to chapters 1—9, with some limited notes on 31.10–31. In the remainder of this chapter I shall examine some aspects of the structure and content of this section of Proverbs in order to gain a sense of the overall shape and character of the writing. However, one theme which is especially prominent – that of woman and wisdom – will be reserved for the next chapter, which will be entirely devoted to that subject. In what follows it is assumed that Chapters 1—9 form, with 31.10–31, the latest part of the whole book of Proverbs, and represent the thought-out views of an unknown (but not insignificant) author who understood the importance of knowledge as both a means to a right relationship with God and a discipline through which the individual would reach maturity.

Some comments on structure

The first verse of Proverbs 1—9 is, I assume, a title for the whole of the book of Proverbs as it was designed by the author largely responsible for these first nine chapters. There follow five verses whose purpose seems to be to provide an explanation of the nature and purpose of the subject matter of the study of wisdom (1.2–6). It is probably best to regard these also as belonging to the preface to the whole book. Thus the specifics of the chapters under immediate examine do not begin until 1.7, where we find the motto or *leitmotif* of Proverbs 1—9: 'The fear of the Lord is the beginning of knowledge.' We have said something about this above (p. 73) when we examined structure in Proverbs as a whole, and noted the *inclusio* with 9.10: 'The fear of the Lord is the beginning of wisdom.'

On the whole these nine chapters present a remarkably coherent and theologically refined position. The material is by no means pedantically structured, for there is a free-flowing character to it which would be quite in keeping, say, with the decision of the author to wind up his or her text not with the predictable 'good goddess *plus* motto' theme, but with the negative and sombre account in 9.13–18, thus displacing the second occurrence of the *leitmotif* from its expected position at the end of chapter 9. While many commentators have divided the text up into ten discourses and three 'hymns to wisdom', these are to some extent arbitrary, and certainly do not offer a neatly balanced textual structure. Nonetheless, this approach does serve to emphasize just how different these chapters are from the main bulk of proverbial wisdom. The pattern is as follows:

First discourse	1.8–19	
First hymn: 'Wisdom the Prophetess'		1.20–33
Second discourse	2.1–22	
Third discourse	3.1–12	
Second hymn: 'Wisdom Personified'		3.13–20
Fourth discourse	3.21–35	
Fifth discourse	4.1–9	
Sixth discourse	4.10–19	
Seventh discourse	4.20–27	

Eighth discourse	5.1–23	
[Editorial intrusion[12]		6.1–19]
Ninth discourse	6.20–45	
Tenth discourse	7.1–27	
Third hymn: 'Wisdom Deified'		8.1—9.6

It is obvious that the distribution of the 'hymns' is very uneven, so that claims that this represents a coherent structure must be regarded with caution. We shall not take up this framework further in our discussion, though others have used it as a basis for an analysis of the themes in the piece. I prefer to note the character of these chapters, but to adopt a different approach to their analysis.

Folly and immaturity

We consider first a group of words around the ideas of 'foolish' or 'scornful' on the one hand, and 'immature' (*pty*) on the other. The latter idea is essentially that of the simple, but teachable individual. All but four of its occurrences are in Proverbs, ten in Proverbs 1—9 and six elsewhere in the book.[13] The former group is more extensively used and represented, occurring in mainly in Proverbs and Ecclesiastes, with a scatter of isolated examples elsewhere. Words relating to foolish are distributed in equal proportions in these two books (51 in Proverbs and 19 in Ecclesiastes), but the mockery motif is confined to Proverbs (21 instances).

While the terms under discussion are deployed throughout Proverbs, there is a special intensity to their use in the first nine chapters. The table below identifies the distribution of these key terms across Proverbs as a whole, based on those passages which include the root *pty*. Shading is used to indicate places where the root for 'immature' is used together with terms for foolish or scornful. It may seem arbitrary to address these particular motifs, but they do reflect what comes across from a general reading of Proverbs 1—9: a clear emphasis on the practical utility of wisdom as a means both of showing up foolishness and of leading those who are willing to learn into right knowledge. With one exception, the terms we are looking at are all used in masculine gender – it seems that in ancient Israel only men were foolish (or, perhaps more realistically in the social context, only men were fit to be educated). The one exception

---

12 The material in 6.1–19 appears to break into a connected theme which originally ran from 5.19 directly to 6.22. There is some textual evidence to support this; and with the removal of the doubtful passage, the whole of chapters 5, 6 and 7 is devoted to reflections on the nature of woman and wise behaviour.

13 Ezekiel 45.20; Psalms 19.8, 116.6, 119.130; Proverbs 1.4, 22(2x), 32, 7.7, 8.5, 9.4, 6, 13, 16, 14.15, 18, 19.25, 21.11, 22.3, 27.12

is the reference to the Woman (called) Folly in 9.13, where it seems likely that a faux-goddess is conjured to contrast with the goddess Wisdom in 9.1. We will return to this motif in Chapter 5.

	Immature	Young	Foolish	Foolish	Scornful	Without sense
	pty	*nᶜr*	*ksl*	*'vl*	*lets*	*chsr-lb*
1.4, 7	✓	✓		✓		
1.22	✓✓		✓		✓	
1.32	✓		✓			
3.34–35			✓		✓	
5.23				✓		
6.32						✓
7.7	✓	✓				✓
7.22				✓		
8.5	✓		✓			
9.4, 6	✓✓					✓
9.7					✓	
9.8					✓	
9.12					✓	
9.13	✓		✓			
9.16	✓					✓
14.15–18	✓✓		✓	✓✓		
19.25	✓				✓	
21.11	✓				✓	
22.3	✓					
27.12	✓					

The difference between Proverbs 1—9 and the rest of the book in respect of this aspect is evident, in that where there are eight such links in the former, there are only three in the remaining 22 chapters. Of the these few, 19.25 and 21.11 express virtually the same sentiment, one which is echoed in the didactic passage which separates the two 'goddesses' in chapter 9 (see vv. 7–9). The remaining piece, in 14.15–18, is of some interested in that it is a short sustained sequence on the specific theme we are looking at; perhaps it inspired the more extensive treatment in chapters 1—9?

The importance of this association of ideas in our chosen text is that it *dramatizes* and *personalizes* what might otherwise be an abstraction: the value of learning. The addition of the poignant 'young man' to the concept of immaturity, and the introduction of four short stories, in each of which this character is put at risk or given a golden opportunity, enables the reader to enter into an imaginative empathy with the author's purpose. The *male* reader, that is; one of the most distancing things about this aspect of the wisdom discourse is the curious invisibility of women and girls, and we cannot avoid the sexism of the morals which follow.

These are the stories

In 1.20–33 Wisdom appears in person and is rejected alike by the simple, the mocking and the foolish – in turn, those who do not (yet) know any better, those who know better and choose scorn instead, and those who have long since settled into the fog of folly.

7.6–23 describes an encounter as old as story-telling itself: the seduction of the gullible by the temptress. Ensnared by his own ignorant mixture of pride and lust (notice how readily he falls for the blatantly improbable claims in v. 15), the young man is left in the end with the bitter taste of a lesson he'd rather not have learned!

There are two contrasting scenarios in chapter 9. In the first, vv. 1–6, Wisdom plays the role of a goddess who sends out her maidservants to attract worshippers. By contrast, Folly (vv. 13–18) uses a similar technique to lead the naïve to their doom. Both, in a sense, play a game, and it is the task of the teacher of wisdom to ensure that his (sic) young men learn the rules and do not (as in v.18) end up as guests of Sheol.

Incidentally, another pedagogical device is illustrated in Proverbs 1—9: the use of the negative threat as a prominent (if not predominant) mode. Like those teachers who believe that telling us we are the worst class they have ever taught is the best way to inspire us to greater efforts, the author of this book ends no fewer than seven of the nine chapters on a sour note (chapters 2, 3, 5, 6, 7, 8, 9), and three of the four stories above are also negative in character.

'Old wisdom' and the language of Yahweh

While the character of Proverbs is largely anonymous and quite general-ized – its language and themes have a universal, even bland character, and could presumably have been propounded as common sense in most societies of the period – there is, nevertheless, an infusion of language that is more appropriate to the religious discourse which is familiar from elsewhere in the Old Testament. McKane suggested many years ago that an older, universal tradition was adopted by and adapted for a more specific religious context, and suggested three types of saying: A – general instruction for the education of the individual; B – a similar content, but with a distinct community focus; C – material with a clearly religious or ethical content characteristic of Yahwism.[14] McKane was careful not to make strong claims for a chronological ordering, and his analysis was confined to chapters 10—22 and 25—29. There is, of course, a degree of subjectivity which must limit the usefulness of such an analysis. Do terms like 'the wicked', 'the good' and 'the upright', for example, belong to religious discourse or to the general appraisal of society which accompa-nies any realistic view of life? Does the mere mention of the proper name 'Yahweh' represent an appropriation of language for religious purposes, or is it simply the case that every society of the time would have addressed its god or gods?[15]

A brief examination of the Egyptian and Aramaic texts suggests that there is a general similarity between these and Proverbs, in that the gods are variously appealed to and good and bad types are compared. There is, however, an intensity of use of '*good* versus *bad*' and '*wicked* versus *righteous*' in Proverbs, which might testify to a particular world view, and there is nothing in the other literature to compare with the exten-sive use of 'Yahweh' (84 times). We might, incidentally, contrast this with Ecclesiastes, where the generic *elohim* is frequently employed, but Yahweh not at all (*elohim* is used only six times in Proverbs).

When we turn to Proverbs 1—9 we find a difference of emphasis which, though subtle, seems significant. Whereas the use of 'Yahwistic' language in the rest of the book is at the level of a widely dispersed sentence-pattern,[16] in 1—9 there are several tightly controlled passages

---

14 *Proverbs*, 1970, pp. 10–22.

15 Weeks in his *Early Israelite Wisdom* (1994, pp. 58–62) is sceptical about McKane's thesis.

16 The only verse which seems to contradict this assessment is 21.2–3, 'All deeds are right in the sight of the doer, But the Lord weighs the heart. To do jus-tice and righteousness is more acceptable to the Lord than sacrifice.' Given that this sentiment is also repeated in the prophetic literature (e.g. 1 Sam. 15.22; Isa. 1.12–17; Hos. 6.6; Amos 5.21–4; Micah 6.6–8) it begins to sound like a popular proverb.

which effect dynamic transformations without affecting the underlying mood of a universally applicable teaching. The table below provides a list of all the occurrences in Proverbs 1—9 of certain key terms (righteous/ ness, Yahweh, justice, fear, upright, law and teaching) which have a claim to religious significance, and highlights those passages where they produce this transformatory effect. The headings in the table give both the Hebrew root and the rough English equivalent. As a footnote, it is interesting to observe that, even if the language can be claimed to have some kind of Yahwistic thrust, it lacks all *national* specificity. Apart from the heading which refers to 'Solomon, son of David, king of Israel', there is no reference anywhere in the book to Israel, Judah or Jerusalem, and only one possible reference to what might be understood as a cultic context – in 3.9–10, the offering of the first fruits. Thus any understanding of Proverbs which gives it a specific Israelite context must be qualified – a point which will gain in significance when we reach the book of Sirach, in many respects very similar to Proverbs, but imbued with a highly specific national consciousness.

Proverbs	*tsdq* etc. righteous (ness)	*YHWH*	*shpt* justice	*yr'* fear	*yshr* up- right	*mitzvah* law	*torah* teaching
1	3	7, 29	3	3 7, 29	3		8
2	9, 20	5, 6	8, 9	5	7, 9, 13, 21	1	
3	33	5, 7, 9, 11, 12, 19, 26, 32, 33		7, 25	6, 32	1	1
4	18					4	2, 4, 11
5		21					
6		16				20, 23	13, 20, 23
7						1, 2	2
8	8, 15, 16, 18, 20	13, 22, 35	16, 20	13	6, 9		
9	19	10		10	15		

Two of the highlighted passages (1.7 and 9.10) refer to the *leitmotif* which we have referred to already on a number of occasions, and need no further discussion at this stage. We shall examine each of the other five briefly to identify their significance in their particular settings.

1 Proverbs 1.3

Proverbs 1.2–6, the introduction to the book as a whole, contains something like a thesaurus of wisdom terms (learning, wisdom, instruction, understanding, insight, wise dealing, shrewdness, knowledge, prudence, discerning, skill, proverb, figure, riddle). They belong firmly to the category of pragmatic and practical erudition, and some hint at the kind of low cunning or street smartness which has nothing to do with ethics and everything to do with survival in a harsh and competitive world – this is particularly true of the terms in v. 4 translated as 'shrewdness' and 'prudence'. The contrastive force of the single half verse, 3b, is therefore particularly strong. In the middle of this catalogue of cunning we encounter the trio 'righteousness, justice and equity' which exerts a hermeneutical force far greater than its numerical strength, coercing the reader into believing that she is encountering a noble and ethical statement – a belief then reinforced by the subsequent placing of the leitmotif 'the fear of the Lord is the beginning of knowledge' immediately after v. 6, in which the cryptic and technical language of proverbs, figures and riddles predominates.

2 Proverbs 1.29

We will return in Chapter 5 to the portrait of wisdom the prophetess in 1.20–33. For the moment we simply note that once again a passage which could function perfectly well in any or no religious context, as a powerful metaphor of the disastrous effects of ignorance, is given 'a local habitation and a name' by the insertion of the half verse 'because . . . they did not choose the fear of the Lord' which draws the reader simultaneously both to the twist in v. 3 and the motif in v. 7.

3 Proverbs 2.5–9

This passage represents a more extensive example of the phenomenon we have noticed in 1.3 and 29. Here too, in a chapter which is impeccably universal in tone, there is an insert which begins with 'the fear of the Lord' and concludes with the same trio as in 1.3 – 'righteousness, justice and equity' – and in between does something which is actually very rare in the wisdom tradition: attributes the gift of wisdom to God. Since by far the dominant message of Proverbs is that wisdom is there for the taking if we will but expend the requisite effort, this brief passage represents an important theological development. Later in the tradition, from Sirach onwards, the idea that wisdom is God-given comes to dominate, and arguably culminates in the Philonic and Johannine concept of the divine Logos who mediates on behalf of the aspiring soul.

4 Proverbs 3.5–7

This little pericope must be one of the best known in the whole of Proverbs, though perhaps for the wrong reason, bearing in mind the comment that the term 'heart' does not have the same metaphoric force in Hebrew as in English (see the box below). This passage is usually taken to be a plea for an emotional commitment to the Lord – a paradigm of Luther's primacy of devoted faith over intellectual acceptance. In truth, however, it is a plea for that dedication of the mind and the will to Yahweh without which wisdom cannot be found; it is, in other words, a form of the theme of Proverbs 1–9: 'The fear of Yahweh is the beginning of wisdom' – a point established clearly in the last line of v. 7, 'fear the Lord, and turn away from evil'.

5 Proverbs 3.32–4

At the end of a passage which employs a technical literary device – 'Do not . . .'[17] – to introduce a series of ethical injunctions of a general nature, we find a passage which turns the material around and fills it with the power of divine outrage. As well as the religious language which we are considering in this subsection, we meet here also one of the terms from 2.2.1 – the *scornful*.

On the terms 'heart', 'commandment', and 'teaching' in Proverbs

Chapter 3 of Proverbs introduces problems of translation and interpretation in respect of three technical terms which merit a separate comment.

The first of these is the word for 'heart' (Hebrew *lev, levav*) which is very common, but is also very commonly misunderstood.

It first appears in Proverbs 2.1, 10, and then in 3.1; but the difficulty it represents is most dramatically seen in traditional translations of 3.5, 'Trust in the Lord with all your heart.'

---

17 We shall encounter this again when we look at Sirach, in Chapter 10.

The key thing to realize is that in the conventions of Hebrew literature, the heart as an organ was understood to be the seat of the *mind*
or the *will* – and *not* of the emotions. Ancient Hebrews (and not without
cause, as anyone who has ever suffered nervous 'butterflies' will know)
associated the emotions with the region of the kidneys and the gut.
Not so romantic, perhaps, but accurate! Hence the literal translation
of *lev* into the English 'heart' leads to a fundamental misinterpretation.
What the metaphor refers to is the mind or the will, and so a much more
accurate reading would be something like 'Trust in the Lord with your
whole mind (or will)'. Trust – and this should not be a surprise in wisdom
literature – is a matter of the intellect.

A similar kind of difficulty surrounds the use of 'commandment'
(*mitzvah*) and 'teaching' (*torah*).

Within Judaism these are very specifically associated with the core
of the rabbinic tradition, representing the fundamental covenant between Israel and God. Thus any reader of Proverbs familiar with Judaism will instinctively interpreted these terms through the halakhic[18]
phrase *torah vemitzvot* ('Torah and Commandments'), and will imagine
themselves to be reading something akin to rabbinic literature. Thus a
later interpretive field is used to read literature which may well not have
been aware of these specific religious connotations.

Almost every occurrence of *torah* in 1–9 is in the context of *human*
teaching (1.8; 6.20 'your mother's torah', 3.1; 4.2; 7.2 'my (i.e. the
father's or the author's) teaching'). In 4.4, 11 the associated verb 'to
teach' is used. Similarly, *mitzvah* is associated with the father or author
(2.1; 3.1; 4.4; 6.20; 7.1,2).

The one exception is 6.23, 'For the commandment is a lamp and
the teaching a light' which is reminiscent of Psalm 119.105. In this
one instance it is just possible that we are coming closer to the later
rabbinic usage – but that is hardly capable of being read back into the
rest of Proverbs 1—9.[19]

---

18 The word 'halakhah' is used to indicate the individual and collective oral
legal traditions which make up Mishnah and Talmud.

19 There are fewer instances of these terms in the rest of Proverbs. Three of
mitzvah are all secular (10.8; 13.13; 19.16). Torah is used very generally in 13.14
and 28.2, 4, 9, and is attributed to the ideal woman in 31.26. There is just one
possible religiously significant instance, in 29.18: 'Where there is no prophecy,
the people cast off restraint, but happy are those who keep the law.'

Some points to think about

One of the main theses of this chapter has been that Proverbs 1—9 together with 31.10–31 are distinctly different from the rest of the book. Read these chapter through without a break, then read any two consecutive chapters from the rest of the book. Does the thesis still seem plausible?

Some scholars have argued that Proverbs 2 provides a kind of summary of all the themes covered in chapters 3—9. This might imply that the whole of chapter 1 is introductory. You might find it interesting to evaluate this proposal.

Does the information about the meaning of words like 'heart' etc. surprise you? Does it suggest a radical reassessment of your reading of certain familiar passages from the Old Testament (For example, Proverbs 3.5–7, Psalm 51.10)?

On p. 83 we set out some stories by means of which the author of Proverbs 1—9 dramatizes his or her teaching. Try to find at least three more such stories and think about how they make the writer's point more effectively.

Further reading

(Those marked with an asterisk are commentaries; you should find helpful information *either* in their general introductory sections *or* in chapters dealing with Proverbs 1—9.)

*Clifford, Richard J. (1999) *Proverbs: a commentary* (Old Testament Library), Louisville, KY, Westminster John Knox Press

*Fox, Michael V. (2000) *Proverbs 1—9: a new translation with introduction and commentary* (The Anchor Bible; vol. 18A), New York; London, Doubleday

Harris, Scott L. (1995) *Proverbs 1—9: a study of inner-biblical interpretation* (SBL Dissertation Series 15024), Atlanta, GA, Scholars Press

*McKane, William (1970) *Proverbs: A New Approach* (Old Testament Library), London, SCM Press

*Martin, James D. (1995) *Proverbs* (Old Testament Guides), Sheffield, Sheffield Academic Press

*Murphy, R. E. (1998) *Proverbs* (Word Biblical Commentary; vol. 22), Nashville, TN, Thomas Nelson

*Scott, R. B. Y. (1965) *Proverbs, Ecclesiastes: introduction, translation and notes* (The Anchor Bible; vol. 18), New York, Doubleday

*Toy, Crawford Howell, (1970 [1889]) *A critical and exegetical commentary on the book of Proverbs* (The International Critical Commentary), Edinburgh T. & T. Clark

*Waltke, Bruce K (2004) *The Book of Proverbs: Chapters 1–15*, Grand Rapids, MI, Eerdmans

Whybray, R. N. (1965) *Wisdom in Proverbs: the concept of wisdom in Proverbs 1–9* (Studies in Biblical Theology No. 45), London, SCM Press

*Whybray, R. N. (1972) *The Book of Proverbs* (The Cambridge Bible Commentary. New English Bible), London, Cambridge University Press

Whybray, R. N. (1994) *The Composition of the Book of Proverbs* (JSOT-Sup 168), Sheffield, JSOT Press

*Whybray, R. N. (1994) *Proverbs: based on the Revised Standard Version* (New Century Bible Commentary), London, Marshall Pickering; Grand Rapids, MI, Eerdmans

Whybray, R. N. (1995) *The Book of Proverbs: A survey of modern study* (History of Interpretation, Vol. 1), Leiden; New York, Brill

5

Wisdom and the Feminine in Proverbs

Wisdom and woman: the human dimension

There is a strong strand of misogyny in the Old Testament, which is hardly surprising given its cultural milieu. Women are regularly abused or sidelined (Sarah is excluded from the episode in Genesis 22 when Abraham proposes to sacrifice Isaac; Hosea's wife Gomer is taken up and cast aside arbitrarily, and is branded a prostitute; Hagar is banished defenceless into the desert with her infant son – the list goes on!). Legally women were possessions – for this reason a married woman who had an affair was guilty of adultery, but a married man who had sexual relations with an unmarried women was not: polygamy was permitted, polyandry was condemned.

The use of women as a source and epitome of wisdom is therefore somewhat surprising. It may reflect a deep ambiguity in the male psyche – the simultaneous fear and envy of the mother figure – or it may arise from a genuine recognition that social and legal norms are not the final word. Proverbs 1—9 and 31 displays this ambivalence strikingly. We meet women who are wise and women who would seduce the innocent from their pursuit of wisdom. We meet ideal wives and 'working girls'. We meet mothers, mistresses and home-makers in an indiscriminate hotchpotch of metaphor. And we encounter, on several occasions, quite earthy language (sometimes masked because of the sensibilities of prudish translators). Our task in this chapter is to try to tease out and clarify the different ways in which 'woman' is used to heighten the dramatic force of the text.

Examples of sexually explicit language in Proverbs 1—9

5.5 'Her *feet* go down to Death; her *steps* follow the path to Sheol.'
This is a problematic verse. The second verb ('follow the path') actually means 'to lay hold of'. 'Feet' is a well-known Hebrew euphemism for genitalia, and there is a similar euphemistic application of 'steps' in the closely related semitic language Ugaritic. It has been suggested that this verse is better understood as a graphic – almost lewd – description

---

of the strange woman offering her sexual favours to the gods of the underworld:

> She gives sexual favours to Death
> and seizes Sheol in her lust.

5.19 Older translations were more coy, but the more recent NRSV gets it right, in this description of the sexually desirable partner:

> May her breasts satisfy you at all times;
> may you be intoxicated always by her love.

7.10–13 Not much is concealed in this sequence describing a woman playing the part of a prostitute for cultic reasons. It may well be that v. 11 ('She is loud and wayward; her *feet* do not stay at home') contains a sexual allusion; and the preceding passage, in which the young man is seen wandering indiscreetly in her direction, includes a verse ('passing along the street near her corner, taking the road to her house') in which the expression 'taking the road' is semantically linked to the 'steps' of 5.5. The word is rare, so the pun may well have been noticeable to an informed Hebrew reader.

A problem of language

First, there is one cautionary linguistic note to be sounded. Various adjectives are used to describe (or damn!) the women whose role is to deflect the young man from the pursuit of true knowledge. These are *not* the same throughout Proverbs 1—9, but translators have fallen into the unforgivable habit of using the English meaning of just one of them and applying it to the woman whenever she appears. This is a serious dereliction, for it pre-empts the reader's own journey of discovery. The terms are *nokriyah*, which means 'foreign', *zarah*, which means 'strange' (or 'foreign') and *zonah*, which means 'a prostitute'. The first two are absolutely not synonymous with the third, nor is it appropriate, as in some versions, to translate either of them as 'adulteress'.[1] To make this clear, the table below provides a list with translations of all the verses in which these terms occur with reference to women. A comparison with the NRSV translation is provided; the reader might find it instructive to compare other standard English versions to get a sense of how pervasive this mistranslation is.

---

1 There is a Hebrew word for *adultery*. It is only used once in Proverbs 1—9, in 6.32 with reference to male behaviour. It is *never* used of the woman in this material. There is just one explicit reference to an adulteress, in 30.20.

Reference	Author's Translation	NRSV Translation	Terms Employed
2.16	You will be saved from the *strange* woman, from the *foreigner* with her smooth words.	You will be saved from the *loose* woman, from the *adulteress* with her smooth words.	zarah nokriyah
5.3	For the lips of a *strange* woman drip honey.	For the lips of a *loose* woman drip honey.	zarah
5.20	Why should you be intoxicated, my son, by a *strange* woman, and embrace the bosom of a *foreigner*?	Why should you be intoxicated, my son, by *another* woman, and embrace the bosom of an *adulteress*?	zarah nokriyah
6.24	To protect you from the evil woman, from the smooth tongue of the *foreigner*.	To protect you from the wife of another, from the smooth tongue of the *adulteress*.	nokriyah
6.26	A *prostitute*'s fee is only a loaf of bread.	A *prostitute*'s fee is only a loaf of bread.	zonah
7.5	That they may keep you from the *strange* woman, from the *foreigner* with her smooth words.	That they may keep you from the *loose* woman, from the *adulteress* with her smooth words.	zarah nokriyah
7.10	Then a woman comes towards him, decked out like a *prostitute*.	Then a woman comes towards him, decked out like a *prostitute*.	zonah

5.10	*Strangers* will take their fill of your wealth, and your labours will go to the house of an *alien*.	*Strangers* will take their fill of your wealth, and your labours will go to the house of an *alien*.	zar nokri
5.17	Let them be for yourself alone, and not for shar-ing with *strangers*.	Let them be for yourself alone, and not for sharing with *strangers*.	zar
6.1	My child, if you have given your pledge to your neighbour, if you have bound your-self to *another* . . .	My child, if you have given your pledge to your neighbour, if you have bound your-self to *another* . . .	zar
	[The adjectives are used in these three verses in their masculine form. It is most interesting that none of the translations suggests a sexual connotation in these cases!]		

One obvious conclusion to be drawn from this survey of language is that the woman whom the author of Proverbs fears, and warns his (*sic*) readers against is *strange, alien* or *foreign*. She is dangerous because she is an outsider, who hints, perhaps, at forbidden knowledge and alien wis-dom. There is undoubtedly also a sexual frisson to this danger, but what she presents is primarily the threat of the other – enhanced by the use of the language of sex which, in many cultures, has its own aura of risk, adventure and illicit pleasure.

Real women as role models

In Proverbs there are a number of passages which deal with 'real' women, using them in a diversity of metaphoric situations as well as appealing to their human nature in order to dramatize the didactic lessons the writer wishes to emphasize. They are 1.8, 2.16–19, 5.1–23, 6.20–35, 7 and 31.10–31. Along with them I shall briefly consider Psalm 128 and Genesis 2—3, in which we find perhaps stereotyped but also indicative presentations of women in domestic settings. The questions we shall put to these passages are:

What are the different roles that a woman is expected to play in this material?

What are their implications for the morality imputed to the women in question?

What do they tell us about the power or influence (or lack of it) of these women?

Is there any sense of a development of the metaphors and rhetoric as we go further into the texts?

We begin in 1.8 with a very simple model: 'Do not reject your mother's teaching.' To a modern ear this might suggest the setting of the school and the teaching profession, dominated as it is by women. And to a Jewish eye it speaks of the world of the rabbis, for the term for 'teaching' is *torah*. Both, of course, are anachronistic: no women taught in Israelite schools (even if such things existed – see Chapter 2), and at this stage the rabbinic Judaism of Torah and Talmud lies several centuries in the future. The immediate context is, obviously, 'your father's instruction' and the opening imperative, 'Hear, my child', which together imply a metaphor of the family in which both parents share in the business of inculcating sound common sense in the children. But even that might be to say too much, for the implication of equality of roles is not certain in a society where women were clearly second-class citizens. To assess the meaning of the language in this simple verse requires a balancing of the 'normal' position of women in Israelite society with the somewhat unusual inclusion of the mother here (and also in 4.3, 6.20 and 10.1), and the introduction to King Lemuel's teaching in 31.1, which is described as 'An oracle that his mother taught him'. On balance, we might be justified in seeing this pattern in Proverbs as going beyond the merely conventional, suggesting a more empowered role for the mother in the process of intellectual nurture. Obviously this particular role model is morally, if somewhat conventionally, positive.

In striking contrast to this benign, if somewhat anodyne, portrait, the next woman who appears is dangerous indeed – and also very powerful, at least in her ability to bring about the most disastrous of outcomes for her victims:

You will be saved from the [strange][2] woman,
from the [foreign woman] with her smooth words,

---

2 The three words in square brackets represent my choice of a more literal translation of the Hebrew – see the remarks above and the table on p. 93.

who forsakes the partner of her youth
  and forgets her sacred covenant;
for her [house] leads down to death;
  and her paths to the shades;
those who go to her never come back,
  nor do they regain the paths of life. 2.16–19

There are textual difficulties with this passage, particularly to do with the phrases 'partner of her youth' and 'her sacred covenant'; for the purposes of this discussion we will not enter into these, but simply confine our remarks to more general issues. The role model here is that of the *foreign seductress* whose lack of moral consistency imbues her with a combination of threat and dangerous attraction. She is probably being denounced as a married woman who is willing to betray her partner; what is interesting is that she herself seems to escape punishment, which is reserved in all its Dantean horror for those who succumb to her. Quite what is afoot is not wholly clear – it may be that the more extended scenario presented in chapter 7 should be understood in tandem with this brief account – but it is by no means a simple condemnation of those who break the seventh commandment. This is where the mistranslation by so many English versions (though not the King James) is also misleading, since it elides the element of foreignness, with its hint at practices devoted to other deities, in favour of a simplistic morality. Does power, then, only appear in the person of the woman who is to be feared and avoided? Let us turn to the next passage.

In chapter 5 we encounter first of all the 'strange' woman whose seeming seductiveness turns rapidly to the bitterness of wormwood and death (vv. 3–6). The author now elaborates further, by insisting that the consequences spread wider, into the community as a whole, with its resources being expropriated by strange and foreign *men* (vv. 7–14). Once again, the dangerous stranger in female form has remarkable powers to deliver on her declared agenda of the destruction of Israelite society through the moral undermining of its young men. But a new element now appears, in the form of the sexy wife: a message which says that it is not necessary to contrast the sexual attraction of the exotic with the dull routine of convention!

Let your fountain be blessed,
  and rejoice in the wife of your youth
  a lovely deer, a graceful doe.
May her breasts satisfy you at all times;
  may you be intoxicated always by her love.
Why should you be intoxicated, my son, by another woman
  and embrace the bosom of a [foreign woman]. 5.18–20

Note in the phrase 'wife of your youth' an echo of 2.17; it may not be far-fetched to read this passage as a deliberate response to the foreigner in chapter 2, as if the Israelite author is engaged in a version of 'anything you can do, we can do better'! More seriously, if seductiveness is a kind of power, then we now see its force being applied to the good, where previously it was exclusive to the forces of immorality. Chapter 5, in other words, extends the power and influence of both sorts of women in the battle for the hearts and minds of the young men of Israel.

In chapter 6 there is a passage which takes up the idea of a mother's teaching again (6.20), emphasizing that 'she' will keep the learner company at all times (v. 22).[3] If this is a viable interpretation it paints a charming picture, if one all too familiar from the literature of mothers and sons! But the narrative soon darkens, as we encounter warnings against a mysterious 'evil woman' (v. 24) who threatens a mans' very life. The disturbing contrast is with the prostitute, who 'only' charges the price of a loaf of bread; again the metaphor is at once effective and reprehensible. By v. 29 the agenda is clearer: the threat is adultery, destructive of both reputation and life itself. Whether the author is still using these images as metaphors for the pursuit of wisdom is doubtful. What appears to be the case at this point is that the perhaps limited morality of the times is presented as the content of wisdom.

Chapter 7, on the other hand, is allegorical in nature. Though it opens with a straightforward homily on obedience (vv. 1–3) which defines the theme, the reference to wisdom as 'sister' (v. 4) indicates that we have entered a metaphoric field in which female personification is important, and the mysterious figure at the window who observes what is to happen (v. 6) further alerts us to the layers of meaning in this text. The whole of this chapter is rich in allusions, and is both sexually and esoterically suggestive. Commentators find references, for example, to Egypt in the trappings of the seductress's boudoir (vv. 16–17), to Canaan in the image of the woman looking through the lattice (v. 6, cf. Judg. 5.28), and to Mesopotamia in the implied importance of the moon to the woman's ritual and her husband's journey (vv. 14, 19–20). I cannot offer a detailed account of this fascinating chapter here; it must suffice for our purposes to observe (a) that the woman 'decked out like a prostitute' represents the fatal charms of alien wisdom, (b) that the woman at the window may well be a representation of the Israelite 'goddess' of wisdom, and (c) that the boldness of the allegory in its use of sexuality ought to remind us that the true woman, the 'sister' of v. 4, might be better construed as a lover (the Hebrew term here translated 'sister' is used in the Song of Songs for

---

3 Many translations amend this verse to make it refer to the 'commandment' and 'teaching' of v. 20; others have suggested that it originally accompanied 5.19 and concluded the description of the loving wife.

the bride). Incidentally, the mistranslation in v. 5 is particularly unfortunate in this case. It is particularly important that the woman is strange and foreign, as many elements of the allegory make clear; for it is the lure of both foreign knowledge and unfamiliar religious rites that constitutes the meaning of the allegory.

The juxtaposition of this chapter with the preceding one reopens the matter of the way we should read chapter 6. If, as some scholars have claimed, the first part of that chapter is a later intrusion – and certainly it is strikingly different in form[4] from the material which surrounds it – then we have in the sequence of chapters 5—7 a series of extended metaphors of the dangers and attractions of both the 'right' and the 'wrong' kind of woman embedded in a string of teachings about the need to learn and absorb the purest forms of wisdom. As we shall see shortly, this material is sandwiched between even more radical presentations of wisdom herself in what seems to be quasi-divine form.

One further woman deserves our attention, though she is outside the direct context of chapters one to nine. I refer to the 'ideal woman' of 31.10–31, a passage which we have already proposed as forming an *inclusio*, with the opening nine chapters, for the whole of Proverbs. Once again it is necessary to begin with a quibble about translation, relating to the writer's likely meaning in 31.10. NRSV has 'A capable wife who can find?' The King James version reads, 'Who can find a virtuous woman?', and most translations offer something similar, such as 'good' or 'of noble character'. Now the word in question is an adjective which, when applied to men, is regularly translated as 'powerful' or 'mighty' or 'warrior-like' or 'wealthy'. It seems reasonable, therefore, to describe her as 'strong' or 'powerful', and in the light of that opening epithet to rethink the description that follows.

Undoubtedly we find many of the virtues and skills which earlier societies would have traditionally seen as the possession of women. Thus v. 13 'She seeks wool and flax, and works with willing hands', v. 15 'She rises while it is still night and provides food for her household and tasks for her servant-girls', v. 19, 'She puts her hands to the distaff, and her hands hold the spindle', and so on. But this is only a small part of the portrait which is drawn. In vv. 14, 16, 18 and 24 there is clear evidence that she has an entrepreneurial role in the economy of the household; her strength (vv. 17, 25) is described in terms elsewhere used of God; her whole family benefits from her powers (vv. 23, 28); she gives alms to the poor (v. 20); she 'laughs at the time to come' (v. 25, compare wisdom herself in 1.26); 'her works praise her in the city gates (v. 31) – surely an indication of pub-

---

4 There are specific linguistic grounds for this proposal, which reinforce the more general stylistic point; these go beyond the scope of this book. Interested readers can look them up in the more technical commentaries.

lic standing; and – the final touch – she is 'a woman who fears the Lord' (v. 30) and who 'opens her mouth with wisdom' (v. 26). This is no mild housewife traditionally described: this is wisdom herself condescending to live with those (her husband and children) who are manifestly her inferiors. A powerful description indeed.

Wisdom and woman: the 'divine' aspect

We come at last to the culmination of our investigation of the wisdom of Proverbs: seven passages in Proverbs 1—9 which to a greater or lesser degree demand that we invoke the idea of the goddess, in various forms, to explain what is going on. This is at first sight strange territory for those whose experience is from within either of the Jewish or the Christian thought worlds. These traditions, as they were definitively shaped in the first centuries of the Christian Era, have taught us to remove all notions of a goddess from our theology, and all hints of any plurality of the divine. But the world in which both of these religions are rooted was a world replete with powerful, sexy and respected goddesses who attracted widespread affection and dedication along with fearful obedience. It is not so surprising, then, that the world of Aphrodite and Diana, of Isis and Ma'at, of Asherah and Ishtar, of Hera and Athena, should have given rise to at least the possibility of a Jewish goddess. Our argument (which will be reinforced when we read Sirach) is that Wisdom was at one time set fair to be that goddess (in partnership with Yahweh, and sharing aspects of her colleagues Ma'at in Egypt and Isis in the Hellenistic world).

Rather than try to formulate a comprehensive portrait, we shall look at the individual passages concerned to see what each has to offer, pairing those which cover similar themes; the concluding exercise will then seek to evaluate what has been uncovered. Even so, what we do now should not be regarded as the end of the matter, for we shall have cause to return to this topic when we encounter the wisdom literature of the second century BC, where the influence of the Hellenistic goddess Isis is stronger, and where elements of Stoic philosophy have a strong bearing. In Proverbs, by contrast, the primary models seem rather to be the Egyptian goddess of wisdom, Ma'at, and the Ugaritic goddess Asherah, consort of El.[5]

---

5 El was the chief god of the Ugaritic pantheon; the name is used in Hebrew literature as one of the titles of the Israelite god.

The scornful prophetess (1.20–31)

In Hebrew literature generally the prophetic books presuppose a public performance in which crowds of people are harangued by charismatic individuals claiming to speak oracles of God on behalf of God. These are characterized by the use of rhetorical questions, accusations of failure and dereliction of duty, threats and warnings about impending disaster, and hopes for the future (both positive and negative). Technical forms like the language of the law court, woe oracles and funeral dirges are often employed to rhetorical effect. The personality of the prophet often forms part of the story – the self-pitying Jeremiah, the professional Ezekiel, the disingenuous Amos – and prophets occasionally resort to a kind of street-theatre in which they act out parables intended to dramatize their message.

In the passage under consideration Wisdom takes on the persona of the prophet. She harangues passers-by in the most public part of town ('Wisdom cries out in the street; in the squares she raises her voice' vv. 20f) and is not shy about raising her voice above the din.[6] She asks impossible questions ('How long, O simple ones, will you love being simple? How long will scoffers delight in their scoffing and fools hate knowledge' v. 22) which, in the manner of the prophets, are designed to force the hearer to realize their predicament. She lays a charge against her victims ('Because I have called and you refused, have stretched out my hand and no one heeded, and because you have ignored all my counsel and would have none of my reproof' vv. 24–5) which sounds very much like the opening speech of the prosecution, and follows it up with a series of threats and warnings ('I will laugh at your calamity'; 'panic [will strike] you like a storm . . . distress and anguish [will] come upon you'; 'they will call upon me, but I will not answer'; 'therefore they shall eat the fruit of their way and be sated by their own devices' vv. 26–31) which include both an element of mockery and a chilling promise that when disaster strikes – as it surely will – they will find themselves utterly alone.

But she is no ordinary prophet, for there are elements missing and an added dimension which conspires to construct a persona of considerably greater authority than that available to the traditional prophet. There is, first, no sign of the introductory 'Thus says the Lord' or 'An oracle of the Lord' which we find throughout the prophets. Wisdom speaks (it seems) on her own behalf, nowhere more strikingly than in v. 23, where she seems to speak as though she were God – or at least, as though she were an independent agent not in need of the approval of God:

---

6 This scenario recurs in 8.1–3, but Wisdom does not there continue in the same vein.

Give heed to my reproof;
I will pour out my thoughts to you;
   I will make my words known to you.

The second twist in the prophetic tale/tail is that Wisdom's revenge takes the form of mockery. She both takes it upon herself to deliver the punishment, and moreover does so in terms elsewhere exclusively the prerogative of God. Verse 26 ('I also will *laugh* at your calamity; I will *mock* when panic strikes you') involves two verbs which are only paralleled in two other places – Psalm 2.4 and 59.8 – and in both of these instances it is God who laughs at and mocks the sinner. Finally, though traditional types of disaster will befall the sinner (v. 27) it is a consequence not so much of the kind of ethical misbehaviour condemned by the prophets (typically, being cruel to widows, orphans and the poor) as a failure to consult the right sources and attend to the true fount of knowledge. Certainly, the 'fear of the Lord' is part of it; but there is no doubt that Wisdom in this passage acts very much on her own behalf.

Practical wisdom: The Ma'at model (3.13–18; 8.1–21)

In these passages Wisdom is presented as a sedate, orderly female[7] figure who is the source of all worldly success and wealth. Superior to mere gold and silver and jewels, she nonetheless promises the good things of life to those who seek her. In particular (8.15f) it is she who gives kings and princes the insight they need to rule wisely (Solomon's prayer for wisdom in 1 Kings 3.5–9 comes to mind here). There is much in this portrayal which is reminiscent of the Egyptian deity Ma'at (whose name means 'truth') who personified the fundamental order of the universe and who guaranteed the regular cycles of the natural world and the proper reward for purity and punishment for sin. An interesting passage from the *Instruction of Ptah-Hotep* (text from the Middle Kingdom, twenty first to eighteenth centuries BC) praises *ma'at* in similar terms:

> If you are a leader and give command to the multitude, strive after every excellence, until there be no fault in your nature. Truth (*ma'at*) is good and its worth is lasting, and it has not been disturbed since the day of its creator, whereas he who transgresses its ordinances is punished. It lies as a right path in front of him who knows nothing. Wrongdoing has never yet brought its venture to port. Evil may indeed

---

7 The reminder that Wisdom is a woman is not redundant. Certain older translations are prone to quietly hide the fact by rendering the pronouns in v. 14 by the use of the neuter form 'its', though the Hebrew is undoubtedly 'her'.

win wealth, but the strength of truth is that it endures, and the upright man says: 'It is the property of my father.'[8]

Explicit iconographic connections with 3.16 have been identified, in that there are representations of Ma'at which show her with symbols of long life, honour and wealth in her hands. There is little doubt that Egyptian materials had some part to play in the shaping of Proverbs as a whole, so that some kind of general awareness of a figure such as Ma'at in post-exilic Jerusalem is not improbable. This is not to imply that any representations of Wisdom existed in Israel, though it is not impossible – there is indisputable evidence for the use of fertility figurines within the period of the Judaean monarchy, and the fifth-century Jewish military community at Elephantine in Egypt worshipped 'Anat-Yahu' (Yahweh's consort). The figurines are almost certainly images of the Asherah who is referred to in inscriptions of the form 'Yahweh and his Asherah'.[9] While there is not (as far as I am aware) any representation that could be identified as Wisdom, there is no doubt that the Jews of that time were both familiar and comfortable with such iconic usage, and would not have been likely to have been disturbed by the idea of a goddess Wisdom. In Ugaritic myths Asherah is referred to as 'She who treads on the sea' (or the day – a similar word), and this might reasonably indicate an active role in creation. This possibility is reinforced by another of her titles, 'She who gives birth to the gods'. She is also paired frequently with El; most scholars interpret this pairing as that of husband and wife. These aspects of the goddess will have a bearing on our account in the next section of Wisdom in creation.

Wisdom and creation (3.19–20; 8.22–31)

Both the brief account in chapter 3 and the extended one in chapter 8 imply (in different ways) a similar conclusion: that Wisdom is in some manner the agent of creation. 3.19–20 uses three synonyms: wisdom, understanding, and knowledge, each of which is stated to be the means by which Yahweh brought into being different aspects of the created order (respectively, the earth, the heavens and the deeps – that is, the waters which the ancients believed to be beneath the solid earth). Chapter 8 is

8 Joseph Kaster, *The Wisdom of Ancient Egypt* (New York, Barnes & Noble, 1993 [1968]), p. 167.

9 Two recent studies have addressed the matter of Asherah in detail. Tilde Binger, *Asherah: Goddesses in Ugarit, Israel and the Old Testament* (Sheffield Academic Press, 1997) and Judith M. Hadley, *The Cult of Asherah in Ancient Israel and Judah* (Cambridge University Press, 2000). Both are highly technical.

more indirect, presenting Wisdom as Yahweh's first creation – or first-born or first acquisition, or wife: the verb is ambiguous[10] – and recording her presence while he carries out the work of creation, which is given in considerable detail. Wisdom's role in this fascinating and puzzling passage seems to be that of celebrant, rejoicing both in what Yahweh does and in the human race which is the summation of that creation ('I was beside him like a master worker; and I was daily his delight, rejoicing before him always, rejoicing in his inhabited world and delighting in the human race' vv. 30–1).

There are mysteries here. Is Wisdom God's consort, or daughter, or simply a cosmic skilled worker? Along with the uncertainty surrounding v. 22, there is further ambiguity in v. 30. The word translated as 'master worker' might also mean 'child' or 'one who is in a close, trusting relationship' – these alternatives clearly match the choices we are offered in v. 22. Finally, just to throw yet another spanner in the hermeneutical works, the verb translated 'rejoicing' is the same as that used in 1.26 to describe Wisdom's mocking laughter.[11] Whatever we make of this passage, it poses more questions than it answers, and opens the way to further speculation about the precise relationship between Wisdom and Yahweh.

Good goddess – bad goddess (9.1–6, 13–18)

Proverbs 1—9 reaches its climax in the presentation of the rival claims of two women to whom we must surely accord the title of Goddess. One is Wisdom, the other Folly. One is good, the other bad. One offers legitimate rewards, the other stolen goods. One offers life, the other nothing but death – the grim picture of a perpetual feast in Sheol. The last verse is surely worthy of Bosch or Faust or Grand Guignol, and must stand as one of the most chilling conclusions to any literary work:

> They do not know that the shades are there,
>   that her guests are in the depths of Sheol.

The two portraits are rich in the kind of allusive writing which is often found in biblical Hebrew, and they add considerably to the effect. In what follows now I have attempted, perhaps somewhat pedantically, and at the risk of diminishing their effect, to compare the two characters and to show what lies beneath the surface of the text. The first comparison is simply to set out alongside each other the parallel accounts in Proverbs 9.1–6 and 13–18. It is, I think, clear from this juxtaposition that the two

---

10 The verb *qanah* can mean 'to create' (Gen. 14.19, 22), 'to acquire' (Gen. 25.10), 'to give birth' (Gen. 4.1), or 'to acquire a wife' (Ruth 4.10).

11 And is also closely related to a cognate verb which has, among its meanings, 'to engage in sexual foreplay'.

are meant to be read in contrast, and this fact persuades me further that the 'foolish woman' of v. 13 ought to be on the same level as 'Wisdom' in v. 1; that is, they are each (for purposes of the metaphor) some sort of supernatural being. The version used is my standard reference point, the NRSV.

Following that simple pairing I have set out an annotated comparison using my own translation which is intended to highlight the 'goddess' aspects of the portraits. The notes attached to this second arrangement should help the reader to follow in some detail the arguments that lie behind the claim that in Proverbs 9, as a culmination of the extended use of both human and supernatural female figures, we are invited (that is, the original 'untutored' readers) to attend the nourishing banquet offered by the goddess Wisdom and to eschew – at the risk of our very lives – the false and empty promises made by Folly.

Comparing the 'goddesses' – NRSV

1. Wisdom has built her house, she has hewn her seven pillars.	13. The foolish woman is loud; she is ignorant and knows nothing.
2. She has slaughtered her animals, she has mixed her wine, she has also set her table.	14. She sits at the door of her house, on a seat at the high places of the town,
3. She has sent out her servant- girls, she calls from the highest places in the town,	15. calling to those who pass by, who are going straight on their way,
4. 'You that are simple, turn in here!' To those without sense she says,	16. 'You who are simple, turn in here!' And to those without sense she says,
5. 'Come, eat of my bread and drink the wine I have mixed.	17. 'Stolen water is sweet and bread eaten in secret is pleasant.'
6. Lay aside immaturity, and live, and walk in the way of insight.'	18. But they do not know that the dead are there, that her guests are in the depths of Sheol.

Comparing the 'goddesses' – New translation and notes

1. Wisdom has built her *Temple* she has carved out her *seven pillars*.	Wisdom's *temple* is matched by Folly's, in v. 14 The word for *naivety* is from the same root as *simple* (vv. 4, 16) and *immaturity* (v. 6)	13. [The woman] Folly is *brash*; Naivety knows nothing.
2. She has *slaughtered the sacrificial beast*, she has *mixed her wine*, her table is well prepared!	The *sacrificial beast* becomes *bread* in v. 5, and matches Folly's *hidden bread* (v. 17). The *mixed wine* is repeated in v. 5, and matches Folly's *stolen water* (v. 17).	(*Note that Folly does nothing, makes no preparations.*)
3. She has sent forth her *acolytes* while she herself *cries out* from a vantage point *high above the town*,	Note that both 'goddesses' *cry out* and sit *high above the town*. The use of *throne* in v. 14 is significant.	14. But she sits at the entrance to her *Temple* on a *throne high above the town* 15. to *cry out* to passers by – people intent upon their *business*.
4. 'You who are simple, turn in here!' To those who lack sense she speaks:	Identical verses.	16. 'You who are simple, turn in here!' To those who lack sense she speaks:
5. 'Come, eat of my bread and drink the *wine I have mixed*.		17. 'Stolen water is sweet and hidden bread tastes better.'
6. *Abandon* immaturity and live, and go *forward* with understanding.'	The Hebrew for 'build' (v. 1) and 'understanding' are similar. There may be a deliberate pun.	18. But they do not know that the shades are there: it is in the depths of Sheol that her guests find themselves.

Notes

vv. 1, 14	Both Wisdom and Folly have a *bayit* which in Hebrew means a whole range of things – house, palace, temple, family, dynasty. The translation 'temple' or 'palace' seems better here than the simple 'house'.
v. 1	No one knows what the 'seven pillars' refers to. There is no archaeological evidence to help, though undoubtedly 'seven' is one of those mystical, complete numbers. T. E. Lawrence (of Arabia) made the phrase famous in his book.
v. 2	The Hebrew here uses the same verb and noun (literally, 'to sacrifice a sacrifice'). This is a common stylistic device in Hebrew, but this particular one only occurs once again, in Genesis 43.16 where Joseph prepares a joyful feast for Benjamin. The word 'slaughter/sacrifice' is also used in Prov. 7.22, where it has a sinister reference to the fate of those who fall prey to the predatory woman. The phrase clearly has a ritual significance.
v. 2	Mixing wine may well have been a religious practice, though the actual phrase is only found in one other place, Isaiah 65.11, where it refers to a feast for the non-gods of Fortune and Destiny – a concept which has some links with the false feast offered by Folly.
v. 3	Literally, 'young women'. The word is often used in plural to refer to the maidservants of various people (Pharaoh's daughter in Ex. 2.5; Abigail in 1 Sam. 25.42; Boaz in Ruth 2.8; Ahasuerus in Esther 2; Esther herself in Esther 4.16; general household servants in Prov. 27.27). It may be of some significance that most of these refer to female servants of people of high status. One reference – Amos 2.7 – appears to indicate cultic prostitution.
vv. 3, 14, 15	Compare the language used of Wisdom as she calls out to people from the high places in 1.21a and 8.2–4, where she adopts a prophetic role.
v. 6	The verb 'to abandon' is often used of Israel's tendency to abandon Yahweh and follow false gods. Elsewhere in Proverbs 1—9 it is used negatively (2.13, 17; 3.3; 4.2, 6). There may be ironic force in its use here to refer to abandoning immaturity.
v. 6	'Go forward'. There is a double word-play here. First, the verb used is almost identical to the phrase 'blessed are', suggesting a blessing on those who make understanding their companion. It is also similar to the verb 'to go straight'

which we is used elsewhere in Proverbs, and which is used in the phrase 'people intent upon their business' – literally, 'those who go straight ahead on their way' – v. 15.

v. 13   The word 'brash' is the same word as one used to describe the woman in 7.11.

v. 14   The word used here almost always refers to the king's throne or God's throne, and is always used with that meaning elsewhere in Proverbs. It seems perverse not to accept that sense in this passage.

Some points to think about

'Though Proverbs 1—9 makes much use of women and feminine imagery, the cultural context is largely misogynistic.' Is this assessment valid, and in any case how does it affect our use of these texts in contemporary discussion?

Do you agree with the author's claim that most of the standard English translations are seriously misleading at certain points, particularly with regard to the language of the 'strange woman'?

How persuasive is the case made for some kind of concept of a wisdom goddess in Proverbs? How does this fit with the traditional understanding of Jewish religion as monotheistic and of Yahweh as 'the only god' (compare Deut. 6.4)?

Further reading

Berrigan, Daniel (2001) *Wisdom: the Feminine Face of God*. Franklin, WI, Sheed & Ward

Brenner, Athalya (ed.) (1995) *A Feminist Companion to Wisdom Literature* (The Feminist Companion to the Bible, 9), Sheffield: Sheffield Academic Press

Brenner, Athalya and Carole R. Fontaine (eds.) (1998) *Wisdom and Psalms* (The Feminist Companion to the Bible. Second series, 2), Sheffield, Sheffield Academic Press

Camp, Claudia V. (1985) *Wisdom and the Feminine in the Book of Proverbs*, Decatur, GA, Almond Press

Camp, Claudia V. (2000) *Wise, Strange and Holy: the strange woman and the making of the Bible*, Sheffield, Sheffield Academic Press

Lang, Bernhard (1986) *Wisdom and the Book of Proverbs: a Hebrew goddess redefined*, New York, Pilgrim Press

6

Theodicy and the Themes in Job

What is Job about? Theodicy and other difficult questions

The problem of suffering

Of all the 'big questions' that confront most of us, however unconcerned we may affect to be, that of the existence and randomness of evil and suffering is arguably the most daunting. It resists satisfactory resolution: believers, agnostics and atheists seem equally bereft of anything other than platitudes or blank resignation. We all cry, 'Why me?' just as we know in our hearts that the honest reply is: 'Why not?' So the presence in the Old Testament of a book whose entire purpose seems to be to debate the question of suffering and the role of God in understanding is promising. Perhaps here the wisdom of the ancients (even if we are not disposed to trust revelation) might lead us to some hidden knowledge, provide some long-lost key to life's most poignant dilemma.

Theologians use a technical term for this: the word *theodicy*; and commentators have often defined it as the central issue of the book of Job. The word is formed from two Greek terms: *theos* (god) and *diké* (justice). Thus, in brief, it defines the debate about the justice of God and how (if at all) we can understand such a thing in view of the evil and suffering which seem so prevalent in the world. Theodicy is a particular problem for what the Qur'an calls 'the people of the Book' – Judaism, Christianity and Islam – because each of these faiths holds firmly to certain beliefs about the nature of God which turn out to be incompatible with our notions of natural justice. Strong claims are made to the effect that the deity is absolute and perfect; in particular, that God's power is absolute and God's love is perfect, and that God is wholly just.

God, justice and suffering

THEODICY

theos	+	*diké*
= God		= Justice
Assumed to be		*Assumed to be*
loving		normal
+ just		+ God's will
+ powerful		+ applicable to all

BUT

Suffering is perceived to be random, unmerited, unfairly distributed

and evil appears to go unchecked,

WHAT IS THE ANSWER?

At the same time most people believe in a system of natural justice which seeks to match suffering with sin, and would prefer to fit the punishment to the crime. In principle, a just, loving and powerful God would have no difficulty delivering on these expectations; but the world, quite evidently, does *not* conform to the paradigm. Natural disasters randomly and effectively destroy innocent lives; all manner of disease afflicts young and old, good and bad alike in a monstrous parody of Matthew's loving God who 'makes his sun rise on the evil and on the good, and sends rain on the just and the unjust' (5.45). Thoroughly corrupt and unpleasant people become rich and flourish, while honest, hard-working and devoted souls earn a pittance and in the end have to scratch a meagre living from a state pension grudgingly given.

In earlier times the solution to this dilemma was seen to lie in the assurance of bliss and reward in the hereafter, where all injustices would be put right, and those who had been guilty of incorrigible sin would be dispatched to eternal punishment in Hell (though viruses and volcanoes would presumably be exempt). Two different critiques have rendered this simple – if not simplistic – solution problematic. The first is that for many people the thought of a God who creates the kind of universe which will inevitably lead to the consignment of an unknown number of its denizens to eternal punishment is morally offensive. The *theodicy* question is, for them, not resolved by heaven and hell; it simply shifted *post mortem*. An

intermediate and superficially attractive way round this was to imagine
that God would ultimately forgive everyone, perhaps after a suitable
period of heavenly chastisement. We are, in short, free to suffer in this
life, or in the next, but eventually all will be well. Once again, however,
the niggling question arises: what is the point? If God can create a just
existence eventually, and God is all we claim God to be, why do we have
to witness the suffering of millions of innocents in this world?

A more recent – though at the same time more ancient – challenge
is to doubt that there is any such thing (place? experience?) as heaven
and hell after death. Death is the end; this life is what we have, and its
blessings the only ones we shall know. Such views are often attributed to
contemporary secularism or atheism, but in fact they reflect what seems
to have been the normal belief of most of those who wrote the Old Testament Scriptures. There is therefore an unexpected congruence between
the world of the likes of Job and Qoheleth (the author of Ecclesiastes) and
many of the Psalmists, and modern western society. The struggles of Job
to understand his unfortunate and unfair situation are *our* struggles, and
he therefore deserves a hearing without the mediation (or intervention) of
the thought world of patristic and medieval Christianity with its elaborate system of punishments and incentives tied to a hypothetical judicial
process after death.

The customary phrase used to characterise this debate – 'The Problem
of Suffering' – seems to presuppose a force of evil working to undermine
the essential goodness of creation. Within mainstream Christian tradition these basic ideas are conflated with a belief in original sin (which
condemns all human beings *by their very nature* to be incorrigibly evil)
and the doctrine of the Fall, which implicates the whole of creation in the
original human act of disobedience. For some Christian thinkers this in
turn enables us to subsume both natural disasters and malignant illness
under a single paradigm: *all* bad things result from *human* sin, so there
can be no such thing as an inexplicable disaster. We suffer (whether as a
result of blind natural forces or human wickedness) for a reason, and that
reason is intrinsically bound up with our fallen human nature. It would
be fair to say that this latter mode of explanation is not now so common;
most people today (whether Christian or not) would now identify *two*
problems: Human evil on the one hand, and naturally caused suffering
on the other.

The biblical world's views on this matter do not fit modernity, though
neither do they reflect the full Augustinian postulate of original sin. It
is, in Job's thinking, entirely possible for a man or woman to be good,
to obey God and to expect to be worthy of an appropriate reward. However, that world made no distinction between natural disasters and events
appointed by the deity. Everything is under God's constant control, and
whether one's affliction is caused by illness, by natural disaster, or as a

result of human action, ultimately God bears the responsibility. Thus, though we are not born with sin in our genes, all that happens thereafter is part of a cause and effect involving good and bad, wickedness and righteousness – and is to be interpreted within the overall divine scheme of things.

The theodicy question in the Bible

There are a number of passages other than Job in which the writers of the Old Testament explore the kind of questions we have categorized as belonging to the problem of theodicy. Several of them are briefly described here; it is clear that the range of opinion they represent is very similar to what would be expected in a contemporary review of the question.

1 Genesis 3.14–19

This is the poetic passage, in the form of a curse, which accompanies the banishment of Adam and Eve from the garden. It attributes the need for back-breaking labour, pain in childbirth, and the prevalence of weeds to the human couple's disobedience, and imposes the ultimate punishment of death. This is, if you like, a theodicy of the commonplace: things which are a natural and inevitable part of the normal order of things are directly attributed to God's displeasure.

2 Genesis 18.16–33

The famous debate between God and Yahweh about the impending fate of Sodom. Various themes are bound up together here: the legend of a violent event, something like a volcanic eruption (19.24–5), is explained on the grounds that everyone who died was part of an unredeemably wicked civilization. The debate reveals an awareness on the part of the biblical tradition that this is an improbable scenario – it would be a very strange society in which everyone was wholly evil; thus Abraham's attempt to reason with God, which culminates in the acceptance of God's starting point. Though there is a curious ambivalence: would not Lot and his entire entourage have constituted the ten righteous people on whose behalf the city might have been spared (18.32)? The theodicy here, which explains natural disaster as a punishment from sin, is a mirror of the flood story, in which God decides to wipe out all human life (Gen. 6.5–7), but spares the righteous Noah and his family (6.8–9).

3   Exodus 23.23–30; Deuteronomy 11.13–17

At the end of the Exodus account of the ordinances which expand upon the Decalogue we find a passage which describes how, in return for their acceptance of the covenant, God will both bless the Israelites in the land and drive out the previous inhabitants by a combination of terror and pestilence. Thus what is a positive theodicy for Israelites is decidedly negative for Amorites, Hittites and the rest. This is a dilemma which often presents itself: how can incompatible good things be delivered by the same just and loving God? If the Lord supports both sides in a war, is the justice of the cause determined simply by whoever defeats the other? The second passage has a similar message, but only from the Israelite perspective: faithfulness to God, it seems, will guarantee prosperity, while apostasy will lead to economic disaster. This is, of course, precisely the argument which informs the case made by Job's adversaries.

4   Psalm 73

There is a pattern common to many psalms in which the writer, while affirming the traditional position (thus 73.1: 'Truly God is good to the upright, to those who are pure in heart'), proceeds immediately to bewail the fact that the brutal reality is exactly the opposite (73.2–14) – the wicked grow fat, live at ease, and gain immoderate wealth. This is similar to Job's dilemma; though it does not necessarily entail suffering on the part of the Psalmist, it makes him/her wonder just what advantage there is to being faithful. The answer, at least in the Psalmist's experience, is that it is in one's duty to the community as a whole and in one's experience in worship that strength can be found to live with the appearance of injustice (73.15–17). Unfortunately, the remainder of the psalm is devoted to a restatement of the traditional view, that in the end the wicked will be punished.[1]

5   Ecclesiastes 4.1–3

As we might expect from this master of melancholy, Qoheleth's view of suffering is uncompromising and without any compensating hope:

> I thought the dead, who have already died, more fortunate than the living, who are still alive; but better than both is the one who has not yet been, and has not seen the evil deeds that are done under the sun.[2]

---

1 For a more detailed analysis of what is going on in this Psalm, see Robert Davidson, *The Courage to Doubt* (London, SCM Press, 1983) pp. 32–7.

2 This is, of course, only part of this writer's more considered view. We shall look more closely at Ecclesiastes in Chapter 8.

What we see here is something like the kind of fatalism which accompanies certain modern secular responses, though perhaps in rather extreme terms: few who call themselves secular today envy either the dead or the unborn!

6 *Luke 13.1–5*

Finally, and by way of a footnote, we turn to a famous passage in which Jesus seems to address the question of unjustified suffering. He refers to two, presumably contemporary, disasters: the murder of some Galileans by Pilate, and the death of 18 people in the collapse of a tower. In each case he asks, rhetorically, whether they died because they were worse sinners than their compatriots. Though the answer is 'no', each saying concludes with a warning to the hearers that, unless they repent, they will perish like the victims in question. Since this appears to reintroduce the connection between suffering and wrongdoing which the examples seem to deny, we are left perplexed. The problem is indeed a complex one, and those who seem to have an answer often turn out, like Jesus, to have performed a kind of verbal sleight of hand.

What question does Job ask?

The book of Job is a more puzzling work than is often realized. Because we so readily consign it to the category of 'discussion of the problem of evil and suffering' its more subtle aspects are lost, and we find ourselves combing through its pages in a desperate search for that most elusive of holy grails – the answer to the problem of unmerited suffering. But what if that is not what the book is about? What if it never pretended in the first place to do anything like that? In order to unpack this proposition, I want to introduce a parallel case. It is drawn from *Through the Looking Glass*, a book which, with its companion *Alice in Wonderland*, set the agenda for a great deal of what the twentieth century puzzled over in philosophy and literary theory.

What's it called? Alice and the White Knight

[Alice was walking beside the White Knight in Looking Glass Land.] 'You are sad,' the Knight said in an anxious tone: 'let me sing you a song to comfort you.' 'Is it very long?' Alice asked, for she had heard a good deal of poetry that day. 'It's long,' said the Knight, 'but it's very, *very* beautiful. Everybody that hears me sing it – either it brings *tears* to their eyes, or else –' 'Or else what?' said Alice, for the Knight had made a sudden pause. 'Or else it doesn't, you know. The *name of the song is called* "Haddocks' Eyes." ' 'Oh, that's the name of the song, is it?' Alice

> said, trying to feel interested. 'No, you don't understand,' the Knight
> said, looking a little vexed. 'That's what the name is called. *The name
> really is* "The Aged, Aged Man." ' 'Then I ought to have said "That's what
> the song is called"?' Alice corrected herself. 'No you oughtn't: that's
> another thing. *The song is called* "Ways and Means" but that's only
> what it's *called*, you know!' 'Well, what is the song then?' said Alice,
> who was by this time completely bewildered. 'I was coming to that,' the
> Knight said. '*The song really is* "A-sitting On a Gate": and the tune's my
> own invention.' So saying, he stopped his horse and let the reins fall on
> its neck: then slowly beating time with one hand, and with a faint smile
> lighting up his gentle, foolish face, he began:

In the course of Alice's encounter with the White Knight the subject of the naming of things comes up. The White Knight (like many other characters in the story) wishes to sing a song to our heroine, but confusion arises when he attempts to identify the song: his precise distinctions between what the name of the song is called, what the name really is, what the song is called and what the song really is leave Alice 'completely bewildered'. In addressing the question of 'meaning' in relation to the book of Job, much the same sense of bewilderment is aroused.

- The name of the text is called 'The Book of Job' (but is it a book at all, or is it a patchwork of ill-assorted and rather seriously damaged reflections on a theme?).
- The name of the text is 'Job' (which rather suggests that it is about this named individual; but then, most commentators have read it not as 'the story of Job' but as a metaphysical debate about the problem of good and evil).
- So what is the text called (to take up the next level of the White Knight's naming process)? Perhaps it could be called 'a dialogue in several stages, with prologue and epilogue', if we are to interpret the problem of naming the text as equivalent to that of *Formgeschichte* ('form criticism') or identification of *genres*. Or perhaps it could better be described as a drama in five acts.
- And as for what the text is – that is surely the famous hermeneutical conundrum that what the text is what you want it to be: the answer to the problem of innocent suffering; a type of the suffering of Christ; a self-deconstructing exercise in postmodern literary criticism; a verse-drama;[3] or a psychoanalytical study of human responses to stress[4] (to name but a few).

---

3 A. MacLeish, *J.B. a play in verse* (London, Secker & Warburg, 1959).

4 As, for example, in *Job's Illness* by Jack Kahn (Oxford, Pergamon Press, 1975).

Behind this brief detour into Wonderland lies a serious purpose: to reflect upon the importance of what questions are asked, and how they are phrased, when deeply life-threatening issues are under discussion. The importance of getting the question right is of course no new emphasis. Plato's application of the Socratic technique, which depends so much on persuading victims (not, I think, an unfair term to use) to arrive at the 'right' answer by means of leading questions, is a well known, if somewhat devious device. Many years ago Collingwood stressed, in *The Idea of History*,[5] the importance for historical investigation of asking questions which are appropriate to the kind of information which is sought, and which you have some hope of answering. 'How long is a piece of string', 'What colour are God's eyes' and 'Where did the universe begin' are clearly (are they not?) inadmissible questions. What is more difficult is to recognize such questions when we enter areas of passionate and vital concern to our individual well-being.

The theological enterprise is at once fascinating and frustrating precisely because the questions it raises are existentially urgent, but at the same time apparently unanswerable. This is why theological systems so often degenerate into dogmatism, because the human mind (like nature) 'abhors a vacuum', and readily propounds formulae which serve to close the gap between the known and the unknowable. The book of Job, which is the focus of our particular attention, has prompted many volumes of speculation in the realm of urgent questions lacking persuasive answers. There exists a bewildering array of literary, psychological, christological, sociological and pious discussions of the book, most of which seek to understand how the problem of suffering – with which Job manifestly deals – can be resolved in the world of a good God and a just universe. Quite clearly, no one has yet successfully squared that particular circle; equally clearly no one ever will, for it belongs to the realm of competing absolutes: the absolutely good versus the absolutely just. It is our Wonderlandish fate to belong to an era which has enthroned the principle of logical precision in all things, forgetting that our whole being is formed of materials which respond to logical argument – if they respond at all – only in the most faltering and fitful manner. It is tempting to ask, therefore, whether we have not been seduced into putting quite the wrong question to the book of Job. For the 'problem' of suffering (as distinct from the physical, mental and spiritual anguish of suffering, all of which are perfectly real) is something of a contrived conundrum, depending as it does on speculative assumptions about the nature of God and the universe. That the universe as we know it ought to be 'meaningful' within the rationalist terms of modernist thinking, and that we are capable of

---

5 R. G. Collingwood, *The Idea of History* (Oxford University Press, 1946), pp. 269–82.

comprehending even *that* form of meaning, are axioms of quite startling audacity. Could it be that there is something wrong with the questions we habitually put; that there is another way to read the dialogues of Job without getting ourselves tangled in the ineluctable net of rationalist discourse?

In the next chapter we shall examine the structure of Job with a view to understanding how the writer has shaped quite a difficult body of material into a coherent pattern. What we shall find is that the *ostensible* pattern turns out (at least on my reading) to be deceptive, and that there is a meaning to be derived from what appear to be flaws or disruptions to this pattern. Part of this study of meaning depends upon the recognition of a number of themes running through the central portion of the book (chs. 4–27). These are not explicitly presented in the book, but emerge through the process of the debate between Job and his interlocutors. The section which follows elucidates the themes as part of a preliminary discussion of the dialogues.[6]

The themes of Job [7]

A superficial reading of the dialogues in Job can give the impression of a rather haphazard, almost inchoate series of harangues in which Job piously defends his unassailable case against the blunt and unsophisticated arguments put by his adversaries (see the box opposite for a comment on the use of this term rather than *friends*). The sheer length of these diatribes makes it difficult to get a good grasp of what is going on, with the result that popular interpretations tend to resort to cliché – Job's patience, his unjust suffering, his faithfulness rewarded, the friends' arrogant refusal to 'think outside the box', and so on. What I hope to do in the analysis presented here is to begin from a closer reading of the themes which are to be found in the speeches of the four protagonists with a view to seeing, first, how they are distributed and second, how (if at all) they interact with each other – and, indeed, with the remainder of the book.

The identification of themes offered here is quite broad-brush and impressionistic, and is not intended to represent a rigorous analysis of the text in detail. In my defence I claim that the reader can best gain access to this lengthy book by means of that kind of general overview, and that the

---

6 See my essay, 'Could not the universe have come into existence 200 yards to the left? A thematic study of Job' in R. P. Carroll (ed.) *Text as Pretext* (Sheffield, JSOT Press, 1992), pp. 142–52, of which the material in the rest of this chapter is a revision.

7 A table is provided at the end of this chapter which shows how the specific themes are distributed through chapters 3—31. Those who wish to look more closely at the arguments in section 4 should consult this table.

themes and motifs identified are sufficiently robust to withstand closer scrutiny. I shall make a case in the next chapter for a kind of mimetic effect in the book whereby the structure and arrangement of the text is part of the way it delivers meaning. The fact that the four participants rehearse themes over again, picking up and abandoning lines of argument, and largely talking past each other can be interpreted as a literary device which mimics the rambling, incoherent and sometimes belligerent manner in which major existential problems of this kind are often in practice debated. The more complex the question the more likely we are to adopt strident and intransigent positions, paradoxically claiming certainty that we would never aspire to on lesser (or more obviously factual) matters. I shall return to this dimension of our study in the next chapter; in the meantime I shall turn to a closer examination of themes and motifs.

'Friend or foe': the status of Eliphaz, Bildad and Zophar

The description of Job's 'sparring partners' as *friends* comes from 2.11, where they are described as getting together to 'console and comfort him' (NRSV). More accurately, this refers (as the King James version makes clear) to sharing in his mourning – a more limited social function than the phrase 'Job's comforters' might suggest. Moreover the Hebrew term which is translated as 'friends' has a more general meaning of 'neighbour', 'associate', 'one who lives in the same community' or 'relative' – again suggesting a less intimate connection than is traditionally assumed.

The relationship between Job and the three is adversarial rather than one of friendship in the sense of solacing or comforting – there is nothing *comfortable* about what the three have to say, nor should they be criticized for this. The formal structure is that of a contest in which rival contenders offer their differing views in the setting of a riddle: 'Is it possible to be innocent and not to prosper?' Indeed, given the clear links that Job has with Wisdom literature more generally, it may not be inappropriate to identify the central issue as primarily an intellectual rather than a moral one. The idea that Eliphaz and the others are 'friends' or 'comforters' thus raises quite the wrong expectations: we are not looking at a pastoral case study.

An overview

Several preliminary observations may be made on the basis of the distribution of themes as set out in the appendix (pp. 128–9 and summarized in the box on p. 119). First, the use of the most deeply negative motifs largely disappears after chapter 19. That is, there is no further expression by Job of the wish to die (3i), or of the brutish nature of life (3h), and both parties cease their preliminary sniping at each other (4j, k). There are two exceptions to this broad conclusion: in 30.24–31 Job resumes his musing on the harsh nature of life, but this is in the context of his final 'summing up', which puts it in a different context; and in 26.1–4 Job makes what are usually taken to be sarcastic comments on Bildad. This is an interesting passage, and I shall argue below that it may not in fact be a negative opinion.

Second, while the most commonly attested theme is, not surprisingly, that of the traditional view of the relationship between suffering and wrongdoing (2f), its distribution is noteworthy. For most of the first two cycles of debate it is addressed by Job's adversaries exclusively; but after Zophar's second speech it turns up just as often in Job's own responses. This links to another important point, namely that for most of the process of dialogue there is a remarkable lack of direct response. Job rarely takes up directly a theme presented by one of the others, and the exceptions are instructive (they are indicated in the appendix by linking arrows). The first is perhaps the least significant: in 4.17–21 Eliphaz speaks of the insignificance of humankind in the eyes of God; Job turns to this himself in 7.17–21, but in a purely pessimistic tone. Human beings, he argues, are insignificant by comparison with God; why, then, does God bother to harass and persecute us? The other two direct responses are both to Zophar (11.5–9 followed by 12.7–16 and 20.4–29 followed by 21.1–34).

Third, we note four themes which have importance for the outworking of the book as a whole. These are: the depiction of God as creator (1c), the relationship of humankind to God (1d) and the philosophical question 'Where is wisdom to be found?' (2g). Each of these has an important part to play in the way the book of Job achieves something like closure. The first two fairly obviously prepare the way for Yahweh's powerful creation-based speeches (38—41) and Job's abject responses (40.3–4 and 42.1–6). The third is more subtle in that it provides, as we shall see, a kind of meta-discourse in which the very methodology of the book is questioned from within. This makes it all the more significant that the first direct response that Job makes to any of his interlocutors is when Zophar takes up this seemingly minor theme. Finally, there is the extensive material relating to Job's personal grievance with God (1a and 1b). None of Job's three adversaries responds in any way to this material – a fact which, while not entirely surprising, does say something about the extent to which these exchanges can properly be described as dialogues.

Themes in Job

1 Themes relating directly to God

a Job's demands that God give him a hearing, or vindicate him
   [9.1–4, 9.13–20, 9.32–5, 13.1–28, 14.13–17, 16.18–21, 19.23–
   9, 23.3–7, 30.20–3, 31.35–7]

b Job's charge against God, of the vindictive use of divine power
   [6.2–7, 7.11–16, 9.21–31, 10.1–17, 12.4–6, 12.17–25, 14.18–22,
   16.6–17, 17.6–7, 19.6–22, 23.2, 30.1–19]

c Recognition of God as creator
   [5.8–10, 9.5–10, 22.12–14, 26.5–14]

d What is humankind?
   [4.17–21, 7.17–21, 15.7–16, 22.1–4, 25.2–6]

e Mysterious presence
   [4.12–16, 9.11–12, 20.2–3, 23.8–17?]

2 Themes relating to general questions

f Suffering, the innocent, and the wicked (in both personal and general terms)
   [4.7–11, 5.1–7, 5.11–27, 8.3–22, 11.10–20, 15.17–35, 18.5–21,
   20.4–29, 21.1–34, 22.5–11, 22.15–30, 24.1–25, 27.1–23,
   29.1–25, 31.1–34, 38–40]

g Where is wisdom to be found?
   [11.5–9, 12.7–16, 28.1–28]

3 Themes reflecting feelings of despair

h Life is short and brutal
   [7.1–10, 14.1–12, 16.22–17.1, 30.24–31]

i Wish for death
   [3.1–26, 6.8–13, 10.19–22, 17.11–16]

4 Mutual responses

j Adversaries' attitudes to Job
   [4.1–6, 8.1–2, 11.1–4, 15.1–6, 18.1–4]

k Job's attitudes to his adversaries
   [6.14–30, 12.2–3, 13.1–12, 16.1–5, 17.2–5, 17.8–10, 19.1–5,
   26.1–4]

The opening soliloquy and the first cycle of dialogues

The opening soliloquy is entirely devoted to a moving expression of the death-wish theme (3i), one of four themes which Job addresses in the first stages of the dialogue (chs. 6—7), the others being the charge that God is vindictive (1b), the brutishness of life (3h), and the hopelessness of the adversaries' advice (4k). We have already noted that these are all strikingly negative in tone, and that their further distribution is significant: The death-wish theme is abandoned after chapter 10 and that of the brutishness of life after chapter 17. The remaining theme (God's vindictiveness) is likewise given considerable coverage in the first cycle, less in the second, and almost none in the third, although it does reappear, as we have seen, in 30.1–19, as part of Job's final soliloquy. This is something of a special case, however, and does not affect the basic observation that there is a clear development from the first to the third cycle; and that, in particular, Job's opening soliloquy and his first response to Eliphaz explore broadly negative themes which are departed from by the middle of the second cycle.

Moving on to chapters 9—10 (the reply to Bildad's first speech), Job begins by introducing the two remaining themes which are addressed directly to God: recognition of God as creator (1c), and the demand for a hearing (1a). The former is a relatively insignificant motif within the dialogues, only clearly appearing in chapters 9 and 26, but is worth listing separately, nevertheless, because it plays a dominant role in the speeches of Elihu (chs. 32—37) and in Yahweh's reply to Job (chs. 38—41). The other new theme – the demand for a hearing – is one of two major themes which are central to the dialogues, recurring in chapters 12—14, 16—17, 19, 22, 23—24 and in Job's closing appeal in chapters 29—31.

With regard to the development of the dialogue, the opening speeches of both Eliphaz and Bildad are devoted predominantly to the general subject of the justice of God: an affirmation of the received wisdom that only the wicked suffer. But we ought to recognize that this point is not made at all in *personal* terms at this stage; rather it is in the form of a general statement of self-evident truth. Job's speeches, on the other hand, are graded. Chapter 3 consists entirely of the death wish, and the reply to Eliphaz in chapters 6—7 is couched in purely negative terms, but covers four themes. In chapters 9—10, however, a new note is sounded. It seems that Bildad may have been the catalyst for a change of tone, although not a direct *response*: there is no meeting of minds. The new themes addressed to God suggest a more positive approach, although this note is not sustained; for the remainder of the speech returns to the death wish and the charge that God is vindictive, producing as it were a falling off as Job returns to the mood of chapters 6—7.

The third stage of the cycle (chs. 11—14) displays some fascinating structural features. Zophar breaks ranks, as it were, by abandoning the 'party line' and opening with a reflection on the contrast between wisdom and folly, and the ineluctable truth that only God has wisdom (for example, 11.5–6a, 7–9), in terms which powerfully anticipate chapter 28. He then proceeds to personalize the claim that only the wicked suffer by charging Job directly with the responsibility for examining his own conscience. As if recognizing this initiative, Job responds in like terms, taking Zophar's second point first by protesting his innocence, and then offering some thoughts of his own on the theme of God and wisdom. This is the first time that Job has responded directly to another participant in the dialogue, and this is the catalyst for further developments. Thus, although Job's first response to Zophar ends, like his replies to the other two, on a negative note, the general effect is of an oscillation between negative and more positive reflection, rather than a simple downward path. Thus ends the first cycle. It began with a death wish and ends with a diatribe, but in between we have seen interesting developments in Job's responses, and (curiously) evidence of a 'special relationship' between Zophar and Job.

The second cycle of dialogues

In the second cycle of dialogues Job's adversaries (perhaps they had held a briefing meeting!) present what appears to be a solid front on the theme with which they dominated the first – that suffering is deserved. Job's first two responses (chs. 16—17 and 19), like their equivalents in the first cycle, give no indication that he is responding to, or wishes to respond to, anything his opponents have to say. As in the first cycle, negative themes appear, but now in a more desultory manner. The brutishness of life is addressed only once (a mere three verses, compared with 22 in the first cycle. It should also be noted that Job's response to Bildad in this second cycle ends on a more positive note – an expression of Job's challenge to God and demand for vindication. Once again, however, we find a striking change when Job answers Zophar. Just as Job responded directly to Zophar in the first cycle, so also in chapter 21 the whole content of Job's speech is a treatment of the theme which he has studiously avoided so far: the theme of the innocent, the wicked and the place of suffering. His argument, not surprisingly, is directly counter to that of Zophar, but it is a clear encounter, not (as in earlier replies to Eliphaz and Bildad) a simple avoidance of the issue.

To sum up our observations thus far, we note the following patterns: (1) A general consensus among Job's adversaries that the important issue is the question of God's justice, mostly addressed in general terms, but on two occasions directed against Job personally. Only Zophar (11.1–12) varies this pattern. (2) A tendency for Job's reflections to be dissociated from those of Eliphaz and Bildad – his 'replies' are not replies in the sense of a response to what they say; rather they represent a further stage of Job's *own* consideration of his situation. But this is dramatically in contrast with the fact that Job makes a direct and genuine *reply* to each of Zophar's speeches. Is this significant? It will be of particular interest to see what happens in the third cycle.

The third cycle of dialogues

We must recognize at the outset that the crucial third cycle is not complete – lacking as it does any contribution from Zophar. But perhaps this might have been expected – given that we have already identified the third adversary as having a distinctive function. In fact, I shall propose that part of the reason for the truncation of this last cycle is that Job now responds directly to Eliphaz and Bildad; the dialogue no longer needs Zophar as catalyst. The cycle is also strange in that chapters 26 and 27 are thought by many commentators to contain material which would have sounded better from the lips of one of the adversaries – the absent Zophar, for example? However plausible such claims may be, and however attractive the possibility of reconstructing a perfect cycle, I shall argue that this is too superficial an approach. Not only the well-known critical principle of *lectio difficilior,* but also the deeper levels of meaning of the third cycle suggest that the apparent difficulties have profound hermeneutical importance.

Following on my remarks about Zophar's role as catalyst, it is of note that in his third speech Eliphaz refers to a major Joban theme – the challenge to God. This is the first time that any of his adversaries has addressed a theme which was first introduced by Job, and the first time also that a response is made by them to Job's arguments. While Eliphaz makes clear his view that Job's demands of God are both futile and evidence of his sinful hubris (22.12–15, 27, 29), it is significant that this is at least evidence of a direct exchange of views. Together with the fact that in chapters 23—24 and 26—27 (with the possible exception of 26.1–4) Job deals only with *positive* themes, this seems to answer in the affirmative the question I indicated above: Does the Zophar intervention at the end of each of the first two cycles prepare the way for a change of mood in the following cycle? For what now ensues is a closer relationship between Job, Eliphaz and Bildad: at last a genuine debate has taken off – though, surprisingly, that debate reflects mostly an acceptance by Job of the agenda laid down by his adversaries. This is *not* the result one would expect from a traditional reading of the book – and it does not imply that Job simply agrees with the others. But the recognition of this development opens up possibilities for the understanding of Job's last response to Eliphaz and Bildad which take account of (rather than being at odds with) the structural patterns to which we referred in the opening paragraph of this section.

With these comments in mind, let us turn to Job's third-cycle speeches. Chapter 23 begins, quite predictably, with a stout defence of his repeated demands to be heard, and when heard, justified. But there then follows a passage (23.8–17) which is surely one of the cruces of the whole cycle of dialogues, a passage which resists any attempt at classification along the lines of the themes which we have so far used (I have tentatively allocated it to the category of 'the mysterious presence'), and yet which seems to allude to several of them. It is also a passage in which we surely detect a movement in Job's thinking in the direction of, if not acceptance, at least a sense of his own inadequacy. Since the passage has a number of puzzling features I will begin by giving my own translation:

> Behold, I go forward but he is not there,
>   and back, but I do not recognize him.
> He is at work on my left hand, but I do not perceive him,
>   he conceals himself on my right hand so that I cannot see him.
> Yet he knows my way:
> He has tried me like gold,
>   and like gold I shall come forth.
> My foot clings to his path,
>   I have kept to his way and will never wander;
> His lips command:
> I will never depart from his instructions to me,
> I have treasured up the words of his mouth.
> For he is single-minded: who can gainsay him?
>   What he desired, he has done.
> He will certainly carry out what he has ordered for me:
>   many such plans are in his mind!
> Therefore I am disturbed by his presence,
>   when I consider, I am afraid of him;
> for El has numbed my brain,
>   Shaddai has troubled me.
> Yet I have not been silenced by darkness
>   though he has covered me in gloom.

The opening theme of this speech – the unsuccessful search for God on all sides – has one very striking parallel in Psalm 139, where the writer speaks memorably of the impossibility of *escaping* God's presence:

> You hem me in, behind and before,
>   and lay your hand upon me . . .

Where can I go from your spirit?
   Or where can I flee from your presence?
If I ascend to heaven, you are there;
   if I make my bed in Sheol, you are there.
If I take the wings of the morning
   and settle at the furthest limits of the sea,
even there your hand shall lead me,
   and your right hand shall hold me fast.   (Ps. 139.5, 7–10)

The reversal is ironic: the psalmist who (like Jonah) longs to flee from God finds that God is unavoidably present; Job, who passionately desires a confrontation with God, finds that the deity remains hidden (though undoubtedly present). But there are further connections with Psalm 139. Verses 11–12 ('If I say, "Let only darkness cover me, / and the light about me be night," / even the darkness is not dark to thee, / the night is bright as the day; / for darkness is as light with thee') also represent an intriguing reversal: Job concludes by insisting that even the darkness with which God surrounds him cannot silence him; the psalmist recognizes that his or her attempts at obfuscation cannot confuse God! Again, vv. 2–4 address the theme of Job 23.10–11, and vv. 13–18 that of Job 23.12–14. The remaining theme of Job's speech (his sense of awe and terror in the presence of God [vv. 15–16]) finds a response in v. 6 of the psalm – and also, interestingly, in Job's concluding confession (42.3). The psalm concludes (vv. 19–24) with a plea that the wicked might receive their just deserts, and that the writer might be vindicated: the themes precisely of Job 24 and of 23.1–7.

The point of drawing out these parallels with Psalm 139 is not to suggest any direct influence one way or another, but to indicate the nature of this crucial passage in Job. It belongs with those personal/liturgical reflections which recur throughout the Psalter and which suggest a coming to terms with the nature of God and humanity, good and evil, *in the context of the cult*.[8] This seems a surprising note: we are not accustomed to think of Job in such terms. But it is undoubtedly a true note, and has importance for the way that the remainder of the book is shaped (or rather, in the way that his thoughts are expressed), for it is at pains to demonstrate the fitness of Job's attitude to God: awe, obedience, the need to be purified, steadfastness of purpose and the recognition of God's power.

After such a sharp change of emphasis it is not perhaps surprising to find in chapter 24 an apparently confused passage on the theme of the wicked, the oppressed, and the indifference of God. Confused because it is not clear whether Job is here continuing his earlier charge (in ch. 21)

---

8 Robert Davidson has an interesting discussion of this point with reference to Psalm 73 in his *The Courage to Doubt* (London, SCM Press, 1983), pp. 33ff.

that the wicked prosper (thus, seemingly, vv. 13–23[9]), deploring the callousness of God in the face of the cry of the oppressed (thus vv. 1–12), or whether he has come to endorse the 'party line' (v. 24). So incoherent is this chapter that many commentators have proposed significant amendments to the text, or have wondered whether an earlier, more radical statement (justifying Job's concluding challenge in v. 25) has been tampered with. Reading meaning from such disarray is difficult; unless of course we take the confusion to be the point;[10] Job's earlier certainties are now under attack, and this is to be dramatically reinforced in the last stage of the dialogue proper (chs. 26—27). It is a feature of the book of Job that, like its principal protagonist, its readers are not infrequently reduced to silence (or speechlessness) – a case of the medium being the message?

Job's last reply to Bildad presents us with real problems. In the first place there is the matter of 26.1–4, which is commonly interpreted as a sarcastic riposte to Bildad (hence the NRSV's exclamation marks). But the text is ambiguous:

> How have you helped one who has no power?
>   You have assisted the arm that has no strength.
> How have you counselled one who has no wisdom,
>   and given much good advice!
> With whose help have you uttered words,
>   and whose spirit has come forth from you?

I believe that these lines may well indicate not a bitter comment but the beginnings of a recognition that there is wisdom other than what Job himself possesses. He is clearly not quite sure of its provenance; but (perhaps reluctantly) is forced to admit its value. This may be surprising (we have after all been trained to expect nothing but antagonism between Job and the others); but it is strangely in tune with what follows. For 26.5–14 consists of a celebration of God's creative powers of impeccable orthodoxy (compare, for example, Elihu in ch. 37 and Yahweh in ch. 38), and a disquisition on the fate of the wicked (ch. 27) which is in substantial agreement with the line put forward by Eliphaz and company. But there remains a personal note which reminds us of the Job with whom we are familiar; for however much he may have been swayed by the intransigence

---

9 Although different translations interpret this passage in different ways: thus NEB treats it as a statement supporting the traditional case, as do the AV and NIV; RSV takes the opposite view.

10 The claim that the confusion of the text is the point is admittedly postmodern. Such a text has, with a real vengeance, deconstructed both authorial intention and readerly control, leaving the interpreter with the difficult task of sailing safely between the Scylla of radical textual emendation and the Charybdis of incoherence.

of his adversaries, they cannot be allowed to carry their case against Job personally. *He* is not unrighteous. This is most powerfully insisted upon in 27.2–6, in words which carry, even in English translation, a vivid sense of the passion with which they are imbued. The passage begins with a telling echo of 23.16:

> As El lives, who has taken away my right,
>> and Shaddai, who has made my soul bitter . . .

and concludes in tones of ringing defiance:

>> till I die I will not put away my integrity from me.
> I hold fast my righteousness, and will not let it go;
>> my heart does not reproach me for any of my days.

These are not the words of the self-pitying, somewhat cringing figure of the first cycle. They are spoken by a man who has now seen the full paradox of his situation: I *am* innocent, I have no regrets. Yet justice must be done and must be seen to be done – to this extent at least the case argued by Eliphaz, Bildad and Zophar carries weight. Hence the passion with which the denunciation of the wicked is made in vv. 7–23. If nothing else, the arguments of the adversaries have forced Job (and his readers!) to confront the paradox squarely: innocence may be affirmed, justice must be done; how can these be reconciled? It is a classic example of an unanswerable question, to which the only constructive response must be: surely the question is wrong.

The poem to wisdom and the closing soliloquy

I do not wish to comment at length on chapters 28 and 29—31. Chapter 28 has been so often and so readily dismissed as a jarring intrusion into Job's private grief that it must seem capricious to insist that it belongs in context and has a purposeful presence there. Nevertheless, I would make this claim, bearing in mind the intellectual nature of the debate and the fact of Job's functioning within the Wisdom tradition. For it turns the spot-light, *at precisely the appropriate moment,* on the underlying principle of the whole debate: the belief that a rational dialogue can succeed in resolving the dilemma which faces both Job and his friends; the belief, in short, that wisdom – *hakam* – is within the grasp of human intelligence. In truth, however, only 'God understands the way to it, / and he knows its place' (28.23); furthermore, picking up a traditional motif of the Wisdom literature, but applying it with peculiar pertinence to Job's situation, we find:

> Behold, the fear of the Lord, that is wisdom;
>> and to depart from evil is understanding. (28.28)

Compare the two key passages in the third cycle, specifically 23.15–16 ('Therefore I am disturbed by his presence, / when I consider, I am afraid of him; / for El has numbed my brain, / Shaddai has troubled me') and 27.3–4 ('as long as my breath is in me, / and the spirit of God is in my nostrils; / my lips will not speak falsehood, / and my tongue will not utter deceit'). Although, as we have seen, Job has acknowledged the necessity of facing up to the adversaries' arguments, at the very points where he does so he demonstrates that he satisfies the conditions for true wisdom and understanding. At the stage the dialogue has reached, these are surely highly relevant connections, and significant indications of the way forward to a resolution within the final chapters of the book.

The dialogues end, as they begin, with a soliloquy. But where the opening soliloquy was wholly despairing, in the end Job defends his personal integrity at some length (ch. 29 and most of 31), attributes his sorry state once again to God (30.1–19), and makes a final dramatic appeal to be heard (30.20–31 and 31.35–7). It seems reasonable to accept a small re-ordering of the text of chapter 31, to reposition vv. 35–7 at the end, as Job's final words; but even if we leave the text as it stands, the contrast between Job's (virtual) last words ('like a prince I would approach him') and his first words ('Let the day perish wherein I was born') could hardly be stronger. And this is clearly demonstrated by the distribution of themes which moves from a heavily negative cluster at the beginning to this note of confident challenge at the end. The one reversion to a theme from earlier sections (the vindictiveness of God in 30.1–19) is a necessary element of Job's 'summing-up': the challenge is to God because it is God who must be held responsible for the situation of crisis in which Job finds himself.

Some points to think about

In the light of what has been presented in this chapter, do you agree that we should think of the meaning of Job without necessarily prescribing a focus on theodicy and the meaning of suffering?

Do the other biblical passages cited in this regard help to clarify the problem?

Do you find the thematic approach to the dialogues helpful? Were the results which emerged from it surprising, and did they assist in the process of managing what seems to be a dauntingly large quantity of material?

Further reading

See the end of Chapter 7.

Appendix

Themes in Job 3—31

	1a Demand for a Hearing	1b God's Vindictiveness	1c God as Creator	1d What is man?	1e Strange Presence	2f Traditional View	2g Where is Wisdom?	3h Life is Short	3i Death Wish	4j Friends on Job	4k Job on Friends
Job									3.1–26		
Eliphaz			5.8–10	4.17–21	4.12–16	4.7–11, 5.1–7, 5.11–27				4.2–6	
Job		6.2–7, 7.11–16		7.17–21				7.1–10	6.8–13		6.14–30
Bildad						8.3–22				8.2	
Job	9.2–4, 9.13–20, 9.32–5	9.21–31, 10.1–17	9.5–10		9.11–12				10.19–22		
Zophar						11.10–20	11.5–9			11.2–4	
Job	13.1–28, 14.13–17	12.4–6, 12.17–25, 14.18–22					12.7–16	14.1–12			12.2–3, 13.1–12
E2				15.7–16		15.17–35				15.2–6	

Job	16.18–21	16.6–17, 17.6–7						16.22—17.1	17.11–16		16.2–5, 17.2–5, 17.8–10
B₂						18.5–21				18.2–4	
Job	19.23–29	19.6–22									19.2–5
Z₂				20.2–3		20.4–29					
Job						→ 21.2–34					
E₃			22.12–14	22.2–4		→ 22.5–11, 22.15–30					
Job	23.3–7	23.2			23.8–17?	→ 24.1–25					
B₃			26.5–14	25.2–6							
Job						27.2–23					26.2–4
Wisdom							28.1–28				
Job	30.20–23, 31.35–37	30.1–19				29.2–25, 31.1–34, 38–40		30.24–31			

Job's contributions are shaded to make the differences between his and his interlocutor's arguments clearer. Arrows indicate where Job directly responds to what his interlocutors have to say. Verses which simply report 'N said' or 'N answered' have been omitted.

7

Structure and Meaning in Job

The structure of Job: in search of the ur-text

Overview

The structures of the book of Job are plainly visible. Beginning with the two dramatic episodes involving Yahweh and Satan in the opening chapters, the book progresses through a series of dialogues involving several named characters followed by a direct intervention by Yahweh in the closing chapters. Finally a narrative epilogue appears to provide closure for the whole drama. Equally plainly, there are problems with these structures. In this chapter I shall first look in some detail at these structures and problems, and consider how scholars have tried to resolve them – what might be classified as a traditional 'redaction criticism' analysis. Having done that, I shall then look at alternatives which make use of the final form of the book as it stands to investigate ways of making sense of the drama.

In defining the overt structure of Job we note that it concerns a group of characters (in the dramatic sense) who interact exclusively in dialogical exchanges. That is, no more than two are ever 'on stage' at the same time. Further, the character whose name is Yahweh ought to be distinguished from the being referred to as 'God'. The former features largely in chapters 1 and 2 and 38—42, where the deity is a participant in the debates. There are only two uses of Yahweh in the rest of the book. One, in 28.28, occurs in the stock phrase which we examined in Chapter 1 (above pp. 17–18), 'Truly, the fear of the Lord, that is wisdom.' The other isolated example is in 12.9: 'Who among these does not know that the hand of the Lord has done this?' While some have concluded from this that these sections belong to a different tradition or author, it is more satisfying to explain this as having dramatic purpose: Yahweh appears in person on stage, God is the remote being whose nature is under question. It is also important to make it clear that the character called Satan is *not* the demonic figure of later Christian and Jewish apocalyptic (see box opposite).

Satan in the Hebrew Bible

The Hebrew root which gives rise to the apparent proper name Satan is found 33 times in the Old Testament.

Once, in Ezra 4.6, it is used to form an abstract noun, 'accusation'.

Both the verb and the personal noun are frequently found (11 times) with reference to human accusers or adversaries (1 Sam. 29.4; 2 Sam. 19.22; 1 Kings 11.14, 23, 25; Pss 38.20; 71.13; 109.4, 9, 20, 29).

Three times the word is associated with a supernatural figure who appears either to give a warning or to provoke. Two of these are in the story of Balaam (Num. 22.22, 32); the other is in 1 Chron. 21.1 where 'Satan' persuades David to carry out a census. This is an interesting passage, because in the parallel in 2 Samuel 24.1 it is God who incites David. This might suggest that in ancient Israel 'Satan' could be seen as a kind of *alter ego* of God, acting as a kind of *agent provocateur*.

Of the remaining occurrences, 14 are to be found in Job 1—2 and 4 in a curious passage in Zechariah 3.1–10. The latter is a cameo scene in which the high priest Joshua is before the heavenly court, being accused by Satan. There are interesting parallels with Job, in that God's role is to defend Joshua and to protest his innocence. It seems, therefore, that the Satan who appears in Job is a sort of divine accuser, but not in any way the embodiment of evil.

The structures of Job

The book of Job affords at first sight a very precise structure, though it soon becomes apparent that there are problems associated with it. In this section we shall set out this structure, identify its flaws, and discuss the solutions that have been proposed to recover a hypothetically pristine version of the book. The details are set out in the box, below. In general terms, the book consists of a long poetic section framed by two narrative pieces. The bulk of the poetic material is taken up with three cycles of dialogues between Job and his three interlocutors (Eliphaz, Bildad and Zophar) followed by a soliloquy from a new character: the younger man Elihu who believes his precursors have let Job off too lightly (32.1–5). The conclusion takes the form of the long-anticipated appearance of Yahweh, who indulges in four chapters of unanswerable challenge to Job. Questions as to the relationship of the prose to the poetry, the purpose and propriety of Elihu's intervention, the fractured nature of the structure, and so on have greatly exercised scholars and commentators. We shall provide a basic review of these and of some proposed solutions, before going on to offer our own tentative explanations.

Structure in Job

(a)	Narrative Prologue	1—2	
(b)	Job's first protest	3	
(c)	Dialogues with Interlocutors		

	First cycle	ELIPHAZ	4—5	
		JOB		6—7
		BILDAD	8	
		JOB		9—10
		ZOPHAR	11	
		JOB		12—14
	Second cycle	ELIPHAZ	15	
		JOB		16—17
		BILDAD	18	
		JOB		19
		ZOPHAR	20	
		JOB		21
	Third cycle	ELIPHAZ	22	
		JOB		23—24
		BILDAD	25	
		JOB		26—27

(d)	Poem to Wisdom		28	
(e)	Job sums up for the prosecution			29—31
(f)	Intermission:			
		ELIHU	32—37	
(g)	Yahweh speaks for the defence:			
		YAHWEH	38—39	
		JOB		40.3–5
		YAHWEH	40.6—41.34	
		JOB		42.1–6
(h)	Narrative Epilogue		42.7–17	

Problems relating to structure and some possible solutions

1 Problems

(a) The prose material at the beginning and end of the book has been questioned. It appears to reflect a more naïve perspective than does the bulk of Job, with its rather simplistic account of the trial of Job and its embarassingly straightforward conclusion in which everything is put right simply by giving Job more worldly wealth at the end than he had at the beginning.

(b) Second, it has often been remarked that the three cycles of three dialogues is incomplete. Zophar does not present his expected third speech, and there are two introductions in Job's last response to Bildad (26.1; 27.1) which might imply some kind of redactional damage somewhere during the process of transmission of the text.

(c) Third, just before Job's final soliloquy – or summing up for the defence, if we use the model of the law court – an unexpected chapter appears (ch. 28) in which what appears to be a stray from a traditional wisdom book is reproduced. Chapter 28 would not be out of place in the book of Proverbs, but it does seem somewhat intrusive in Job. It has often been thought to constitute an independent composition which found its way into Job after the original cycle had been disrupted (perhaps through the prior insertion of the speeches of Elihu). It could, of course, form part of Job's comments in 26–27, but there is a very wide consensus that this is a quite distinct composition, not to be attributed either to Job or to any of his adversaries, but inserted by some later editor for reasons unknown.

(d) Finally, there is the 'problem' of Elihu. He plays no part in the earlier dialogues, is not mentioned in the epilogue, though the others are (42.7–9), and is thought by many commentators to be both derivative as to content and inferior as to style. A significant number of scholars regard him as an unworthy intruder, and wish to send him packing!

2 Solutions

(a) Attempts have been made to 'recover' a third cycle, on the assumption that it was once present, but has been damaged, perhaps through part of a scroll having gone missing at some time. There are *some* signs that this might have happened: there is in 27.1 a second introduction to Job's last speech in response to Bildad, and commentators have argued that the content of chapter 26 is more typical of the adversaries than of Job, so it might therefore be reasonable to continue Bildad's speech through to the end of 26. It is further of note that 27.7–23 seems to adopt a 'traditional' position as regards the punishment of evil and rewarding good – could it be that this was originally Zophar's (now missing) speech? Finally, if we agree that chapter 28 is a later addition, Job's 'summing up' in the version which has come down to us would become his contribution to the third cycle in the 'restored' edition. The result of these various suggestions is to produce a revised third cycle as follows:

Eliphaz		22
	Job	23–24
Bildad		25 + 26
	Job	27.1–6
Zophar		27.7–23
	Job	29–31

(b) The character and speeches of Elihu are subject to the fiercest attacks by modern commentators, who broadly agree that his intervention serves no useful purpose. Marvin Pope sums up their views in a terse paragraph:[1]

> The Elihu speeches . . . are rejected as interpolation by many critics who regard them as having scant value either as literature or as a solution to the problem of evil. Their style is diffuse and pretentious, nearly half of the contents of the four discourses devoted to prolix and pompous prolegomena. For the most part Elihu's arguments merely echo what the friends have already said repeatedly, yet he has the effrontery to offer them as if they were novel and decisive.

Whatever the objective value of such remarks, it seems unduly harsh to apply them to Elihu exclusively. Surely similar charges could easily be brought against the speeches of the three adversaries – or Job himself – which raises the questions of just how reliable is our understanding of how such literature works, and whether there is not some prior animus against Elihu which results in specially negative pleading. I suspect that scholars are too readily tempted into value judgements of the quality of ancient literature, whether positive or negative, without due recognition of the way that material might have functioned for its primary audience. I am not claiming to have privileged knowledge of that presumed audience; I simply want to enter a caveat against too ready a process of redactional excision on the basis of stylistic opinions.[2]

(c) While few would want to detach the prologue and epilogue entirely from the body of the book, there is a significant opinion which holds that these represent the remains of a folk-tale of international origin which has been put to good use as a means of framing and dramatizing what otherwise might have been a rather dense set of arguments. No one has ever produced the original independent folk-tale, but the setting – the mysterious land of Uz – and the names of all but Elihu are resistant to interpretation within the normal Hebrew range of personal names. Also, the theme of a wager between the urbane character of Satan and a remarkably malleable God is surely best understood in the light of, for example, the trickster folk-tale form.[3] In the end, there is no significant

---

1 Marvin Pope, *Job* (Anchor Bible; New York, Doubleday, 1965), p. xxvi.

2 There is a parallel in scholarly work on the Psalms, which used regularly to amend stichs and cola with the excuse 'm.c.' (*metri causa* – because of the metre). This is less often found now, because of a general recognition that we have effectively no knowledge of how metre, rhythm and verse or line length worked in ancient Hebrew poetry.

3 On this type of folk-tale see further in Chapter 11, below.

move to propose a form of Job in which only the dialogues appear, since at the very least they need to be motivated by *something*, and it would be perverse to remove the obvious frame in favour of something purely hypothetical. The 'tidy' structure which results from these various observations is given below.

Job: A revised and simplified structure

Prologue	1—2	
Job's opening lament	3	
First cycle		4—14
Second cycle		15—21
Third cycle		22—31
Yahweh's speeches		38—41
Job's response	42.1–6	
Epilogue	42.7–17	

This is *almost* chiastic. If we interpret Job's lament in chapter 3 as a response to what Yahweh has orchestrated through Satan, we could perhaps link Yahweh's speeches with Job's response in a similar cause-and-effect manner.

The fractured structures of Job: an exercise in reading

In this section I want to make the case for a meaningful interpretation of the structure *as it is* in the book of Job, or – to use a now familiar technical term – a reading of the *final form* of Job. In practical terms this means that I shall assume that all of the 'problems' identified by critical scholarship should be disregarded: whatever may actually have happened in the process of transmission of the text, I intend to discuss it now *as if* what we have before us is the form that demands to be explained.

The dialogues

Job is a man we all want to feel sorry for. He has been afflicted with the most awful and undeserved horrors – including the loss of the whole of his family apart from his wife. He sits, famously and apocryphally – the text of 2.7 actually refers to ashes, a sign of mourning – on a dung heap and scratches the sores which Satan, with Yahweh's permission, has added to his other suffering. At length, after a week's silence, he speaks – but only to curse the day he was born (ch. 3). This is a grim but majestic poem which uses the most powerful of language to deny life: indeed, it has been described as an anti-creation song.

Immediately following Job's cry of despair the cycles of dialogues begin. And go on . . . and on . . . and on . . . For, despite the reader's willingness to sympathize, there is something wearisome about Job's continued protestations of innocence. Despite the proverbial saying about the patience of Job, there is in truth little sign of that virtue in his responses to his situation. Like those people who lose our compassion by never letting up on how awful everything is, Job too seems bent upon driving us away. For 18 full chapters between 4 and 31 he expands at length upon his misfortune, his innocence, and the deity's refusal to attend a tribunal at which God could be held to account. Thus one of the ways in which the flawed structure of Job feeds into a reading of the book is that, just as the sympathetic ear tires of the victim's story, so does the text itself grow tired. After two full cycles, and no sign of a resolution, it is as if the third cycle collapses under its own inertia.

This breakdown is not simply a mimesis of reality, for it has another fascinating effect: it points to the ultimate failure of dialogue – there is no way that an unending cycle of cycles will ever reach closure, and there is no way that the indefinite continuation of intellectual argument will bring the participants to an agreed conclusion. No concordat will issue from this set of dialogues, no matter how firmly everyone asserts that a full and frank exchange of views has taken place. This second level of meaning is further affirmed by the immediate presence of the (apparently) intrusive wisdom poem in chapter 28. But of course, it is *not* intrusive; its presence is *not* accidental. What it constitutes is a reminder to *all* the participants (and that includes the reader) that wisdom and understanding are not to be found through mere cerebral activity. Wisdom is ultimately beyond our grasp unless we also grasp the importance of 'the fear of the Lord' – the awe and respect which is due to Yahweh, even while that same god inflicts upon us seemingly meaningless and unmerited pain. It is important to realize that, standard translations apart, the words of this chapter should *not* be attributed to Job, but rather seen as the work of the anonymous author through whose words we are given insight into the predicament of the book.

This theme differs in an interesting way from the core teaching of Proverbs, where the emphasis is precisely on the individual's potential to acquire wisdom and duty to become wise. No doubt Proverbs sees the task as one to be conducted from the context of a proper relationship with God, but it is still a *possible* quest. The remoteness of wisdom, as described in Job 28, has closer affinities with the philosophy of Philo, for whom *sophia* (wisdom) and the *logos* (word) belonged to that intermediary realm between the absolute God and the human which could only be reached by the most advanced spirits. In its stress on the divine origins of wisdom there are anticipations of the theology of Sirach – particularly chapters 1, 24 and 51.13–22 – which we shall consider in Chapter 10.

A few notes on chapter 28

Despite the tendency to regard this orphan chapter as an isolated example of wisdom, it is in fact quite closely connected to later motifs in Job. While some of its language – in particular vv. 12, 20 and 28 – has parallels in Proverbs (1.7; 3.7) and Qoheleth (7.23, 24), most of the chapter is in fact an anticipation of the kind of arguments which will be found in the speeches of Yahweh. In particular this is true of the language of nature, both physical and animal (v. 26 is actually repeated in 38.25). Thus it would be a mistake to dismiss this passage as an intruder from another genre.

Job's long speech in chapters 29—31 forms the conclusion of his case, and contrasts interestingly with the death wish of chapter 3. Far from wishing he had never been born, he now has the strength of mind and will to put his case firmly before God in the hope (however vain) of a fair hearing. The model of the court action is reflected also in the fact that the adversaries now keep silent. The final word (it seems) goes to the accused – who is also, of course, prosecuting council. How does Job reach this point of rational argument from the starting point of despair in chapter 3? I believe that a closer examination of the various themes with which we engaged in Chapter 6 shows that, far from being a simple process of repetition, there is in fact movement within the dialogues – a movement that constitutes a real shift in Job's thinking and prepares the way for the final stages of the book.

Elihu, Yahweh and the Epilogue

Job himself is much given to asking questions (many of them rhetorical), and much of the irony of the book lies in his being suddenly faced with a response to these questions – and that from a God who demolishes Job's case by means of equally rhetorical language. I have attempted to show in the first part of this section that the very structure of the book is arguably designed to undermine Job's own starting point and to lead him (and us as readers) into a new perception of the relationships involved. But what of 'the question', the 'problem of suffering'? What in the end is the contribution of Job to this long-standing riddle? I believe that just as the cycle of dialogues both structurally and in terms of content succeeds in subverting Job's initial set of priorities, so the book as a whole may be read as a dramatic or deconstructive analysis of the propriety of asking such questions in the first place. There is also a certain wry humour to be found in the fact that the epilogue quietly unstitches everything that Job has earlier argued by restoring to him twice as much as he had before as a 'reward' for his righteousness!

But surely the clearest *intellectual* implication of our study of Job is that the question as traditionally put is simply misconceived. It leads either to paradox or to incoherence; a result which in any other field of rational enquiry would immediately prompt the response, 'You're asking the wrong sort of question.' The defining of God's nature is not an abstract exercise which can be carried out in isolation from our position as thinking life-forms within a universe about which we postulate certain general truths (including the observation that individuals who appear to us to be 'innocent' also appear to us to 'suffer'). The theodicy question is thus subject to the *intellectual* objection that it presumes a knowledge of God which is in fact dependent upon the definition of terms like 'justice' and 'innocence' which appear in the question. This, in the end, is why the drama of Job renders the hero speechless, and is precisely the point of his response in 42.3:

> Therefore I have uttered what I did not understand,
>   things too wonderful for me, which I did not know.

But of course Job is far more than an intellectual exercise (though it is undoubtedly at least that). It is a spiritual odyssey and a psychological journey into self-knowledge. The parallels between 23.8–17 and Psalm 139 which we examined in Chapter 6 suggest – perhaps surprisingly – a cultic experience not dissimilar to that of the psalmists. As to the latter, there is room here only to hint at what might be at work. Jack Kahn[4] has already provided a major contribution to this approach; I would wish only to add a further dimension (perhaps best described as 'literary-psychological') in terms of a phrase familiar to Scots: the self-righteousness of the 'unco guid'. Burns's 'Holy Willie's Prayer', and Hogg's *Confessions of a Justified Sinner*[5] will serve as potent symbols of what I mean: the alienation of the individual whose self-awareness is that they alone exemplify personal probity in a world of otherwise mediocre

---

4 Jack Khan, *Job's Illness* (Oxford, Pergamon Press, 1975).

5 James Hogg, *The Private Memoirs and Confessions of a Justified Sinner* (London, Panther, 1970 [1824]). Hogg's hero is convinced that, being predestined to salvation, he can act in whatever way he pleases. Burns's poem 'Holy Willie's Prayer' celebrates the hypocritical self-righteousness of a notorious elder of the Church of Scotland. See *Chambers Poetical Works of Robert Burns* (Edinburgh, W. & R. Chambers, 1990), p. 63.

individuals. It is an alienation born of arrogance masquerading as piety – something that is as contemporary as it is ancient. Might not the drama of Job as a whole be interpreted as a journey from a peculiarly egocentric notion of righteousness to an integrated, balanced view of one's role as servant of God in relationship to others? The drama begins by describing an almost impossibly idyllic scene (one may suspect here some ironic hyperbole) which is rapidly destroyed by various calamities as a result of which Job is left alone and suffering, but protesting his innocence. In a dramatic sense, we then follow through the dialogues the process by which a man whose instincts are to proclaim that everyone (including God) is wrong but him is brought to a quite different sense of his status. It is only when Job abandons his isolation and slowly discovers how to relate to those who challenge him that he can find some meaning in his situation. The last sections of the book (Elihu, 32—37, and Yahweh, 38—41) signal a significant reversal: Job is now the thoughtful listener, rather than the stalwart debater. His final confession completes the process – he is now reconciled not only to God but to his fellows (note his prayers for his adversaries in 42.8–10) – and this is spelled out in graphic terms by the extravagant restoration of his fortunes in the epilogue.

These final comments are, of course, sketchy in the extreme. But they do have one virtue, that of taking the prologue and epilogue seriously as vital elements of the whole work. And what does that work describe? A psychological journey from solitary righteousness (1.1) to a proper understanding of religion as a celebration of the community of men and women and God together (42.10–11). In other words, the ultimate religious question of the book of Job is not, 'How do we reconcile the justice of God with the suffering of humanity?'; it is rather, 'How do we rediscover and redefine ourselves as individuals in relationship with others within the community of faith?' In the last section of this chapter I shall present an interpretation of Job which was originally published in 1985.[6]

A reading of Job

Job is frequently described as the finest example in the ancient world of an individual's lonely fight with the soul-destroying effects of unjust suffering. Where the Psalmist spoke within and for the faithful community, Job speaks as one who is outcast, whose very suffering is taken to be proof of his rejection by God and society alike. Yet, as we have seen, a close reading of the book as a whole produces a disturbing effect: Job's complaints become wearisome after a time. His constantly

---

6 Alastair G. Hunter, *Christianity and Other Faiths* (London, SCM Press, 1985), pp. 134–9.

reiterated protestations of innocence, touching at first, gradually begin to nag at the reader like a decaying tooth and we find ourselves more in sympathy with Job's adversaries than would have seemed possible at first. This increasing disenchantment is an important part of the drama. It is an example of a familiar effect in which the way something is presented becomes part of the meaning itself. The alienation of the reader from Job and his problems is part of the message of that troublesome book. He is *utterly* alone: not even posterity has sympathy with him. In 19.23–25 Job gives voice to a prayer which has become one of the most memorable passages in the whole book:

> Oh that my words were written down!
>   Oh that they were inscribed in a book!
> Oh that with an iron pen and with lead
>   they were engraved on a rock for ever!
> For I know that my Redeemer lives,
>   and at the last he will stand upon the earth.

The first part of this prayer, though literally fulfilled, is by a dark dramatic irony negated by the effect his words have on those to whom he appeals for vindication. And the second part of the prayer is in Hebrew which has become so damaged and distorted that it is virtually impossible to know what its original meaning was.[7] Thus Job is twice silenced, once because we understand his words and find ourselves out of sympathy with him, and again because we can no longer understand his words. Christian piety has been content to see in the mysterious 'redeemer' (Hebrew *go'el*) a prophecy of Christ; but this is unsubstantiated by the text which belongs, in so far as it can be reconstructed, to the domain of the law (while the word *go'el* is used poetically of ransoming from death, its major use is as a legal term). Job anticipates that if his testimony is preserved and read, some counsel for the defence will come forward to acquit him. But none such appears and from now on it is clear that the gap between Job and his advisers is unbridgeable, as his complaints increase and his speech becomes increasingly fretful (see in particular ch. 31). He is ultimately unlovable. Our hearts do not warm to him and though he deserves our understanding, he fails somehow to win our sympathy.

Now this is a man who has without any shadow of a doubt pursued the injunction to 'get wisdom, get insight' (Prov. 4.5) with unremitting ardour. He has asked and asked, he has been grossly importunate in his demands of God. He has sought (as men seek for wisdom in ch. 28)

---

7 See almost any modern version of this passage, and note the number of alternative translations and reservations made. NRSV, for example, says of v. 26, 'Meaning of Heb of this verse uncertain'. That is certainly an understatement!

high and low, day and night. He has knocked and beaten his fists against closed doors until they bled with pain, but to no avail. His God remains resolutely silent and hidden. His friends tell him to see sense. His wife offers hard-headed advice: 'Do you still hold fast your integrity? Curse God and die' (2.9). His modern readers might find it hard to believe that anyone could be quite so pure, and be inclined rather to interpret his protestations as a sign of guilt than of innocence. Jack Kahn, as we have already noted, has even analysed the dialogues as a record of psychological illness[8] – a peculiarly modern solution.

Job has alienated himself from all human support, and his intellect serves only to demonstrate more forcibly the vanity of his beliefs and the hopelessness of his case. Even in such extremes, however, a dialogue can take place, and this is what the final chapters of the book of Job are devoted to. At the beginning of chapter 32, when Job's complaints have finally ended, a new character enters the story. This man's name is *Elihu,* and he speaks for six chapters – longer by far than any of the other friends, half as long again as God himself, and equalled only by Job's last set of speeches in chapters 26—31. There are a number of important points to be noted:

1 Elihu's name can be interpreted to mean 'He is my God', and it is quite clear that 'He' refers to Yahweh, the personal name of the God of Israel, and the name used for God when he finally addresses Job in chapter 38. Thus immediately we find a significance in the name which is not present in the case of the other three advisers.

2 Although Job responds volubly to the criticisms of his other advisers, culminating in the lengthy speech which ends in chapter 31, he makes no response to Elihu at all. Elihu has done what hitherto seemed impossible: he has rendered Job speechless. It is not without significance that only Yahweh himself is able to force out of Job the admission that he has no reply to make (40.3–5; 42.1–6).

3 There are a number of features of Elihu's speech which foreshadow the arguments to be used by Yahweh. (a) He appeals to the character of God as creator and sustainer of the created order, as the all-powerful at whose word the most unruly elements are obedient (36.24—37.13). (b) His manner of hurling unanswerable questions at Job (for example, 37.14–20) is exactly mirrored in God's speeches (cf. ch. 38). (c) The direct challenge to Job, who up until now has been asking all the questions, is that he should answer – if he can! (33.5, compare Yahweh's challenge in 38.1–3 and 40.1–2).

---

8 I would not wish it to be thought that I was dismissive of this book, which is, within its terms of reference, a most interesting and stimulating study.

Following immediately upon Elihu's exhortations, with no word of reply from Job, no opportunity indeed for any reply, the drama concludes with the speeches of Yahweh in person, 'out of the whirlwind'. The language used here is designed to convey the awesome and terrifying aspect of the presence of the Almighty, whom to see is death, whose least word causes the whole earth to shake to its very foundations. The whirlwind accompanies God's appearances, or is used by God as a weapon of terror, in all but a few of its occurrences in the Old Testament.[9] At the end of his first speech, Yahweh gives Job an opportunity to speak (40.1–2):

And the LORD said to Job:
  'Shall a fault-finder contend with the Almighty?
  Anyone who argues with God must respond.'

At last! This is what Job has asked for: 'I would speak to the Almighty, and I desire to argue my case with God. . . . I have indeed prepared my case; I know that I shall be vindicated. . . . Call, and I will answer; or let me speak, and you reply to me' (13.3, 18, 22). But here is a strange thing: this great man of words, this furious debater, has become strangely tongue-tied (40.3–5):

Then Job answered the LORD:
  'See, I am of small account; what shall I answer you?
    I lay my hand on my mouth.
  I have spoken once, and I will not answer;
    twice, but will proceed no further.'

Still this is not the end. Yahweh goes on to illustrate his power in the figures of the two great monsters Behemoth and Leviathan (40.15—41.34), a passage which has produced more than a little disagreement among interpreters. Some want to 'demythologize' the two beasts by identifying them as the hippopotamus and the crocodile respectively. This seems to me to misunderstand both the theology and the poetry of the passage. Surely the point is that Behemoth and Leviathan should be creatures which human beings could *never* conceivably master, creatures from the primordial nightmares of the human race and therefore a vivid expression of the mythical powers of raw untamed nature. It is in his control

---

9 It is used by God against Jonah (1.4, 11, 12, 13), it is the means by which Elijah is carried up to heaven (2 Kings 2.1, 11), and is found in a number of prophetic books (Isa. 28.2; 29.6; 40.24; 41.16; Jer. 23.19=30.23; 25.32; Ezek. 1.4; 13.11, 13; Nahum 1.3; Hab. 3.14; Zech. 7.14; 9.14) and features in several Psalms (50.3; 55.8; 83.15).

of them that God makes dramatically clear his absolute dominion over creation.

Having thus convincingly asserted his unique claims, Yahweh holds his peace. Now at last Job finds his voice. No longer does he argue and fume and fret. Yet there is more than just the somewhat sullen response of chapter 40, which might have been expressed in colloquial language as 'What's the point of saying anything? I've obviously said too much already, and I'd best keep my mouth shut from now on.' In his final confession he admits God's two specific charges against him ('Who is this that hides counsel . . .' and 'Hear, and I will speak . . .') and fights through to the realization that his mourning and his self-abasement have been an indulgence of self-pity rather than noble suffering: 'I despise myself, and repent of[10] dust and ashes.' Far from being a portrayal of a chastened and humiliated man, we have here something more like a shout of praise as the dark begins to fade and the light dawns (42.1–6; my translation):

> At last Job answered Yahweh:
> I know that you have power to do anything,
>   that nothing you intend can be thwarted.
> ['Who is this who hides wise advice without knowledge' (cf. 38.2)]
> Therefore I declare! – though I do not understand;
>   wonders far beyond me! – though I do not comprehend.
> ['Listen, and I will speak;
>   I will question you, and you will explain to me' (cf. 38.3)]
> I knew of you by hearsay,
>   but now I really see:
> Therefore I reject my complaints,
>   and repent of dust and ashes!'

It was no easy answer that Job found, though if he had *begun* with that sort of statement we might justifiably have found him guilty of superficiality. It was only after he had gone through all the process of grief and protest, of wild railing against the fates, that the healing mechanism could begin. The book presents it as an external debate, though we might in modern terms express it as an inner dialogue. First Elihu, a human figure who clearly stands *in loco dei,* prepares Job for the inevitable: it is as if Job has for the first time become aware of issues beyond his own immediate circumstances. The voice of conscience, perhaps, has found

---

10 Other translations have 'Repent *in* dust and ashes', which of course gives a completely different meaning. My translation follows that indicated by Lester J. Kuyper in *Vetus Testamentum* IX, 1959, p. 91 and Dale Patrick, *Vetus Testamentum* XXVI, 1976, p. 369, and much earlier by Maimonides in *The Guide for the Perplexed*, III, 23.

personification in Elihu. Fittingly, the hero is silent at this juncture; words would be premature, and protest is past. Then comes the revelation, the gradual dawning of insight. That the process is a slow, reluctant one is demonstrated by Job's first response in 40.3–5. We do not abandon cherished beliefs lightly; and even if the final 'conversion' seems sudden, it only marks the last small step in what has been a long and eventful journey. So for Job the journey ends as we have seen with a new hope: the answers may never be found, but God remains, and with that realization there comes a kind of peace – *shalom* – that no 'outrageous fortune' can disturb.

But that cannot be the last word; for however satisfying this conclusion may be in artistic terms, the book of Job does not end there. It sums things up in a narrative passage which in a way makes a nonsense of the preceding drama, for it reverts to the old dogma that righteousness can be measured by prosperity: the very doctrine that Job had sweated blood to deny! 'The Lord restored the fortunes of Job, when he had prayed for his friends; and the Lord gave Job twice as much as he had before' (42.10). This abrupt return to the status of Job at the beginning of the book seems to undermine, to deconstruct, what we have witnessed and shared in the progress of the debate. What, in the end, is the point of exploring and probing conventional wisdom if it turns out that the whole thing was an elaborate trick? It could be that the restoration described in 42.10–17 is a metaphor for the wholeness of soul which Job has achieved, and is not meant to be taken literally. But this stretches credulity to unreasonable lengths. Perhaps, on the other hand, this is the signature of a somewhat frivolous God who, taken by Job's boldness in challenging the very Lord of the Universe, takes a perverse pleasure in taking his – and the reader's – breath away by imposing a trite but nonetheless provocative closure to the book; and by so doing, bringing us right back to the beginning, our questions unanswered, our journey but a circle round an unmoving centre.

Some points to think about

Chapter 3, in which Job expresses very negative feelings, is sometimes described as an 'anti-creation poem'. Evaluate this claim by comparing it with the standard creation liturgy in Genesis 1.

The material often described as the 'confessions' of Jeremiah (Jer. 11.18–23; 12.1–6; 15.10–21; 17.9f, 14–18; 18.18–23; 20.7–18) provides another example of an extended discourse not unlike that of Job.
Look at the Jeremiah passages in this light and evaluate whether the comparison is valid.

In the light of the interpretations of Job we have offered in this chapter, what might a reading of the hypothetical reconstruction of Job given in the information box on p. 135 look like?

Can you improve on the explanations of 42.1–17 provided in this chapter?

Further reading

Clines, D. J. A. (1989) *Job 1–20*, Waco, Word Books

Cook, A. S. (1968) *The Root of the Thing,* Indiana University Press, 1968

Cook, Stephen L., *et al.* (eds) (2001) *The Whirlwind: essays on Job, hermeneutics and theology in memory of Jane Morse*, London, Sheffield Academic Press

Dell, Katharine J. (1991) *The Book of Job as Sceptical Literature*, New York, de Gruyter

Duquoc, C. (1983) *Job and the Silence of God*, Edinburgh, T. & T. Clark

Eaton, J. H. (1985) *The Book of Job*, Sheffield, JSOT Press

Fyall, Robert S. (2002) *Now My Eyes have Seen You: images of creation and evil in the book of Job*, Downers Grove, Ill.; Leicester, Inter-Varsity Press

Glatzer, N. H. (1969) *The Dimensions of Job*, New York, Schocken Books

Gordis, R. (1965) *The Book of God and Man*, Chicago, Chicago University Press

Gordis, R. (1975) *The Book of Job,* Jewish Theological Seminary of America

Habel, N. C. (1985) *The Book of Job*, London, SCM Press

Hartley, J. E. (1988) *The Book of Job*, Grand Rapids, MI, Eerdmans

Hofman, Yair (1996) *A Blemished Perfection: the book of Job in context*, Sheffield, Sheffield Academic Press

Janzen, J. Gerald (1985) *Job*, Atlanta, GA, John Knox Press

Jones, E. (1966) *The Triumph of Job*, London, SCM Press

Kahn, J. (1975) *Job's Illness*, Oxford, Pergamon Press

Murphy, Roland E. (1999) *The Book of Job: a short reading*, New York, Paulist Press

Newsom, Carol A. (2003) *The Book of Job: a contest of moral imaginations*, Oxford; New York, Oxford University Press

Penchansky, David (1990) *The Betrayal of God: ideological conflict in Job*, Louisville, KY, Westminster/John Knox Press

Pope, M. H. (1965) *The Book of Job*, New York, Doubleday

Rodd, C. (1990) *The Book of Job*, London, Epworth Press

Scheindlin, R. P. (1998) *The Book of Job*, New York, W. W. Norton

Whybray, N. (1998) *Job (Readings)*, Sheffield, Sheffield Academic Press

Wolde, Ellen van (ed.) (2004) *Job's God*, London, SCM Press

Zerafa, P. P. (1978) *Wisdom of God in the Book of Job*, Rome, Herder

Zuckerman, Bruce (1991) *Job the Silent*, Oxford, Oxford University Press

8

Sceptic, Realist or Cynic?
The life and philosophy of Qoheleth

Qoheleth: an overview

Introduction

The book of Ecclesiastes, known in Hebrew as Qoheleth, is an unlikely candidate for membership of the Hebrew canon. Its chief attitudes, on first acquaintance, appear to be cynicism, realism, fatalism, atheism, and despair – approaches to life which would not seem to be entirely in harmony with the rest of Scripture. The rabbis were unsure of its value, and continued to debate whether it 'contaminated the hands'[1] (their technical term for the defining quality of sacred Scripture) into the second century AD. That it was in the end accepted, along with the equally problematic Song of Songs, owes something to its attribution[2] to Solomon. But that acceptance was enhanced by the presence within it of a contrary mood which was tolerant of a much more conventional reading of the book.

Many readers have found in Qoheleth not a counsel of despair but a pious, faithful, believing and God-fearing attack on the kind of negative attitudes that are listed above. Such a reading is based primarily on two phenomena: first, the fact that the last verses of the book (12.13–14) are quite conventional in their teaching ('The end of the matter; all has been heard. Fear God, and keep his commandments; for that is the whole duty of everyone. For God will bring every deed into judgement, including every secret thing, whether good or evil'), and, second, that there is a regular scattering of traditional advice among the undoubtedly despairing language. Chapter 5 is a good example of this mixed signalling. The

---

1 By long convention, the books which were fully canonical Scripture were held to 'defile the hands' on the grounds that, as sacred Scripture, they belonged to the realm of the holy. Whenever a mortal handles the sacred books, he or she must wash their hands afterwards to prevent any improper contact between the holy and the secular worlds.

2 As we shall see, the name Solomon is never used; but the reference to 'son of David' in 1.1 can be interpreted that way.

first seven verses, describing how we ought to approach God, could easily find a place in a book like Proverbs:

> Guard your steps when you go to the house of God; to draw near to listen is better than the sacrifice offered by fools; for they do not know how to keep from doing evil. Never be rash with your mouth, nor let your heart be quick to utter a word before God, for God is in heaven, and you upon earth; therefore let your words be few. For dreams come with many cares, and a fool's voice with many words. When you make a vow to God, do not delay fulfilling it; for he has no pleasure in fools. Fulfil what you vow. It is better that you should not vow than that you should vow and not fulfil it. Do not let your mouth lead you into sin, and do not say before the messenger that it was a mistake; why should God be angry at your words, and destroy the work of your hands? With many dreams come vanities and a multitude of words; but fear God.

Verses 8–12 sound an uncertain note: the brief narrative about oppression in a particular province (vv. 8–9) could be an exercise in cynicism, suggesting that endemic injustice makes life easier for kings!

> If you see in a province the oppression of the poor and the violation of justice and right, do not be amazed at the matter; for the high official is watched by a higher, and there are yet higher ones over them all.[3] But all things considered, this is an advantage for a land: a king for a ploughed field.

But then the next three verses propound unremarkable truisms (money and wealth can never satisfy those who pursue them, and peaceful sleep is the special prerogative of those who perform honest hard work). The chapter ends with some reflections of a rather despairing nature on the fact that at the end we all return to the earth as naked as the day we were born (v. 15) and therefore that the best we can do is to 'eat and drink and find enjoyment in all the toil with which one toils under the sun the few days of the life God gives us' (v. 18). The judgement as to the writer's ultimate intention is more than usually difficult, and this chapter is not unrepresentative; is not surprising, therefore, that opinion as to the value of Qoheleth has varied widely.

---

3 I am irresistibly reminded here of the familiar ditty, 'Big fleas have little fleas upon their backs to bite 'em, and little fleas have littler ones, and so *ad infinitum*'.

Authorship, date and name

In chapter 1 the claim is twice made that the writer of the book is a king in Jerusalem (vv. 1, 12). In v. 1 he[4] is described also as 'son of David', and in v. 12 additionally as 'king over Israel'. Thus, though the name 'Solomon' is never mentioned, there is a clear implication (at least in v. 1) that we are meant to think of him. It is, however, odd that the postscript in 12.9–10 describes him simply as 'Teacher' (see below for a discussion of the meaning of the Hebrew 'Qoheleth' which lies behind the translation 'teacher' found in modern versions), and gives the strong impression that he was a scholar and not a monarch. It is possible that the mention of the son of David in v. 1 is simply the kind of titular attribution that is normal in wisdom literature (compare the introduction to Proverbs), and that the more nebulous 'king over Israel in Jerusalem' in v. 12 is simply a metaphor – or pose – which sets the scene for the kind of opulence described in chapter 2. After all, if the point is to demonstrate the vanity of the most indulgent of human pleasures and possessions, what better model to use than that of the petty oriental or Hellenistic despot familiar to the writer?

This brings us to an unavoidable, but probably fruitless discussion: when was the book written? Though the short answer is, 'Of course we don't know' there are nevertheless some clues. There are more than a few signs of familiarity with the material in the first chapters of Genesis – this is particularly obvious in chapter 3 – and the so-called 'primeval' material in Genesis is likely to be among the last to have been added to the Torah. The sceptical pose adopted in the book, whether or not the final attitude is one of faith, seems to many to reflect the Hellenistic thought world of the late third or early second centuries; moreover, the way that the writer adopts and then criticizes a number of sayings of a proverbial kind would seem to imply a composition later than the book of Proverbs. But by far the most conclusive evidence lies in the character of the Hebrew in which the book is written. It has many features common in later forms of the language, in particular those found in Mishnaic Hebrew (the language, as its name suggests, of the Mishnah, which was published around AD 200 but was certainly the result of at least 100 years of tradition), and lacks aspects common in biblical material from earlier periods. It is quite different, for example, from Proverbs, even though the mode of discourse is similar.

We know that the date of the non-canonical book with a similar name, Ecclesiasticus, is almost certainly early second century BC.[5] The author

---

4 There is a problem about the gender of the writer's name or title; see the box below.

5 See Chapter 9 for a detailed examination of the dating of Ecclesiasticus/ Sirach.

of that book was evidently a teacher and scholar who lived and worked in Jerusalem. It is a much more traditionally pious work, but is also clearly imbued with the religious and philosophical thinking of Hellenism. Both of these books reflect a kind of calm and unhurried approach to their subject which suggests a relatively peaceful context – even the sufferings and civil disturbances described in Ecclesiastes have the feel of a theoretical use of examples rather than something drawn from the writer's own experience. This suggests, without trying to place the two in any order, that they come from the period just before the Maccabean revolts which followed the accession of King Antiochus IV in 175 BC.

And what of the name which most readers of the English text associate with the author? The first thing to say is that the translation 'Preacher', which seems to have been introduced by Martin Luther and is found in older versions like the King James, is most inapposite. The mind behind the book is decidedly not that of a preacher in any sense which modern people would recognize. That title comes from a misinterpretation of the Greek term *ekklesiastes* which means something like 'the one who summons', but suffers by association with the later term *ekklesia* – 'the Church'; that is, 'the people who have been called'. That is why, in scholarly and Jewish circles, the word is often left untranslated in its Hebrew form Qoheleth (sometimes written as Koheleth). It is a strange term to use for the writer, whether he is indeed a king, or simply an honest teacher. In the first place, it is not a proper name – it describes a function; and in the second place, it is a feminine form. There is no real solution to this puzzle – hence the use of the word Qoheleth – but some of the background, and one intriguing suggestion, is set out in the box opposite. In fact the author is anonymous, and if we take 1.1 and 12.9–10 to be editorial additions, and perhaps even the references in 1.2 and 12.8, there are in the end only two uses of the term in the body of the book, in 1.12 and 7.27, and in the latter case it is explicitly feminine! The somewhat confusing conclusion is that the writer presents him/herself (or is presented) as perhaps male, perhaps female, perhaps a king and possibly a son of David. Nothing certain follows from this 'evidence'!

The meaning of Qoheleth

(a) Grammar

The basic Hebrew root[6] is *qahal* which is a noun, meaning 'gathering, assembly'.

There is a verb derived from the noun, meaning 'to gather'. In Hebrew the verb can take any one of a number of different forms. The root *qahal* only appears in what is called the *niphal* form.

The word *qoheleth* is technically a feminine participle, meaning 'she who calls'. Oddly, it belongs to a form of the verb – the *qal* – which is not used anywhere else with this root. However, with the exception of 7.27, it is always used with *masculine* verb forms in the book.

(b) In the titles and postscript

'Qoheleth' is used in 1.1, as if it were a proper name, in apposition to the further name/title 'son of David, king in Jerusalem'. In 1.12 the sense of a proper name is even stronger: 'I, Qoheleth, was king over Israel in Jerusalem.'

In 1.2 and 12.8, the text gives us 'Vanity of vanities, said Qoheleth'. In 12.8 the definite article is used: 'the Qoheleth'.

It is also used by whoever added the material in 12.9–10 which describes the qualities of the author.

(c) In the main body of the text

In 7.27 we find this: 'See, this is what I have discovered, said Qoheleth.' No other title is used, and the verb 'said' is also feminine – thus in this one case reinforcing the gender of Qoheleth.

(d) A solution to the puzzle?

Paul Nadim Tarazi[7] has proposed an intriguing solution, to the effect that there is a double identification going on. The passage in the middle of the book where Qoheleth appears is one in which wisdom

---

6 Hebrew grammar packages meaning in parcels called 'roots' – normally groups of three consonants – out of which all kinds of derived forms with various related meanings are constructed.

7 *The Old Testament: An Introduction. Volume 3: Psalms and Wisdom* (Crestwood, NY, St Vladimir's Seminary Press, 1996) pp. 133–7.

is discussed and (in a manner reminiscent of Proverbs) the seductive woman is encountered. Might Qoheleth therefore be a concealed persona of Wisdom? Following this through, the identification of Qoheleth as king suggests not a simplistic reference to the conventional Solomon (who is not in fact mentioned), but a more eschatological indication of the time when Wisdom and the Law[8] will rule in Jerusalem (note how 1.16 and 2.7, 9 describe Qoheleth as surpassing all who previously ruled in Jerusalem).

As we shall see in Chapter 9, Ben Sira, who almost certainly wrote and taught in the same period as 'Qoheleth', combined the concepts of Wisdom and Law (Torah) in a single personification of God's purpose for the people of Israel.

Language unique to Qoheleth

There are four linguistic expressions that are repeated in the book and which seem to have an important contribution to our understanding of it. They are also, within the Hebrew Bible, unique to Qoheleth. The first – *Vanity of vanities, all is vanity* – seems to serve as the theme or motto of the writer's thesis, since it is found only at the beginning and the end, in 1.2 and 12.8 (compare in Proverbs 'The fear of the Lord is the beginning of wisdom'). It is just possible that this motif has been extrapolated from the body of the text and used by an editor as part of the framework of the book,[9] given that these are third person references in what is a predominantly first person discourse. If so, it is clear that it is nonetheless sympathetic to and in harmony with the main thrust of the book itself.

This then forms the basis of a repeated leitmotif – *All is vanity and chasing the wind* – which is used several times in the first half of the book (specifically, in 1.14; 2.11, 17, 26; 4.4, 16; and 6.9); modified forms are found in 3.19 ('all is vanity') and 11.8 ('all that comes is vanity'). The simple expression 'vanity' continues throughout the book – indeed, of the 73 occurrences of this term in the Old Testament, 38 (52 per cent) are

---

8 Tarazi admits that the word *torah* does not occur in Qoheleth. However, there is a possibly significant accumulation of other key terms in 8.5: 'He who keeps (*shomer*) the commandment (*mitzvah*) will know no harm, and the mind of a wise man will know both the time and the judgement (*mishpat*).' The same terms turn up in the pious conclusion in 12.13–14: 'Fear God and keep (*shimor*) his commandment (*mitzvah*) . . . For God will bring every deed into judgement (*mishpat*) . . .'.

9 A similar argument could be made for the two framing instances in Proverbs, since they occur in 1.1–7 which seems to be a prologue, and 9.7–12, which interrupts the pairing of the two women in that chapter, and may have been added.

found in Qoheleth. It is not clear why this particular phrase is confined to the first half; perhaps it has some structural significance. Qoheleth is notoriously difficult to analyse formally, but some have seen chapter 7 as a crux, with its discussion of wisdom and the curious use of the feminine verb form in v. 27.

There is a well-known saying which seems to sum up the fatalism of Qoheleth's world view. It occurs four times – in 2.24; 3.13; 5.18; 8.15 – with some variations each time, though the essential set of ideas is the same: *There is nothing better for a man than to eat, drink and take pleasure in his toil.* It is striking that this is always a positive injunction in Qoheleth, for a similar phrase is found in Isaiah 22.13, 'Let us eat and drink, for tomorrow we die.' Here, however, it forms part of a condemnation of people who are so obsessed with material pleasures that they cannot hear God's warning. Luke 12.19–20 puts a similar phrase in the mouth of the rich farmer who foolishly believes his wealth will give him peace of mind ('I will say to my soul, Soul, you have ample goods laid up for many years; relax, eat, drink, be merry'), but here too the sense is darkly negative ('But God said to him, "You fool! This very night your life is being demanded of you. And the things you have prepared, whose will they be?"').

Finally, there is the phrase which occurs so often that we must consider it almost a cliché – at least of Qoheleth's writing style – *Under the sun.* (See 1.3, 9, 14; 2.11, 17, 18, 19, 20, 22; 3.16; 4.1, 3, 7, 15; 5.12, 17; 6.1, 12; 8.9, 15, 16; 9.3, 6, 9, 11, 13; 10.5.) Its most familiar use is in the celebrated observation, 'There is nothing new under the sun'; just one of a number of proverbial sayings which this ancient teacher has contributed to the world. The likely intention of this phrase is a reference to the quotidian, the relentless sameness of the sun's daily circuit and the inevitability of our own patterns of life and behaviour.

The combination of these idiosyncratic and striking turns of phrase with the late – almost Mishnaic – form of the Hebrew in which the book is written strongly reinforces the sense that we are in touch with a powerfully individual mind. The bold and radical nature of much of what he has to say is given an extra edge by his linguistic style, and by the fertility of his coinages. Unlike the writers of Proverbs and Sirach, whose generalities could be exchanged without most readers being aware of the fact, it is almost impossible to mistake the voice and tone of this supremely elegant, almost elegiac writer.

What does 'vanity' mean?

The Hebrew term *hebel* commonly translated as 'vanity' defies definitive interpretation.

It could perhaps better be rendered 'emptiness' or 'futility' – it is associated with words like 'nothingness' (Isaiah 30.7), 'desert' (Isaiah 49.4) and 'shadow' (Psalm 144.4) – but there is also a consistent association with the theme of lies or falsehood (Jeremiah 16.19; Zechariah 10.2; Proverbs 31.30).

In its plural form it is used sometimes as a synonym for idols or 'no-gods' (Deuteronomy 32.21; 1 Kings 16.13, 26; Jeremiah 8.19; 14.22).

Within Qoheleth it is frequently linked to *ruah* ('wind', 'breath' or 'spirit'), and a couple of times with 'shadow' and 'darkness' (6.4, 12). It turns up 38 times in the book, a frequency perhaps designed to numb the reader into acquiescence: the vain repetition of the word 'vain' surely has a powerfully mimetic effect!

Examples of the way translations and commentaries have rendered the term:

1 Translations

NRSV, RSV, KJV	'vanity'	NIV	'meaningless'
Tanakh, REB, NJB	'futility'	NEB	'emptiness'
GNB	'useless'	Knox	'shadow'

2 Commentaries

Most go with the traditional 'vanity', but Lohfink adopts the reading 'a breath' and Krüger has 'futile and fleeting'.

The canonical status of Qoheleth

Why is such a sceptical, even cynical book given space in the canon? It was certainly one of the books whose status the rabbis debated until well into the second century (the kind of discussions which went on are analysed in the box below), and its themes offer little comfort to those who hold a traditional view of theology. Its dubious status is shared with two other Old Testament books – the Song of Songs, which is in truth an erotic love poem, and was probably accepted because, from an early date, it was read allegorically; and Esther, which famously makes no mention of God, but has a powerful role as a Jewish nationalist tract and the foundation story for the festival of Purim. Ecclesiastes does not obviously fit either of these categories. To some extent, whether or not a book was received into the canon depended on a technicality: could it be regarded as having been composed within the prophetic period which came to an end at the time of Ezra? Books admittedly written late were excluded (thus, as we shall see in Chapter 9, Sirach). But while that may be a necessary condition, it is hardly sufficient. We know, for example, of Psalms attributed to David and found in the Dead Sea Scrolls material, but which are not included in the authorized editions of the Old Testament.

The rabbis and the canon[10]

Rabbinic tradition makes a distinction between *inspired Scripture* and *authoritative canonical books*. Not all canonical books fulfill the first criterion, and not all inspired scripture was included in the canon. This is because of the specifically halakhic purpose of the canon: it is primarily designed for use in the elaboration of the customs and traditions which guide Jewish life. The formula 'books which render the hands unclean' is used primarily to designate inspired Scripture, and discussions attributed to the rabbis about whether Qoheleth and Esther had that quality need not reflect on their canonical status. Equally, the fact that Sirach is not in the canon does not deprive it of potentially scriptural status as a source suitable to be cited for ethical and religious purposes, though not for halakhic decisions.

It is sometimes claimed, and used to be regularly stated, that there was a rabbinic council at Yavneh in the 90s AD which defined the Jewish canon. This is an overstatement: rabbinic discussions about particular books took place in the setting of Yavneh, but also continued into the second century, and it is most likely that the final shape of the canon was the result of long use and tradition rather than the specific decision of a 'council'. Indeed, that particular form of decision-making forum belongs peculiarly to the Church, and should probably not be read over into Judaism where decisions were far more likely to evolve through a gradual consensus.

In respect of Qoheleth, three points may usefully be made: First, the imputed authorship of Solomon should not be ignored for its significance in antiquity. The use of pseudonymous attribution to lend authority to a work is widely attested in the period from 200 BC to AD 200 (several of the books in the New Testament are attributed to people of status who

---

10 See in particular Sid Z. Leiman's 1976 study, *The Canonization of Hebrew Scripture: The Talmudic and Midrashic Evidence*. Full details of this and other relevant studies on this topic are given at the end of the chapter.

almost certainly did not write them). Second, we should not forget that
the writer himself may well have been a familiar and important figure in
the Jerusalem community in which he lived and taught (it is clear, by way
of a parallel, that Ben Sira was such a character). Thus the survival and
preservation of his work may, at first, have been an act of both piety and
respect. The postscript in 12.9–14 seems to bear this out. It consists of
three separate notes which in various ways pay tribute to the author and
embed him firmly within the context of orthodox wisdom:

1 Verses 9–10

A biographical addendum which is highly flattering, and portrays
Qoheleth as a fine and subtle scholar and teacher.

2 Verses 11–12

A general observation about wisdom which applies the new title 'Shepherd' to Qoheleth – the significance of this is explained below. In this
passage there is also a clear sense of 'enough', a warning against adding
to the existing body of teaching. This kind of message was in an earlier
age often added to treaties and public proclamations with a warning that
anyone who interfered with the text would be subject to the wrath of the
gods! Here the feeling is rather one of weariness and surfeit (the writer
should be alive now!).

'Shepherd' in Hebrew metaphor

The term 'Shepherd' is often used metaphorically in the Hebrew Bible.

The prophets often use the term of those who should have been
shepherds of the people but failed in their responsibility – a lack poign-
antly reflected in the phrase 'sheep without a shepherd' which is found
in Numbers 27.17 and 1 Kings 22.17. Perhaps Qoheleth is here identified as a *true* shepherd who imparts harsh but necessary teaching.

A second use applies the term to God (in Ps. 23.1; 80.1; Isa. 40.11
and Ezek. 34) and once to Cyrus in his god-given role as messiah (Isa.
44.28). In view of the suggestion above that 'Qoheleth' might refer to
Wisdom, this is an interesting dimension.

There is, however, a third unique reference: in Genesis 4.2 Abel is
described as a shepherd, and as it happens the Hebrew for 'Abel' is
identical to the word for 'vanity' which is so characteristic of Qoheleth.
Perhaps, then, this is a clever pun – but perhaps more, because, as we
shall see in 4.2, it is possible that Qoheleth refers to the legend of Cain
and Abel in chapter 4 of Genesis. Did Qoheleth (the Shepherd) like Abel
lose his life 'in vain' (Hebel)?

3 Verses 13–14

A very conventional epilogue which brings the book firmly under the aegis of traditional wisdom and conventional piety, and makes it clear that by the end of this particular journey we are meant to feel safely at home in the world of the pious teachers of Jerusalem.

Third, there is much that could count as traditional wisdom in Ecclesiastes (for example, 2.13–14, 26; 3.14; 5.1–2, 12). We are likely, from a modern perspective, to read the weariness of the book as a negative commentary on traditional piety. But the reverse reading is possible: age-old truths are adduced as a corrective to the kind of cynicism which is reflected in 'vanity' and which may have been endemic in the 'sophisticated' world of late Hellenism.

Overall structure

As we have seen, there is in Qoheleth, like Proverbs 1–9, a very sharply defined motto which opens and closes the book. It is customary to separate out the title and postscript as being part of a metatext which encloses the actual words of Qoheleth. This seems fairly uncontroversial: titles are found in a number of books, and it is only in the title that the phrase 'son of David' implies the conventional link with Solomon. The postscript quite clearly speaks of the author of the book in the third person, whereas the book itself adopts largely a first person stance.

Apart from these clearly marked features, there is not much overt structure to the text, though some have identified the reference to Qoheleth in 7.27 as a mid-point between two different sorts of discourse. I do not believe there is any clear justification for this, and so I have in preference suggested a very broad account of the contents, together with a separate list of what can plausibly be seen as key themes of the book.

Content

Title	1.1	
Motto	1.2	'Vanity of vanities! all is vanity'
Satire on Hymns in Praise of Order		1.2–11
An Exploration of Wisdom and Folly		1.12—2.26
Man and the Animals: on Futility		3.1—4.16
General Reflections on God, the World and Life		5.1—11.4
Life and Death		11.5—12.7
Motto	12.8	'Vanity of vanities! all is vanity'
Postscript	12.9–14	

Themes

    1   The three elegies

            The vanity of creation   1.2–11

            The vanity of work   3.1–9

            The vanity of life   12.1–7

    2   Qoheleth's anthropology: Qoheleth and Genesis (3.16—4.16)

    3   Qoheleth's theology

    4   The deconstruction of wisdom

Qoheleth: an essay in interpretation

The three elegies

There is a powerfully poetic dimension to Qoheleth. Two of his compositions are particularly well known: the meditation on 'A time to . . .' in chapter 3, and the solemn but yet curiously humorous meditation on the vicissitudes of old age in chapter 12. The third, in chapter 1, has more of the feel of a satire, taking many of the motifs of the creation myths of the Old Testament and reducing them to a weary cycle of inevitability. While this poem is not so well known, it has nonetheless contributed a phrase to the language which everyone (surely) has used at one time or another: 'There is nothing new under the sun'. In this section I shall offer a preliminary interpretation of these three elegies ('The vanity of creation', 1.3–11; 'The vanity of work', 3.1–8; 'The vanity of life', 12.1–7) from the point of view of their poetic structure, psychological emphasis, and theological position.

1 The vanity of creation (1.3–11)

The basic pattern of this poem is a listing of circularities which are directed to the question posed at the outset: 'What do people gain from all the toil at which they toil under the sun?' The first is the generations of people themselves, which are quickly shown to be transient in the face of the solid and permanent earth (v. 4):

> A generation goes, and a generation comes,
> but the earth remains for ever.

This comparison is immediately shown to be ironic, as the poet continues his reflections by imposing upon creation precisely the same circularity which is the fate of humankind (vv. 5–7):

The sun rises and the sun goes down,
   and hurries to the place where it rises.
The wind blows to the south,
   and goes round to the north;
round and round goes the wind,
   and on its circuits the wind returns.
All streams run to the sea,
   but the sea is not full;
to the place where the streams flow,
   there they continue to flow.

The purely descriptive mode of these verses gives way to a more reflective passage (vv. 8–10) in which the grandeur of creation – the view of the world which would be expected in wisdom – becomes a matter of mere weariness. Just as the dramatic elements of the earth are doomed to endless repetition, so is our view of them (v. 8). And just as the creation turns endlessly on itself, so does history (vv. 9–10):

What has been is what will be,
   and what has been done is what will be done;
   there is nothing new under the sun.
Is there a thing of which it is said,
   'See, this is new'?
It has already been,
   in the ages before us.

The conclusion is almost inevitable, but nonetheless stark: just as the cycles of nature and the repetitions of history leave no trace, so do the lives of those who ask, 'What is our gain?' Poetically, as with much of Qoheleth, form mimics sense and structure drives the outcome. The repetition of similar forms is itself circular, just as are the events portrayed. Psychologically, we are thrust right at the beginning of his book into the most uncompromising presentation of his philosophy. The innocent, reading his opening question, might expect something different – and rightly so, for there is an established tradition in which the dramatic features of creation are used both to display the power of God and to reassure the worshipper that he or she is in the same safe hands that hold the whole world. For example, consider the opening of Psalm 24:

The earth is the LORD's and all that is in it,
   the world, and those who live in it;
for he has founded it on the seas,
   and established it on the rivers.

Or the first, scene-setting words of Ben Sira (1.1–4):

> All wisdom is from the Lord
>   and with him it remains for ever.
> The sand of the sea, the drops of rain,
>   and the days of eternity – who can count them?
> The height of the heaven, the breadth of the earth,
>   the abyss, and wisdom – who can search them out?
> Wisdom was created before all other things,
>   and prudent understanding from eternity.

Compare also the famous celebration of wisdom's role in creation in Proverbs 8.22–31. These parallels cast into sharp relief the uncompromising nature of Qoheleth's vision which, if it is a celebration of creation, smacks more of the Epicurean philosophy of Lucretius than of the Jerusalem elite. And if these words deliver a psychological punch, they also bring to the fore a theological point: nowhere in this dramatic opening does God appear. This is a creation on auto-pilot, a deistic watch running on its own without any need for God and with equal lack of interest in its children. Whether Qoheleth himself was an atheist is unknown, but it is unlikely; thus the almost Derridean absence of 'god' from this passage, as from so much of the book, suggest not non-existence but deliberate absence. God does not need to enter into the equation because God *is* the equation, the tautological fact behind the mute wonders that this elegy describes. We take it for granted that both sides of an equation are equal: we take it for granted that God is (as we discover in 5.2) 'in heaven' and *ipso facto* cannot be expected to participate just to make us feeble souls feel better.

Lucretius (Titus Lucretius Carus)

A Roman poet and the author of the philosophical epic *De Rerum Natura* (*On the Nature of the Universe*), a comprehensive exposition of the Epicurean world view. Very little is known of the poet's life, though a sense of his character and personality emerges vividly from his poem. The stress and tumult of his times stands in the background of his work and partly explains his personal attraction and commitment to Epicureanism, with its elevation of intellectual pleasure and tranquillity of mind and its dim view of the world of social strife and political violence. His epic is presented in six books and undertakes a full and completely naturalistic explanation of the physical origin, structure, and destiny of the universe. Included in this presentation are theories of the atomic structure of matter and the emergence and evolution of life forms –

ideas that would eventually form a crucial foundation and background for the development of western science. In addition to his literary and scientific influence, Lucretius has been a major source of inspiration for a wide range of modern philosophers, including Gassendi, Bergson, Spencer, Whitehead, and Teilhard de Chardin.[11]

2 The vanity of work (3.1–8)

Poetically this second elegy combines the utmost simplicity with maximum impact as it tests almost to destruction the principle that the whole is greater than the sum of its parts. Its overt meaning is stated straightforwardly and without fuss right at the beginning, almost as if the writer wants to challenge the more familiar idea that a poem should reveal its secrets slowly and should require serious effort on the part of the reader: 'For everything there is a season, and a time for every matter under heaven.' There follows what is in effect a catalogue in a strict pattern whose relentless repetition is like a solemn drumbeat accompanying a state funeral procession. I am reminded a little of the famous opening words of Dickens's *A Tale of Two Cities*: 'It was the best of times, it was the worst of times' – and there too there is an ominous quality to the words which effectively anticipates the sombre themes of the story. In Qoheleth's poem the structure refuses any kind of ordering principle. While it begins with birth and death followed by a metaphor for fertility ('a time to plant and a time to pluck up what has been planted'), there is thereafter no visible pattern, as if to remind the reader that the events of life similarly resist meaningful interpretation.

Parallels to this elegy are not evident in the Old Testament, though there are some echoes to be found in Sirach. Thus 18.25–26 and 20.1:

In the time of plenty think of the time of hunger;
    in days of wealth think of poverty and need.
From morning to evening conditions change;
    all things move swiftly before the Lord.
There is a rebuke that is untimely,
    and there is the person who is wise enough to keep silent.

A more extended parallel may be cited in Sirach 33.7–9, but here the theological emphasis is quite different, and as the passage continues beyond v. 9 its didactic purpose becomes much clearer:

---

11 http://www.iep.utm.edu/l/lucretiu.htm

Why is one day more important than another,
   when all the daylight in the year is from the sun?
By the Lord's wisdom they were distinguished,
   and he appointed the different seasons and festivals.
Some days he exalted and hallowed,
   and some he made ordinary days.

The text 3.1–8 is interesting psychologically in the way that it combines several different effects which work insidiously on our perception.
The variety of experience it contains is energizing, a reminder of the
kaleidoscopic nature of life at its best. At the same time it conveys a sense
of urgency: the regular rhythm and beat impel us onward, reminding us
that we do not have unlimited time at our disposal. And the accumulative
force of the repeated forms serves as a sign that there is – always – much
more to life than can be summed up in a single individual's experience,
so that however relentless the poet's form may be, it points to a depth
and range of excitement which transcends the mere statement of the obvious. In short, the emphasis of the opening verse should be placed now
on 'everything': 'For *everything* there is a season' – there is room (as
Polonius remarked) for 'more things . . . than are dreamt of in your philosophy',[12] and as a result the poem takes on a strongly affirmative mode.
This is perhaps what inspired the famous folk version of the passage sung
by Pete Seeger, 'Turn! Turn! Turn! (To everything there is a season)'.

Is there a theological dimension to this poem? It can, of course, be read
as supporting in broad terms a deterministic view of human life which
has the characteristics of some forms of Calvinism. But this does not
seem to me to be an accurate reading, as the previous paragraphs will
have shown. Much more apt is, I think, a deist approach which recognizes materialistic determinism along with scope for human choice and
free will. That is, the *mechanics* of the universe are fixed (thus Qoheleth
1.3–11), but the range of possible events is so great that each individual
has effective freedom. Whether God (in Qoheleth's philosophy) has any
part in this is a moot point. In 3.17 there is a reference to the poem under
discussion:

I said in my heart, God will judge the righteous and the wicked, for he
has appointed a time for every matter, and for every work.

But in the very next verse he goes on the say that 'God is testing
[human beings] to show that they are but animals', a sentiment which
appears to negate the implied significance of judgement in v. 17. For
Qoheleth, it would seem, God is either absent or without special regard

---

12 *Hamlet*, Act 1, Scene v, Line 167.

for humankind; the elegy under discussion, on that view, becomes a powerful humanist anthem.

3 The vanity of life (12.1-7)

If the first elegy, on creation, could be taken to indicate *birth*, and the second *life* in all its richness, the final one is undoubtedly a meditation on *death*. Though exegetical opinion has varied as regards the way this allegory is to be interpreted,[13] and indeed as to whether it constitutes a single coherent allegory, I shall confine my reading here to the convention that it describes old age and the inevitable death of the individual. There is in Sirach 14.11–19 a reflection on old age with some similarities to Qoheleth 12, though once again there is an ethical dimension to the former which is quite absent from Qoheleth, and the meaning is conveyed explicitly rather than through metaphor.

That this piece should be read as a poem I take to be obvious, though it is not set out poetically in most English versions (NEB, REB, RSV, NRSV, KJV). Only in Tanakh, NJB and NIV is the poetic structure recognized typographically, as it is also in the principal Hebrew edition, BHS. Structurally it consists of one long, breathless sentence wending its way from youth and the creator to the return of the spirit to God and the dust to the earth. The journey takes in a startling range of metaphors, some apparently easy to decode, others more than a little mysterious. 'When the guards of the house tremble, and the strong men are bent, and the women who grind cease working because they are few, and those who look through the windows see dimly' (vv. 3–4) can easily be related to fairly obvious signs of physical decay. But what is the meaning of 'the almond tree blossoms, the grasshopper drags itself along'(v. 5)? It appears to have something to do with loss of desire, but the exact link is unclear, as indeed is the precise reference of the silver cord and golden bowl of v. 6. In the end what this produces is an effect like that of an impressionist painting, a celebration of vocabulary and sounds which combine to paint a word picture of startling clarity, even if its individual pieces cannot be separately analysed.

What is the psychology employed here? I like to think it is a kind of meandering stream of consciousness which serves to represent both the thought processes of age and the actual haphazardness of life which is, for most of us, a process of getting from A to Z without much of an idea how we managed it, and without any explicit design! More seriously, it encompasses both a distinct pleasure in the inventiveness of language and a reckoning with fate which is neither pessimistic nor resigned. For, if we

---

13 For a thorough discussion of the problems and possibilities of interpreting Qoheleth 12.1–7, see Krüger, *Qoheleth*, pp. 198–205.

look closely at the opening sentence, it is a call to enjoy and celebrate the good things *before* 'the days of trouble come'. There is an implied invitation to whoever reads this passage to defy the lyrical description of decay which follows, to endorse life and its pleasures for as long as possible; but to look the end squarely in the face without fear or regret.

And God? Unlike the other two elegies, God is explicitly present now, as 'creator'[14] in v. 1 and as the point of final return, of ultimate destiny, in v. 7. Does this constitute a theologically more significant presence than the overt absence of 'God' from the other two? I would suggest not: that we come from God and return to God is the least that could be said without professing overt atheism, at least in Qoheleth's world. The elegy on death is otherwise no more concerned with the role of the deity in the detail of life than were those on birth and life. It must be concluded, I think, that in Qoheleth we have three magnificent poetic reflections on life lived, in practical terms, without benefit of divine involvement. This is a startlingly modern conclusion, very much in keeping with western secular reality, where life is to be lived but surveys consistently report surprisingly high levels of belief in God.

Qoheleth's anthropology: Qoheleth 3.18—4.16 and Genesis

If Qoheleth is a humanist, he represents a particularly bleak form of that philosophy – one which holds out little hope of a rewarding outcome to life's endeavours, and which sees humanity's loneliness as particularly ineluctable (see, as a typical example, 5.13–17). Perhaps then it is best to define him as a sceptic – a man who can never be disappointed because he expects nothing from life – and a fatalist, in that he knows the futility of all our hopes and dreams and plans (2.12–23) and therefore settles in the end for the simple pleasures that come from our basic needs: to eat, drink and enjoy your work (2.24 etc.)! He is not, however, an atheist – and in that respect he differs radically from most of those modern readers who might be inclined to accept his acerbic take on life. No doubt the God he acknowledges is remote and austere, characterized as much by indifference to the human condition as by any of the more committed features which belong to Israel's post-exilic covenantal theology. But before we look further at Qoheleth's theological position, let us first consider one of the most interesting passages in the book. I refer to 3.18–22 in which he muses on a topic – the nature of the human 'soul' – which appears to have been the subject of some controversy in his own day.

---

14 There is an alternative view which suggests that the somewhat unusual form translated 'creator' could be modified to read 'pit' or 'grave', which would give the poem an altogether different emphasis.

The context of this specific point is the broader one of Qoheleth's use of Genesis – something that has been noted frequently by commentators. Katherine Dell gives a good summary of this in her book, 'Get Wisdom, Get Insight', (p. 62):

> The book of Ecclesiastes also shows the influence of a thought-world beyond strictly wisdom circles. A number of parallels have been noted . . . between Ecclesiastes and Genesis 1—11. For example, the idea of humans being made of dust and returning to dust (Eccl. 3.20; 12.7; cf. Gen. 2.7; 3.19); . . . the need for companionship (Eccles. 4.9–12; 9.9; Gen. 1.27; 2.18f.); the limitations on human knowledge (Eccles. 1.13; 8.7; 10.14b; Gen. 2.15f.); the idea of life as toil (Eccles. 1.3; 2.22; Gen. 2.15; 3.14–19); a preoccupation with death (Eccles. 3.20; 9.4–6; 11.8; 12.7; Gen. 2.17; 3.3f., 19–24; 6.13); and the idea that God is sovereign (Eccles. 3.10–14; 5.7; Gen. 1.28–30; 3.5, 22; 6.6). There is also a link with Genesis in ideas of the order and regularity of nature (Eccles. 3.11–12; Gen. 8.21f.) and of life being essentially 'good' (Eccles. 2.24; Gen. 1).

Some of these connections are more persuasive than others – I am, for example, not convinced that the last is accurate; and the idea that God is sovereign is surely too generally accepted to constitute a specific connection between Genesis and Qoheleth. The others, however, are strong enough to stand as evidence of more than a merely coincidental link (though it is a pity that the word for toil – 'amal – which is used frequently in Qoheleth is not found in Genesis 1—11). Combined with the reading of Qoheleth 1.2–11 as a kind of anti-creation hymn, this suggests a more than passing interest in the opening chapters of Genesis in the circles in which Qoheleth worked. Once again – as we shall see in subsequent chapters – there is an interesting overlap with Ben Sira, who also makes detailed use of the early chapters of Genesis in one of his meditations on creation (16.26—17.14). I want to look at two specific examples in more detail.

1 The common fate of humankind and the animals

In Ecclesiastes 3.18–22 there is a brief discussion of the ultimate fate of humanity (literally *bene ha'adam* 'children of adam') and the animals (*behemoth*) in which the point is firmly made that there is ultimately no difference in the fate of each. 'Who knows', asks Qoheleth, 'whether the human spirit goes upward and the spirit of the beast goes down towards the earth?' (v. 21). But the question is rhetorical, for the author knows very well (or is convinced) that we should not anticipate any special treatment after death. The reason is to be found directly in Scripture, in the myth of Adam and Eve. There we are told quite explicitly that 'the LORD God formed man of dust from the ground' (Gen. 2.7) and later, that 'out of the ground the LORD God formed every wild animal and every bird of the air' (Gen. 2.19). The fate of 'adam' is made equally clear in Genesis 3.19:

> In the sweat of your face
>   you shall eat bread
> till you return to the ground,
>   for out of it you were taken;
> you are dust,
>   and to dust you shall return.

Thus, Qoheleth's literally dusty answer to the speculation that the human spirit might survive is fixed firmly in a plain interpretation of the plain words of Scripture. If the dating of Ecclesiastes is indeed in the late third or early second century, it may well be that this passage is part of a conscious polemic against a new fashion; for we know that by then a belief in resurrection and judgement was emerging (for example, in Dan. 12.1–4). It is of particular interest, then, that the *terms* in which his refutation is carried out are those of a deliberate application of a hermeneutical principle – that the Scriptures we already possess can be worked into a sustained argument, which does not use them as proof texts, but makes them an integral part of the debate. Once again I have occasion to note that the same thing is true of Sirach, whose theological insights derive from a similar implied use of Scripture as a foundation upon which to build.

In defence of these claims I want to refer to some significant vocabulary which Qoheleth shares with Genesis 1—11 in general, and 2—3 in particular. I shall not engage in a detailed word search, though for those interested there is a list of the uses of the most important of them ('*aphar* = 'dust') in the box below.

Dust – an Old Testament word search

The Hebrew word '*aphar* ('dust') is used in a number of quite specific ways, as well as in rather general terms. To determine if the use in Qoheleth has links with Genesis, the following analysis may be helpful.

1 Meaning 'From the dust and to the dust'
  Gen. 2.7; 3.14, 19; Isa. 26.19; 29.4; Ps. 7.5; 22.15, 29; 30.9; 44.25; 103.14; 104.29; Job 1.9; 19.25; 20.11; 21.26; 34.15; Eccles. 3.20; 12.7; Dan. 12.2

2 Used as a sign of humiliation or mourning
  Gen. 18.27; Josh. 7.6; 1 Sam. 2.8; 1 Kings 16.2; Isa. 41.2; 47.1;
  49.23; 52.2; 65.25; Ezek. 27.30; Micah 1.10; 7.17; Ps. 72.9; 113.7;
  119.25; Job 2.12; 7.21; 16.15; 30.19; 42.6; Lam. 2.10; 3.29

3 Indicating Israel's multitudinous inheritance
  Gen. 13.16; 28.14; Num. 23.10; 2 Chron. 1.9

4 Miscellaneous
  Gen. 26.15; Ex. 8.16, 17; Lev. 14.41, 42, 45; 17.13; Num. 5.17;
  19.17; Deut. 9.21; 28.24; 32.24; 2 Sam. 16.13; 22.43; 1 Kings
  18.38; 20.10; 2 Kings 13.7; 23.4, 6, 12, 15; Isa. 2.10, 19; 25.12;
  34.7, 9; 40.12; Ezek. 24.7; 26.4, 12; Amos 2.7; Hab. 1.10; Zeph.
  1.12; Zech. 9.3; Ps. 18.42; 78.27; 102.14; Prov. 8.26; Neh. 4.2,10;
  Job 4.19; 5.6; 7.5; 8.19; 14.8,19; 22.24; 27.16; 28.2,6; 30.6;
  38.38; 39.14; 40.13; 41.33

The other expressions are 'to return' (*shub*), 'spirit' (*ruach*) and 'earth' or 'ground'[15] (*'eretz*), and the two mentioned at the beginning of the section – 'children of adam' and 'beast'. What we find is that Qoheleth brings together in one short passage this series of terms in a manner that is closely matched in certain sentences in Genesis and in no other place in the Old Testament. Nor is there any similar closeness between any other Old Testament passage and this material in Genesis. The Genesis references are:

> Then the LORD God formed man from the dust of the ground, and breathed into his nostrils the breath of life. (2.7)

> By the sweat of your face
>   you shall eat bread
> until you return to the ground,
>   for out of it you were taken;
> you are dust,
>   and to dust you shall return. (3.19)

> all flesh in which is the breath of life (6.17; 7.15, 22)

The development of these themes in this chapter is Qoheleth's unique interpretation, and it is certainly not a merely incidental aspect of his thinking, because it returns right at the end, in 12.7: 'and the dust returns

---

15 In Genesis the phrase 'out of the ground' uses a different word, *'adamah*, which has a punning link with the word *'adam*.

to the earth as it was, and the spirit returns to God who gave it'. This observation leads in turn to a supplementary structural gracenote relevant to the book as a whole. If 'vanity' is the motto which brackets the whole book, perhaps 'return to dust' represents a secondary *inclusio*:

Motto 1	'vanity of vanities' (1.2)
Theme 1	The futility of creation and the endless cycle of life (1.3—3.17)
Theme 2	The inevitability of death (3.18–22)
Motto 2	'dust to dust' (3.20)
Theme 2	The inevitability of death (12.1–6)
Motto 2	'dust to dust' (12.7)
Motto 1	'vanity of vanities' (12.8)

Clearly this does not constitute a neatly symmetrical pattern, but it does contribute to the shaping of what at times might seem to be a rather formless sequence of variations on a theme.

2 Qoheleth, Cain and Abel

In view of the connections with Genesis 2—3 that we have established, I want to look more closely at the next section of Qoheleth where I believe further – though less clearly signalled – reflections based on the Genesis material are to be found. In particular, I want to propose that it is possible to identify a thematic reworking of the Cain and Abel story (Gen. 4.1–16) in the opening verses of chapter 4 (bearing in mind also the curious fact – noted above – that Abel's name is identical with the word *hebel*, 'vanity'. This word play effect is in itself a notable link with the opening chapters of Genesis, where puns are regularly deployed to reinforce the mythic points being made. We have already noted 'Adam' out of the ground (*adamah*); to that we might add the 'marriage vow' in Genesis 2.23 ('this one shall be called Woman – *ishshah* – for out of Man – *ish* – this one was taken'), the fact that the words for 'crafty' (describing the snake in 3.1) and 'naked' (3.7) are the same, and Adam's naming of his wife 'Eve, because she was the mother of all who live' (3.20) which puns on a similar word meaning 'living'. What more appropriate, in a reflection on Genesis, than to introduce another piece of word play based on the central motif of Qoheleth as a whole? The table opposite shows how elements of the Genesis story might be linked with the details of Qoheleth 4.1–4.

	Ecclesiastes 4.1–4	Genesis 4.1–16
A	I considered all the acts of oppression here under the sun. (v. 1)	Cain said to his brother Abel, 'Let us go into the open country.' While they were there, Cain attacked his brother Abel and murdered him. (v. 8)
B	I saw the tears of the oppressed. (v. 1)	The Lord said, 'What have you done? Hark! your brother's blood that has been shed is crying out to me from the ground.' (v. 10)
C	I saw that there was no one to comfort them. Strength was on the side of their oppressors, and there was no one to avenge them. (v. 1)	The Lord said to Cain, 'Where is your brother Abel?' Cain answered, 'I do not know. Am I my brother's keeper? (v. 9)
D	I counted the dead happy because they were dead, happier than the living who are still in life. (v. 2)	Now you are accursed, and banished from the ground which has opened its mouth wide to receive your brother's blood, which you have shed. When you till the ground, it will no longer yield you its wealth. You shall be a vagrant and a wanderer on earth' (vv. 11–12)
E	I considered all toil and all achievement and saw that it comes from rivalry between man and man. (v. 4)	The Lord received Abel and his gift with favour; but Cain and his gift he did not receive. Cain was very angry and his face fell (vv. 4b–5)

The development of the Cain and Abel story in Qoheleth which is here proposed takes the form of a reversal of the legend as we usually receive it. (1) Qoheleth *begins* with a general observation, and only refers to the specific cause of the oppression at the end. (2) It is the dead who are blessed, the living who are cursed. But this is, of course, true to the Cain legend – the myth of the first murderer marked for unwanted and pitiless survival. Given that God's design is for humankind to return to the ground whence we were shaped, the fact that Cain is banished from the ground which received his brother's life-force (blood) is a travesty of our true end. (3) Though in the Cain and Abel story no one hears the cry of the oppressed, in Ecclesiastes we know that Qoheleth sees their tears.

But – in another ironic shift – we also know (from the rest of his writing) that no justice will be forthcoming. The tears of the oppressed which are seen are as unavailing as the cry of the victim which goes unheard. At least Abel was avenged by God; Qoheleth's God would be unlikely to take any interest in the matter. A point which leads us neatly into the next section: some reflections on Qoheleth's beliefs about God.

Qoheleth's understanding of God

It would be misleading to suggest that Qoheleth presents a theology, though he certainly has things to say about God. More importantly, he often *fails* to say anything about God at points where that might be anticipated. Perhaps, therefore, we should descibe this section as 'Notes towards an anti-theology'. I want to begin by returning to the opening creation hymn in 1.3–11. We have already noted the absence in it of any reference to God; the effect is to de-sacralize the creation process, suggesting that it is a kind of automatic process, quite unlike its counterparts in other places (surely familiar to ancient readers of Qoheleth) where the active involvement of the deity is the *sine qua non* of any successful ordering of chaos into creation. We could argue, perhaps, that Qoheleth is mischievous in his deliberate omission, which has the effect of forcing a re-examination of traditional theology and raising awkward questions. Ironically, the only reference to God in chapter 1 comes when Qoheleth laments that it is a thankless task the deity has given him to carry out – the study of wisdom (v. 13).

It is instructive to compare chapter 2 with the same chapter in Sirach. The latter sees life as a kind of test, a process of purification which refines the pursuer of wisdom just as gold is refined in the furnace. It conceives of a God who is to be trusted, who will reward and punish in accordance with the faithfulness of the individual. Consider, for example, his v. 10:

Consider the generations of old and see:
    has anyone trusted in the Lord and been disappointed?
Or has anyone persevered in the fear of the Lord and been forsaken?
    Or has anyone called upon him and been neglected?

Compare this with Qoheleth 2.15–16:

Then I said to myself, 'What happens to the fool will happen to me also; why then have I been so very wise?' And I said to myself that this also is vanity. For there is no enduring remembrance of the wise or of fools, seeing that in the days to come all will have been long forgotten.

The two writers both draw lessons from life and from the past, neither has a belief in an afterlife to lend consolation, yet how different in tone and content are their conclusions! Once again, it is the absence of God which startles us in our reading of Qoheleth – as if we are part of a cosmic experiment that God monitors from a safe distance, but does not interfere with. And when God does appear, in the concluding verses of the chapter, it is to provide sanction for the doctrine that 'there is nothing better for mortals than to eat and drink' (vv. 24–5)! That said, there is a sudden reversal in the concluding verse, as though our intrepid explorer in the realms of scepticism had taken cold feet (v. 26):

For to the one who pleases him God gives wisdom and knowledge and joy; but to the sinner he gives the work of gathering and heaping, only to give to one who pleases God.

This is the precise negation of Qoheleth's comment in v. 21:

. . . sometimes one who has toiled with wisdom and knowledge and skill must leave it all to be enjoyed by another who did not toil for it. This also is vanity and a great evil.

We observed above that one of the interpretative cruces of Qoheleth is how to understand the occasional outbursts of orthodoxy to which he is prone. This seems to be one such example – but perhaps it provides its own answer, for immediately after this seemingly traditional epigram there is a resounding disclaimer: 'This also is vanity and a chasing after wind.' If, as I suspect, the final phrase refers to the theology of the preceding sentence rather than the action it implies, then it can stand as Qoheleth's riposte to what he must have regarded as trite and superficial.

I have commented already on the theological aspects of the second elegy, so let me proceed immediately to the meditation which follows it, in 3.9–22. The first part of this section (vv. 9–17) is in fact an exegesis of the elegy. It begins with the touching observation that god 'has made everything beautiful in its time' (v. 11) and concludes (v. 17b) with a clear echo of the words of v. 1: 'he has appointed a time for every matter, and for every work.' In between we encounter a rather sad observation: God 'has put eternity (or "the universe") into our minds', but has at the same time made it impossible for us to comprehend anything God does. Thus, though there is a time for everything, not everything and not every time is available to humanity: what is fitting for us is the third motto, 'eat, drink and rejoice in your work'. The reference to eternity serves a dual purpose – on the one hand it expands upon the elegy to Fate, but on the other it anticipates the discussion in vv. 18–22 which we have already examined. For if, on the one hand, we cannot comprehend eternity (though we have a sense of it), on the other hand we are utterly barred from experiencing it. We may have more *knowledge* than the animals; but in the end that may be a curse rather than a blessing, since our knowledge will do us no good. Our breath vanishes as does that of the beasts, and our bodies return to dust as do theirs, and our intimations of immortality prove to be as insubstantial as the early morning mist. Hosea 13.3 offers a particularly poignant expression of this theme:

> Therefore they shall be like the morning mist
> or like the dew that goes away early,
> like chaff that swirls from the threshing-floor
> or like smoke from a window.

Two passages in chapters 5 and 6 (5.1–7 and 5.18—6.2) deal in different ways with God. The second reverts to a now familiar theme, and adds little to what Qoheleth has already had to say in chapter 2 about the essential unfairness of life. However, the first passage is interesting and rather revealing. Its understanding of our relationship to God, while remote and bleak, is not in the end unorthodox, though its orthodoxy is that of the Stoic's faith, or Pascal's when he offered his wager[16] as a starkly intellectual ground for taking God seriously. It contains one memorable and often-quoted maxim ('God is in heaven and you are on earth, so let your words be few') – though like Polonius in *Hamlet* ('since brevity is the soul of wit, and tediousness the limbs and outward flourishes, I will be brief'[17]) he seems ill-disposed to take his own advice! The passage includes an implicit self-criticism, in that it strongly advises something pretty much like silence before God – even denouncing the role of dreams (which elsewhere in the Old Testament are highly regarded as a source of divine revelation).

However much of a sceptic Qoheleth may have been, it seems certain (given his time, status and occupation) that he would not have been an atheist; but what we gain from this reflection on God and humanity is the sense of a kind of practical atheism. We should do what convention and propriety prescribe, but we need not expect either merit or reward as a result. However, we should also note the introduction of a familiar wisdom theme at the end of v. 7 – 'fear God' (the verb used is the one found in the same motif in Proverbs). We may note that Qoheleth's editors introduced

---

16 Pascal gave a pragmatic reason for believing in God: even if God's existence is unlikely, the potential benefits of believing are so vast as to make betting on theism rational. For if God does *not* exist, you lose nothing by supposing that he does; but if God *does* exist and you opt for disbelief, punishment is certain. What the wager does *not* take into account is the possibility that God might punish those with a purely cynical reason for professing belief!

17 *Hamlet*, Act 2, Scene ii, Line 90.

the fear of God in 12.13; so what is the status of this instance within the text – ironic, realistic, fatalistic or pious? See also the highly conventional passage 8.12–13,[18] which raises the same problem regarding Qoheleth's inner belief, but which may, like the last verse of chapter 2, be included in order to be undermined.

Deconstructing wisdom

1 Chapter 7

Chapter 7 begins with a poem that reads as if it could have been drawn from such stalwarts of 'mainstream' wisdom as Proverbs or Sirach, but ends with a comment which turns the usual logic inside out: 'Consider the work of God; who can make straight what he has made crooked' (7.13). Crookedness and deviousness are elsewhere so consistently associated with evil and the wicked[19] that it is startling to find them here laid at God's door. The reflections which follow in vv. 14–29 are a mixture of conventional attitudinizing ('how terrible and deceitful women are'; 'God made us straight but we have sought out ways to be devious') with Qoheleth's own 'twisted' take on life ('God has deliberately designed things so that we remain in ignorance' 'Don't be *too* righteous'). At the heart of the passage is a motif similar to that at the beginning of chapter 5 – the ultimate remoteness of knowledge (vv. 23–4):

> All this I have tested by wisdom; I said, 'I will be wise', but it was far from me. That which is, is far off, and deep, very deep; who can find it out?

This sentiment, combined with the warning in v. 29 ('See, this alone I found, that God made human beings straightforward, but they have devised many schemes'), paints a dark picture of our attempts to know God (see also 8.17—9.1; 11.5).

But there is, perhaps, another dimension to this passage, relating to the possibility we explored above (see the box on 'The meaning of *Qoheleth*,

---

18 'Though sinners do evil a hundred times and prolong their lives, yet I know that it will be well with those who fear God, because they stand in fear before him, but it will not be well with the wicked, neither will they prolong their days like a shadow, because they do not stand in fear before God.' But then Qoheleth goes on immediately to remark: 'There is a vanity that takes place on earth, that there are righteous people who are treated according to the conduct of the wicked . . .'.

19 For the same verb see Pss. 119.78; 146.9; Job 8.3; 19.6; 34.12; for the theme of the twistedness or perversity of the wicked, see Deut. 32.20, Prov. 2.12, 14; 6.14; 8.13; 10.31, 32; 16.28, 30; 23.33.

p. 151 above). What if, here at the heart of the book, the writer is (at least for the moment) taking on the persona of Wisdom (hence the uniquely feminine gender of the verb in v. 27)? This might have the ultimate effect of forcing us to read Ecclesiastes as a deeply anti-Wisdom book, in that not only does the *author* find 'emptiness' in the end, but this is also Wisdom's own experience. If Qoheleth is Wisdom, then ultimately understanding is too hard for her also. In short, we meet with a deconstructive process at the centre of the book in which the goddess figure (to know whom is the ambition of every wisdom writer) turns out to have feet of clay or, more aptly, to be an air-head; and hence, perhaps, the misogynistic comment in the verse which immediately follows: 'One man among a thousand I found, but a woman among all these I have not found' (7.28).

2 Chapter 12.1–8

The concluding meditation in Ecclesiastes is a bleakly realistic view of aging, or loss of faith, or the failure of the intellectual quest, or of the coming apocalypse.[20] Here too there is a passing but perplexing reference in 11.9 to God, where the thought seems to be (a) enjoy life while you are young, but (b) remember you'll have to pay for it. And so to bed . . . 'Remember your Creator' – or, as some have suggested, 'your grave' – the word used is rare, and might in fact be a form of a Hebrew word which means 'pit' or 'hole' or, indeed, 'grave'. So the last word is this: remember, while you are still young, that you are mortal, presumably so that you make the most of life before it is too late and you no longer have the time or the ability. It seems, therefore, that the punishment hinted at in 11.9 is nothing other than the decline of old age and the (welcome?) return of the spirit to God and the flesh to the earth.

There is no comfortable conclusion to this book. At the heart of Qoheleth's dilemma there appears to be the absence that is death, the eternal silence that offers neither punishment for the wicked nor reward for the righteous. Yet he is not an atheist: God exists, God originates, but why and how remain inexorably mysterious. The bottom line is to make the most of life (small comfort to those who lack the resources even to make the least of life!). This could be seen, in the end, to be an arrogant book, the idle work of an idle man with too much time on his hands and not enough real cares to occupy him. Is that a harsh judgement? Or yet another attempt to evade the issue?

---

20 Yvonne Sherwood, ' "Not With a Bang but a Whimper": Shrunken Eschatologies of the Twentieth Century – and the Bible', in Christopher Rowland and John Barton, *Apocalyptic in History and Tradition* (Sheffield Academic Press, 2002), pp. 94–116, offers an interesting reading of this dimension of Ecclesiastes 12.

Some points to think about

At various points we have suggested links between Qoheleth and certain Greek and Latin philosophical perspectives, particularly those of a somewhat fatalistic bent. Does this now strike you as fair; and if so, is there really room for such a work in the canonical collections which belong to Judaism and Christianity?

I have argued that where Qoheleth seems orthodox, it is only in order to undermine traditional positions. Do you agree with this interpretation?

A practical exercise: it has been proposed that a significant part of the book of Qoheleth bears comparison with parts of Genesis, in particular the creation accounts in Genesis 1—3. A list of possible influences, cited from Dell's book, was given on p. 165: examine them in the light of what we have said in this chapter to see how plausible they are.

Dylan Thomas, writing on the death of his father, penned these striking words:

> Do not go gentle into that good night,
> Old age should burn and rave at the close of day;
> Rage, rage against the dying of the light.

Could Qoheleth have endorsed such a sentiment?

Further reading

Crenshaw, James L. (1988) *Ecclesiastes: a commentary*, SCM Press

Dell, Katharine (2000) *'Get Wisdom, Get Insight': an introduction to Israel's wisdom literature*, London, Darton, Longman & Todd

Fox, Michael V. (1999) *A Time to Tear Down and a Time to Build Up*, Grand Rapids, MI, Eerdmans

Fox, Michael V. (1989) *Qohelet and his Contradictions*, Sheffield, Almond Press

Frydrych, Tomas (2002) *Living under the Sun: examination of Proverbs and Qoheleth*, Leiden; Boston, Brill

Gordis, Robert (1968) *Koheleth – the Man and his World: a study of Ecclesiastes*, New York, Schocken Books

Gordis, Robert (1976) *The Word and the Book: studies in Biblical language and literature*, New York, Ktav Publishing House

Krüger, Thomas (2004) *Qoheleth: a commentary*, Minneapolis, MI, Fortress Press

Longman, Tremper III (1998) *The Book of Ecclesiastes*, Grand Rapids, MI, Eerdmans

Miller, Douglas B. (2002) *Symbol and Rhetoric in Ecclesiastes: the place of Hebel in Qohelet's work*, Atlanta, GA, Society of Biblical Literature

Murphy, Roland E. (1992) *Ecclesiastes*, Waco, Word Books

Murphy, Roland E. (1999) *Proverbs, Ecclesiastes, Song of Songs*, Peabody, MA, Hendrickson Publishers

Perry, T. Anthony (1993) *Dialogues with Kohelet: the Book of Ecclesiastes: translation and commentary*, University Park, PA, Pennsylvania State University Press

Schoors, A. (ed.) (1998) *Qohelet in the Context of Wisdom*, Leuven, Leuven University Press, Uitgeverij Peeters

Scott, R. B. Y. (1965) *Proverbs, Ecclesiastes* (Anchor Bible), New York, Doubleday

Seow, C. L. (1997) *Ecclesiastes*, New York, Doubleday

Sherwood, Yvonne (2002) ' "Not With a Bang but a Whimper": Shrunken Eschatologies of the Twentieth Century – and the Bible', in Christopher Rowland and John Barton, *Apocalyptic in History and Tradition*, Sheffield Academic Press, pp. 94–116

Tarazi, Paul Nadim (1996) *The Old Testament: an introduction. Volume 3: Psalms and Wisdom*, Crestwood, NY, St Vladimir's Seminary Press

Whitley, Charles Francis (1979) *Koheleth: his language and thought*, Berlin, Walter de Gruyter

Whybray, R. N. (1980) *Two Jewish theologies: Job and Ecclesiastes*, Hull, University of Hull

Reading on the history of the canon

'Bible: Canon' in *Encyclopedia Judaica* Vol. 4, pp. 816–31

'Canon' in *The Anchor Bible Dictionary* Vol. 1, pp. 837–52

Chapman, Stephen B. (2000) *The law and the prophets: a study in Old Testament canon formation*, Tübingen, Mohr Siebeck

Davies, Philip R. (1998) *Scribes and Schools: the canonization of the Hebrew Scriptures*, Louisville, KY, Westminster John Knox Press

Leiman, Sid Z. (1976) *The Canonization of Hebrew Scripture: the Talmudic and Midrashic evidence*, Hamden, CN, Published for the Academy by Archon Books

McDonald, Lee Martin and James A. Sanders, (eds) (2002) *The Canon Debate*, Peabody, MA, Hendrickson Publishers

Sundberg, Albert C. (1964) *The Old Testament of the Early Church*, Cambridge, MA, Harvard University Press; London, Oxford University Press

9

A Man for the Time: Ben Sira of Jerusalem

Sirach: an overview

In contrast to almost every other Old Testament book, we are remarkably well informed about the author of Sirach and the time and circumstances in which he wrote. In the main this is a consequence of the happy accident that when the work was translated into Greek the translator left a preface that includes significant biographical detail. In order to appreciate what it tells us, it will be useful first to say a little, in very general terms, about the historical, social and cultural circumstances of the Judean state in the period from around 300 BC.

The historical context of the Book of Sirach[1]

1 Alexander and Hellenism

In the late fourth century Alexander the Great and his Macedonian armies created a vast, if short-lived, empire stretching from Egypt in the West to North India in the East – a military achievement only surpassed in extent by that of the Romans. The existence to this day of towns and cities named after Alexander at both extremes of his empire is tribute to his influence (Alexandria in Egypt, Iskunderun in Turkey and Sekundera-bad in Pakistan are three examples); but of more significance is the cultural world that he confirmed, even if he did not originate it: the world of Hellenism. From the Greeks' own word for themselves – *Hellenes* – it denotes a political, cultural and religio-philosophical system which idealized the world of Athens in its heyday and transformed it into a flexible social organism which was to survive until the fall of Constantinople to the Turks in 1453. Based on a threefold foundation consisting of

---

1 In this volume I shall use the name *Sirach* for the book in question. This name is a Greek version of the Hebrew personal name of the author, which is *Ben Sira*. I shall use the latter form when referring to the author rather than his book. The name *Ecclesiasticus*, by which the book was traditionally known, means in Greek something like 'a payment made to an ecclesial official'; it is from the same Greek root as *Ecclesiastes*, the older name of the book of Qoheleth.

the city (*polis*) as the social space, education (in the *gymnasium*) as the ideal preparation for life, and the Greek language as the purest mode of expression of the highest intellectual achievement, it offered a cultural milieu in which those at the top could prosper and rule knowing that across the whole of the Hellenistic world similar ideas and social norms would prevail.

The language, the city and the gymnasium

The institutions of Hellenism

From as early as the tenth century BC the process of Greek colonization was well under way around the Mediterranean. While the primary impulse may have been economic, as colonies became independent of their founding cities, links of an intellectual, cultural and religious nature persisted. This resulted in the establishment from an early period of a remarkably widespread Greek cultural and linguistic presence from Italy to Asia Minor. While other societies spread in a similar fashion, only the Greeks seem to have given birth to a culture of worldwide significance. The reasons for this are complex; but to a degree they may be encapsulated in three phenomena: the city (or *polis*) as the preferred social context; the *gymnasium* tradition of education; and the language itself.

The Greek language

Greek notions of the superiority of their language are well documented, perhaps to some extent based on the presumed differentiation of the cultured life of the city-colony with its *politeis* (citizens) from the rough existence of the illiterate farmer. A sign of this sense of superiority may be found in the word 'barbarian' which was originally used for non-Greeks, and may have had the meaning 'to speak bad or incomprehensible Greek' (some have suggested it may have been mimetic: 'to say "baa baa"'!). Whatever the reason, the existence of an extensive body of poetic, dramatic and philosophical work in Greek by the fifth century combined with the wide distribution of cities owing their origin (real or imagined) to Greek colonization, meant that by the time of Alexander the language itself enshrined a whole culture and philosophy which could hardly be avoided. To be civilized was to speak Greek.

The city

At the heart of the Greek idea lay the city, in which a relatively small group of landowning aristocrats carried out the functions of government, serviced by a slave and serf class, and by women, who had few rights. Such communities were oligarchic rather than democratic; but they shared a number of physical features and aspired to a similar degree of education and civilization.

The *acropolis* of a town served both as a point of defence and as the high place where temples devoted to the tutelary deity of the place would be built. Perhaps the best known is the one in Athens, on which stands the well-known temple of Athena called the Parthenon.

The *agora* (loosely equivalent to the *forum* in Rome or the main square of a medieval town) was the public heart of the city. Here nearly all aspects of public life took place: business, shopping, public debate and discussion, and simple socializing.

Within the *agora* would be found the *stoa* – a pillared building, open on the side towards the square, which provided both shelter from sun and rain, and a place for stalls, offices and storerooms. It gave its name to a philosophical movement – the stoics – who used to teach and debate in the stoa.

The *gymnasion* and the *stadion* (for purposes of education and athletics) were located wherever suitable, perhaps on the outskirts of town. Other public buildings would include a theatre and religious shrines.

The gymnasium

As its name suggests, a major aspect of the gymnasium education in cities like Athens was directed to the development of physical skills which would prepare citizens for participation in war, even if an individual never in fact saw service. Exercising in the nude was normal – something which posed a problem for young Jewish men who wished to adopt Hellenistic fashions, but were embarassed by their circumcision. Intellectual studies such as grammar, rhetoric, logic, philosophy and mathematics were also available, though more advanced studies of this kind tended to be for only a few and took place in other institutions, such as Plato's Academy.

Hellenism was primarily an urban phenomenon, in that it depended upon the existence of a literate class of citizens with disposable income, freedom from the need to work, and the benefits of a good education. Moreover it was from this class that the political leadership of society was drawn. If this portrait sounds familiar, it is perhaps because since the nineteenth century the upper classes in England have modelled their lives on a (possibly romanticized) account of life in Athens in its classical heyday. It was Alexander, who seems to have held a similar romantic notion of Athenian civilization, who facilitated the triumph of Hellenism as a cultural norm which was to survive for almost two millennia. The longevity of Hellenism, and the good fortune of its major source texts having been preserved by Arab scholars of the medieval Islamic empires, facilitated its rediscovery in Renaissance and Enlightenment Europe. Greek thought, both philosophical and scientific – albeit filtered through the lens of renaissance humanism – became in turn the basis of the nineteenth-century ideal of the well-rounded individual. This may appear to be a somewhat curious digression, but it makes the point that Hellenism was a remarkably powerful cultural phenomenon which influenced every society within its milieu. It further reminds us that the dominance of urban elites is nothing new in human history. For while the rural population in antiquity was a larger proportion of society than is the case today, it was true then as now that it is in the social and political 'buzz' of the city that ideas flourish and fashions take hold. Whether or not this is a good thing is beside the point; for better or worse, these are the forces which energize society and enliven its cultures.

Though Alexander's career was brief, if spectacular (336–323 BC), and his empire broke up immediately upon his death, nonetheless his Hellenistic vision persisted through the two kingdoms of Egypt and Syria which were established by his successors. One of Alexander's generals, Ptolemy, established a Greek succession in Egypt – known as the *Ptolemaic* dynasty – which survived until 44 BC. Its last ruler, Cleopatra, and her lover Anthony were defeated by Octavian (the future Augustus) at the Battle of Actium in 31 BC. In Syria the eventual victor was Seleucus who likewise saw the establishment of a Hellenistic dynasty (the *Seleucids*) which remained independent until it was annexed by Pompey in 63 BC. Thus for a period of about 250 years the Jews were flanked by two powerful independent kingdoms representative (though in different ways) of the same Hellenistic political, cultural and religious ideals that had inspired Alexander.

2 Seleucids and Maccabees

The history of Judea and the wider Levant during this period is complex in the extreme, in part a result of the fact that Ptolemaic Egypt and Seleucid Syria waged regular, and at times highly destructive campaigns against each other for most the third century – with most of the fighting taking place in the territories of Samaria and Judea, which formed a kind of buffer state between them. It is quite unnecessary, for the purposes of this background introduction, to examine it in detail;[2] it is sufficient to note that for most of the third century the Jews answered to the Ptolemies as their overlords, with a switch to Seleucid rule occurring

---

2 Those who are interested could start from the relevant parts of Lester Grabbe's *Judaism from Cyrus to Hadrian* (London, SCM Press, 1992), pp. 204–20, 269–312.

around 200 BC, as a result of Syrian victories over Egypt. The change had few practical consequences for the Jews at first – external powers tended not to interfere with Jewish local rule and custom as long as the appropriate taxes were forthcoming! But in 175 one Antiochus IV (known as 'Epiphanes', meaning something like 'God revealed') seized the Syrian throne and soon revealed himself to be a much more repressive and interfering overlord.

The situation rapidly deteriorated, and by 167 BC Judea was in open revolt under the leadership first of Mattathias and then of his sons. The oldest, Judas, took on his father's role when Mattathias died in 166, and led a successful guerrilla operation which culminated in the recovery of Jerusalem and the restoration of the Temple service in 164 – a victory celebrated to this day in the Jewish festival of Hanukkah.[3] Judas himself acquired the nickname 'Maccabeus' or 'the Hammer', no doubt in tribute to his military prowess, and in due course the Maccabean revolt led to the establishment of a kingdom and a royal dynasty, that of the Hasmoneans,[4] which ruled an independent Israel for the best part of 100 years. Pompey finally imposed direct Roman rule as part of his Syrian campaign of 64–3, thus bringing to an end the last independent kingdom of Israel.

Hannukah

In order to return the Temple to its former glory after its desecration by Antiochus much work had to be carried out. A bottle of oil, enough for one day, was found with the seal of the High Priest still on it, and this was used to light the perpetual lamp in the Temple. Maccabees tells how when they returned the next day the oil lamp continued to burn, and did so for the next eight days, by which time a fresh supply of oil had been prepared.

Hanukkah celebrates the restoration and rededication of the Temple. The symbols of the festival pay close attention to the miracle story. To begin with the festival lasts for eight days. Each day a lamp is lit to represent the oil that lasted eight times longer than it should have, so that on the last night eight lamps would be lit all at once. Traditionally these were oil lamps, with olive oil in them, but nowadays people tend to use candles in a holder with eight arms called the *menorah*, and a ninth 'server' candle. The candle on the farthest right is always lit first by a servant candle. The other candles may not be used to light anything else because they are sacred.

---

3 The deutero-canonical books of 1 and 2 Maccabees tell the story, with many legendary accretions.

4 The name comes from Mattathias's ancestral family name, *Hasmon*.

3 Babylon or Athens? The challenge to tradition

Within the small, religiously defined community of Jews in Jerusalem
and its environs, the principal effect of these larger conflicts was to constitute an interference with the rather unremarkable life they had led
throughout most of the Persian period (from 535 BC up to the arrival of
Alexander). During the two Persian centuries the community was largely
self-contained, with its cultural connections more to the east and Babylon than to Greece and the western Mediterranean. The Jewish diaspora
was a significant presence in both Egypt and Babylonia, but it was the
latter group that had played the major defining role in the return from
exile and the constructing of the priestly and Torah-based religious re-
forms of Ezra and Nehemiah.[5] While historical evidence is quite limited
for the period, there is reason to believe that Persian rule was relatively
benign – or at least, disinterested – when it came to matters of Jewish
belief and practice.

With the rise of the two Hellenistic kingdoms of Egypt and Syria, however, new pressures and influences appeared. Of course, Greek culture was
no new thing: the ubiquity of Greek traders and colonies throughout the
eastern Mediterranean over several centuries must surely have impinged
on Jewish life. But this was probably minimal: Judah had no sea ports,
and trade would therefore have largely been through intermediaries.
Interestingly, there are only a very few words in classical Hebrew that
are shared with Greek; but when we come to the Hebrew of the Mishnah
and later, loan words from Greek are much more frequent – and are often
associated with items of trade and everyday life. Both the Ptolemies and
the Seleucids actively pursued policies of Hellenization, though in different ways. The former established a Greek elite class which governed
Egypt and adhered to Greek language, custom and religion (this is the period when the Hellenistic cult of the goddess Isis emerges – based on the
older Egyptian mother/wife of Osiris). But there was no extensive plant-
ing of Hellenistic cities, and the indigenous population was kept in a subservient position. The Seleucids, on the other hand, absorbed the existing
elite into their ruling system, and engaged in a programme of building
that led to the development of a network of Hellenistic cities throughout
their realm (towns called 'Antioch' are typical: Antiochus was a regular throne-name of Seleucid kings). Jews in Egypt under the Ptolemies

---

5 It is interesting to note that this remained a dominant trend in Judaism. It
was the rabbis of Palestine and then Babylonia who shaped both Mishnah and
Talmud, giving what we now recognize as Judaism its characteristic 'feel'. An
alternative tradition, based on the Greek-speaking disapora in Egypt and represented most strikingly by Philo of Alexandria, failed to take root in mainstream
Judaism. By contrast, Philo's thinking came to dominate a major trend in early
Christianity.

seem to have occupied a 'most favoured nation' position – not despised as native Egyptians were, but neither were they in the upper echelons. Their quarter in Alexandria was relatively prosperous, and they seem to have become Hellenized from an early period. Evidence for this may be found in the translation of the Hebrew Bible into Greek, the prologue to Sirach (which we shall examine in due course) and the life and thought of Philo, who was clearly conversant with the major Greek philosophical systems. (Though Philo dates from the late first century BC, he was scarcely the first such Jewish thinker, and must have himself learned from a longer tradition of study of the Greek classical writers.)

These external changes, together with regular communication between Jews in Judea and Egypt, meant that the Jerusalem elite did not remain impervious to the attractions of Hellenism. Greek-style cities had been built, or older ones reconstructed, in Palestine itself: thus, Philadephia, Ptolemais, Gaza, Philoteria, Nysa and Scythopolis. In Jerusalem itself a gymnasium was set up by the High Priest Jason (175–2); there is a description in 2 Maccabees 4.12–17 which, while the writer clearly disapproves of the move, cannot hide the fact that it was a popular development. In general, the majority of cultured Jews seems to have found no difficulty in reconciling their Jewish identity with a Hellenized lifestyle, and leading families such as the Tobiads and the Oniads worked closely with both Ptolemies and Seleucids to ensure their own prosperity without thereby denying their own Jewish identity. What we do not know is the extent to which the kind of awareness of Greek religion and philosophy which was widespread in Egypt had permeated intellectual circles in Jerusalem. In our discussion of Sirach this will be of major significance. An outline of the relevant philosophical positions is provided on pp. 118–200. It was only when Antiochus IV interfered directly in religious matters, attempting to ban 'the traditions of the fathers' and desecrating the Temple, that outright rebellion broke out.

Authorship, date and name

The book of Sirach is unique in the Old Testament in that it contains significant internal evidence as to the name of its author and his life and times. The verse which gives his name (50.27) offers variants in Greek and in Hebrew; the name which is commonly used (Jesus ben Sira) is essentially that of the Septuagint,[6] though with a Hebrew pronunciation. The convention which will I will follow more or less consistently in this

---

6 The LXX has 'Jesus son of Sirach Eleazar the Jerusalemite'. The Hebrew version has 'Simeon son of Joshua (=Jesus) son of Eleazar son of Sira'. The author's grandson refers to him in the prologue as 'My grandfather Jesus'.

chapter will be that of employing 'Sirach' when the book is intended, and 'Ben Sira' for its author.

1 Looking for Ben Sira

There are a number of passages within the book which seem to provide information about the life and character of its author. These are in addition to the prologue which, as we shall see, reveals the high regard in which Ben Sira was held by his grandson. It may be that this *appearance* of being in touch with a real person encourages a less sceptical reading of the autobiographical fragments within the text itself; *caveat lector* – let the reader beware.

The first is 38.24—39.5, a lengthy passage (some sixteen verses in all) which describes, to their detriment, a variety of trades and skills which, however essential, cannot be compared with the high calling of the man of wisdom. This whole section has some similarities with an Egyptian text which we listed in Chapter 3, and this ought to sound a certain warning, for it is possible that what we have here is a literary trope rather than a reliable account of the author's own experience. However, the brief section which concludes this discourse has a certain ring of truth about it. After the lengthy description of the trades (38.24–34a) and a rather predictable account of the sage's duties (38.34b—39.3) we come to the following:

> He serves among the great
> and appears before rulers;
> he travels in foreign lands
> and learns what is good and evil in the human lot.
> He sets his heart on rising early
> to seek the Lord who made him,
> and to petition the Most High;
> he opens his mouth in prayer
> and asks pardon for his sins.   (39.4–5)

If this is more than boasting, there might be an indication here of the profession of the sage (to act as a kind of government adviser) and the life of Ben Sira himself: he has travelled (and in respect of this, see the box on Ben Sira's location on p. 187), perhaps after the example of Herodotus who informed his history with curious information gained from his journeys; and he is a naturally pious and somewhat ascetic individual (note the emphasis on rising early and prayer). The devotional side of Ben Sira is further supported by the poem in the last chapter of the book, and by his enthusiasm for the cult, on which see below (pp. 194–8).

We have already commented on the fact that the author in effect signs his book, in 50.27, and we need not dwell further on that fact. What follows that signature (which, as with Qoheleth, we might expect to conclude the book) is a brief coda (50.28–29) which is reminiscent of Qoheleth 12.13–14, and a variable collection of prayers and personal reminiscence. If this is personal to Ben Sira – and that is a significant reservation – then we have, particularly in 51.13–30, a quite revealing insight into the man himself. It is a shame that its position forces us to doubt its authenticity; perhaps it represents a separate testimony which was latterly collected with the main body of the book. I shall assume something of the sort as a working hypothesis.[7] I delay a detailed examination of this passage for treatment in Chapter 10; suffice it to say at this point that we meet here a man who has dedicated himself both to the pursuit of wisdom through prayer and to the communication of that wisdom, by means it seems of a formal school (51.23), to those who can benefit from an education.

One final passage might be relevant to our quest for the man himself. In 25.13—26.18 there is a quite egregiously misogynistic diatribe against 'wicked' and 'upstart' women who are the bane of their husbands' lives, and headstrong and impudent daughters of low morality. It may be that this material is simply the traditional advice aimed at controlling women in a highly patriarchal society, but the strength with which it is expressed leads me to fear – sadly – that this may reflect the true feelings of Ben Sira.

2 Date and place

We can give a rather accurate date for the book, based partly on information in the prologue, and partly on internal evidence. The former is unique among biblical books, in that it provides an external narrative of the transmission of the text from one context to another. The closest parallels are to be found in the prefaces to the Gospel of Luke and to Acts; but these are *internal* statements made by the author, Luke – who is in fact not mentioned in the body of either text – and not *secondary* commentary of the type found in the prologue to Sirach.

Ben Sira's grandson provides us with a specific date: the thirty-eighth year of king Euergetes. This is in fact Ptolemy VII, whose full title is Ptolemy Phycson VII Euergetes II. He reigned twice – first from 170 to 164 and then from 145 to 117. The reference to the thirty-eighth year of

---

7 John G. Snaith, in *Ecclesiasticus* (Cambridge University Press, 1974) thinks that the passage is an afterthought, but probably from Ben Sira himself. Skehan and DiLella, in the Anchor Bible *Wisdom of Ben Sira* (New York: Doubleday, 1987) do not question the attribution to Ben Sira. However, R. A. F. MacKenzie, *Sirach* (Michael Glazier, 1983) regards it as an appendix composed by someone else not unsympathetic to Ben Sira.

his reign assumes that he was king continuously from 170 to 117, thus placing the grandson's arrival in Egypt at 132 BC. He tells us that having 'stayed for some time [he] found opportunity for no little instruction', and it seems reasonable to deduce that part of that instruction came from Ben Sira's work.

While we do not know when the translation was effected, that is less important when we are trying to date Sirach, for what we do know is that by 132 Ben Sira had an adult grandson. This enables us to define some parameters for Ben Sira's life and work. At one extreme, if we assume that both Ben Sira and his son were 45 before they became fathers, and the grandson was 30 when he reached Egypt, the author would have been in late middle age 75 years prior to 132: that is, around 210 BC. At the other extreme, if we assume both were 25 when the relevant offspring were born,[8] and that the grandson was 20 when he journeyed to Egypt, we should count back 45 years, making Ben Sira a young man in about 180 BC. The book appears to reflect a lifetime's work, which would suggest that the author was at least 50 when he produced it. All of this adds up to the strong probability that Sirach was composed between 205 and 155 BC.

Turning to the evidence that may be derived from Sirach itself, we note first that there is a eulogy to the High Priest Simeon II (known as 'the Just'), which comes at the end of the section of the book known as 'The Praise of the Fathers' (44.1—50.21) in which ancestors of Israel are celebrated, and which, as I noted above, seems to stand close to the end of the book as a whole. It seems clear that Ben Sira writes after the death of Simon, in 190; this then would enable us to bring the earlier date of writing down to 190 BC. Turning to the lower limit, Simeon's successor Onias III was a man who would have equally merited Ben Sira's praise, since he too adhered to the 'traditions of the fathers'; more importantly, there is no hint in the book at the tumultuous events that followed the accession of Antiochus IV and the deposition of Onias, and no reference to the desecration of the Temple in 167 or the Maccabean revolt. While silence is never a complete proof, the whole tone of Sirach implies a stable and unperturbed Temple ritual which provides the solid basis for Ben Sira's personal piety and intellectual apologia. It is hard to believe that he could have written the book he did after Antiochus's direct assault on precisely those 'traditions of the fathers' which are so fulsomely celebrated in chapters 44–50.

I conclude, therefore, that by far the most probable period for the composition and publication of Sirach is the decade 190–180 BC – a period

---

8 There is evidence for somewhat late marriage among the educated scribal classes. If this is not persuasive, the reader may reduce the figures to 20 and perform the relevant calculation!

of relative calm before the Maccabean storm, and a period when the Seleucids were still pursuing the relatively liberal policies of their Ptolemaic predecessors towards the Jewish people.

Ben Sira's location

It is always assumed that Ben Sira was a scribe and teacher in Jerusalem, and that his book represents a review of his life's work, perhaps intended for those who were and had been his students – the sons of the educated elite of Jerusalem. However, there is an alternative view, which has recently been argued by Paul McKechnie, 'The Career of Joshua Ben Sira' in *Journal of Theological Studies* NS51, April 2000, pp. 3–26.

What Ben Sira's grandson seems to imply is that *it was when he came to Egypt* that he first became interested in study. This might mean that he only found his grandfather's work in Egypt: in other words, that Ben Sira was a Jew of the Egyptian diaspora, writing in Hebrew for that community. We know that with the passage of time Greek became the language of the Jews in Egypt; hence the need for the grandson's translation. McKechnie supports his argument with observations based on the content of Sirach.

Certainly, there is widespread agreement that Ben Sira is well informed on matters of Greek philosophy, and may have modelled his portrayal of Wisdom on hymns to Isis (known as *aretalogies*). While such knowledge need not imply residence in Egypt, it does tend to make it at least plausible. We will return to these points later.

The structure of Sirach

It is a moot point whether there is any overall structure to Sirach. In some ways it is tempting to see it as the somewhat rambling musings of a retired teacher, determined to incorporate all his old lecture notes regardless of their relevance. Chapters 25 and 26, for example, sound like the curmudgeonly rant of a stereotypical misogynist, and there are long stretches (chs 8–15, for example) which are reminiscent of the more soporific pages of the book of Proverbs. It is also rather long, which further militates against the likelihood of there being any neat structure to be found.

But this is by no means the whole story. For one thing, Ben Sira displays both a profound skill in the matter of intertextual reading and the shaping of his own scripture-like material, and a distinctive and original theological voice which gives his work a significance far beyond the super-

ficial appearance of a routine wisdom book. Further, he works into his
writing at regular intervals sections which display a striking poetic voice
and a dramatic sense which transcend the mundane material in which
they are embedded. These features of the book will become clearer as we
study specific selected passages; let me for the moment simply draw your
attention to the bold conclusion to chapter 24, in which Ben Sira enters
his own poem in person, and dramatizes his personal role in the grand
mission of bringing wisdom to the world. The river in question is the river
of divine wisdom which has been described in the preceding verses:

> As for me, I was like a canal from a river,
>   like a water channel into a garden.
> I said, 'I will water my garden
>   and drench my flower-beds.'
> And lo, my canal became a river,
>   and my river a sea.
> I will again make instruction shine forth like the dawn,
>   I will make it clear from far away.
> I will again pour out teaching like prophecy,
>   and leave it to all future generations.
> See how I have not laboured for myself alone,
>   but for all who seek wisdom.   (24.30–34)

In their Anchor Bible Commentary[9] Skehan and DiLella provide a
rough structure which is helpful in organizing this somewhat unwieldy
book. I have expanded upon their outline by making use of a series of
poetic sections within the traditional proverbial material to characterize
most of the divisions. The book then falls into two parts, with chapter 24
marking the beginning of the second part.

PROLOGUE		The grandson's testimony
A I	1.1—4.10	Hymn 1 'In praise of wisdom' (1.1–30)
A II	4.11—6.17	Hymn 2 'Wisdom's rewards and warnings' (4.11–19)
A III	6.18—14.19	Hymn 3 'Strive to find Wisdom' (6.18–31)
A IV	14.20—23.27	Hymn 4 'The search for Wisdom' (14.20—15.10)
B I	24.1—35.20	Hymn 5 'In praise of wisdom' (24.1–33)
B II	36.1—38.23	Hymn 6 'The enemies of Israel' (36.1–17)

9 Patrick W. Skehan and Alexander A. DiLella, *The Wisdom of Ben Sira*
(Anchor Bible, Vol. 39, New York, Doubleday, 1987), pp. xiii–xvi.

B III   38.24—43.33   Hymn 7 'The true scholar' (38.24—39.16)
B IV   44.1—50.24   Hymn 8 'Praise of the ancestors' (44.1–15)
          EPILOGUE   The grandfather's testimony

Whether this structure can be used as a significant hermeneutical tool is doubtful; it might be better seen as a means of managing a rather unwieldy text rather than as a framework controlling the author's thinking.

Themes in Sirach

While the structure of the book does not suggest a single overarching thesis to which the author addresses himself, there are nonetheless a number of themes which either receive a special emphasis in the book or emerge as important aspects of the modern exegesis of Ben Sira's work. In this section I shall explore a number of these.

Sirach and the canon

It seems strange at first sight that a book as orthodox as Sirach should have been excluded from the Hebrew canon (in the Catholic and Orthodox tradition it is included in the Deutero-canonical section which was formally excluded by the reformers). The book was undoubtedly composed in Hebrew: we know this not only from the testimony of the prologue but from the survival of significant parts of the original Hebrew in diverse places (a total of about 35 chapters). It was influential in rabbinic traditions, which sometimes quote it as if it were Scripture, and has numerous echoes in the New Testament. There is no doubt that Sirach was esteemed widely, both for its piety and for its quotability, and in terms of its content it would seem to have better claims to be canonical than such books as Qoheleth, Esther and the Song of Songs. It contains little of the sort of nationalistic rhetoric (such as we find in Maccabees), which might be a source of fruitless rebellion against authority. It is not eschatological or apocalyptic – other genres of which the rabbis were deeply suspicious – and was in fact written *earlier* than Daniel, which did succeed in gaining canonical status.

To find the answer to this puzzle we turn to a famous passage from Josephus' *Contra Apionem* (Against Apion), 1.8, in which he gives us an account of the Hebrew canon and the principles underlying its selection. He writes:

We have not an innumerable multitude of books among us . . . but only twenty-two books, which contain the records of all the past

times; which are justly believed to be divine; and of them five belong to
Moses, containing his laws and the traditions of the origin of mankind
until his death . . . As to the time from the death of Moses till the reign
of Artaxerxes . . . the prophets, who were after Moses, wrote down
what was done in their time in thirteen books. The remaining four
books contain hymns to God, and precepts for the conduct of human
life. [History has been recorded since Artaxerxes] but has not been
accorded the same authority . . . because there has not been an exact
succession of prophets since that time.

The reference to Artaxerxes implies that the last prophets were of the
period of Ezra and Nehemiah. Josephus was writing around AD 90, when
the rabbis were beginning to firm up the shape of the Jewish canon, at
least in part in response to the emergence of Christian texts which might
have claimed to be part of the Jewish scriptural tradition. What this implies is that at some time between the writing of Daniel and Sirach the
idea that prophecy came to an end with Ezra was formalized. Daniel,
of course, professes to describe the adventures of an exilic hero of the
sixth century – certainly early enough to qualify under Josephus' test.
The problem with Sirach lies in its prologue. The precise dating implied
there, while it is of great interest to modern readers, successfully puts the
composition of the book significantly later than the period of prophetic
inspiration. Sirach, in short, was ruled out on what seems now to be a
technicality!

Apart from the matter of Sirach's own canonicity there is to be found
in the book and its prologue considerable evidence for the shape of the
canon and of Scripture in the third and second centuries BC. Starting with
the passage from Josephus quoted above, we note that he refers to the
books of Moses, the prophets, and the writings ('hymns and precepts').
It is clear that the second group contains what the Christian canon lists
as histories. Thus, by AD 90 we have explicit evidence for a threefold
canon typical of Jewish Scriptures, together with a prophetic criterion for
validation of individual books. It is noteworthy that Josephus later in the
same passage claims that 'during so many ages as have already passed, no
one has been so bold as either to add anything to them, to take anything
from them, or to make any change in them'. This gives us an upper limit
of c. AD 90 for something like a fixed canon of the Old Testament. It is
striking therefore to note that both in Sirach and in its prologue there is
certain information which suggests the existence of a considerable body
of Scripture not dissimilar to that described by Josephus. We also know,
from the Dead Sea Scrolls, that the text of the various books of the Old
Testament was by no means in a fixed form even as late as the end of the
first century BC. Thus Sirach affords us valuable information from an
intermediate stage in the process.

It seems likely that Sirach and his grandson were in possession of both Torah and Prophets, and there are strong indications of a third group of other books which may be presumed to line up with the third, miscellaneous section: the Writings. Thus, from the Prologue (emphasis added):

Many great teachings have been given to us through *the law and the prophets and the others that followed them* . . . *instruction and wisdom*

. . . my grandfather Jesus, after devoting himself especially to the reading of *the law and the prophets and the other books of our fathers* . . . was also led to write something pertaining to *instruction and wisdom* . . .

. . . not only this work, but even *the law itself, the prophecies and the rest of the books* differ not a little as originally expressed.

And in Sirach itself, in 38.34—39.1:

[He] who devotes himself
    to the study of *the law* of the Most High . . .
seeks out *the wisdom* of all the ancients,
    and is concerned with *prophecies*;

There seems little doubt that by 180 BC there existed a recognized body of Scripture,[10] though we know that it cannot have been closed, since the book of Daniel cannot yet have been included, and it is highly probable that a number of psalms were added in the second and first centuries.

Another striking point is the combined witness of both the book and the prologue that it was still possible to write 'Scripture'. The phrase emphasized ('instruction and wisdom') in the quotations from the Prologue, above, seems to be a standard description of the nature of the scriptural texts; it is applied both to the existing threefold collection *and to the work of Ben Sira himself*. We can go further: at the end of chapter 24, where Ben Sira celebrates his own vocation, he writes:

I will again make *instruction* shine forth like the dawn,
    I will make it clear from far away.
I will again pour out *teaching like prophecy*,
    and *leave it to all future generations*.
See how I have not laboured for myself alone,
    but for all who seek *wisdom*.

---

10 In using this term we should resist applying to it the ideas of inspiration and authority which it entails in Christian thinking. I mean simply, an acknowledged collection of traditional religious texts deemed to be of central importance to the community.

Both Ben Sira and his grandson appear to have no problem with the idea that Scripture is open and can be added to, and that those who study and teach and reflect upon the ancient texts are well qualified to make their own contribution. Together with the freedom with which Ben Sira deploys existing Scripture creatively in the body of his text, this suggests something akin to the later rabbinic process by which earlier materials are commented on and expanded in a highly diverse manner. The Talmud emerged from Mishnah in precisely this fashion. Finally, the fact that Sirach explicitly names its author implies that Josephus' assertion that Scripture ended with Ezra is not yet in force.

To sum up: Sirach provides evidence for a threefold proto-canon by 200 BC at the latest, but one which is still growing, and whose materials may be regarded not so much as authorities to be obeyed as a resource for reflection, study and further inspiration. It must be emphasized that there is no suggestion, in making this observation, that a formal canon was in place or that even the concept of an authoritative canon was yet in place. On this subject, see further the reading list at the end of Chapter 8.

Intertextuality in Sirach

There is considerable evidence in the pages of the Old Testament of what has come to be known as *intertextuality*: the use of quotation of, and reference or allusion to one text within another in order to create or sustain an argument or to illustrate a narrative. Jonah 4 makes reference to the story of Elijah in 1 Kings 19, and quotes the saying (which turns up in a number of places in the Bible) that 'God is gracious and merciful, slow to anger and abounding in steadfast love'. The psalm in chapter 2 is a pastiche of familiar phrases from a wide variety of scriptural sources. There are hundreds of such examples in a wide range of texts – indicating that the Bible is very far from being a series of discrete unrelated books, but is rather an evolving process.

Ben Sira participated in this process. He not only knew of the existence of Scripture, but quoted it and used it as the literary and theological basis of his own reflections. But he did not do so slavishly: he has things to say about wisdom and Torah, for example, that will not be found in the canon. Thus he pictures wisdom as existing from eternity and having a specific link with the cult (24.8–12); and in 24.23 he virtually identifies wisdom ('all this') with Torah. Elsewhere, in his 'Praise of the Fathers' (44—50), he changes the balance of emphasis (much more space is devoted to Aaron than to Moses), and adds significant comments of his own to the received tradition. The placing of Enoch at the head of the list, given the importance of that mysterious figure in the Intertestamental period, is highly significant, as is the final acclamation of Adam

– another figure of eschatological importance in Jewish tradition of the time. Ben Sira's additions include:

44.16 Enoch as an example of knowledge for succeeding generations
44.17 Noah as a remnant
44.20 Abraham as one who observed the law of the Most High

There is one possibly significant omission: Ezra nowhere figures in the list of the fathers who receive praise in 44—49. Given the central importance of Ezra for Judaism as it emerged from the late second century BC, this is very odd. There is no entirely satisfactory explanation. Did Ben Sira have a version of Ezra/Nehemiah which omitted the former? Was Ezra – as some radical scholars have suggested – a later fictional addition to the canon? Or, more mundanely, is the text of Sirach corrupt, with a piece referring to Ezra having somehow dropped out?

We shall attend to this aspect of Ben Sira's writing when we turn to close reading of selected passages in Chapter 10. In the meantime, it is enough to observe that the level of intertextuality in Sirach supports the comments we have already made about the status of Jewish Scriptures at the time as an evolving body of work within an already established framework, rather than as a fixed collection already canonized.

Ben Sira: prophet and scribe

Sirach sees himself as having a significant part to play in the purposes of God. Only two contemporaries are named at the end of the 'Famous Men': the late High Priest Simeon the Just, and Ben Sira himself. While the former stands as last in the succession of priests and kings, Ben Sira belongs to the line of prophets and wise men. He presents himself as the last in a long sequence ('Now I was the last to keep vigil; I was like a gleaner following the grape-pickers' 33.16). His role is exalted and important (33.17–18):

by the blessing of the Lord I arrived first,[11]
   and like a grape-picker I filled my wine press.
Consider that I have not laboured for myself alone,
   but for all who seek instruction.

Moreover, his high calling gives him the right to make prophetic-type appeals to the great ('Hear me, you who are great among the people, and

---

11 He means, of course, that he was the first of his generation, those who belong to the latest stage of the wisdom tradition.

you leaders of the congregation, pay heed!' 33.19; cf. 35.18–20; 36.1–22; 47.22; 50.25f). Ben Sira, as a scribe, regards law, wisdom and prophecy as the source of God's revelation and the fit subjects of study (39.1, 7–8). But this is no academic matter: to study these subjects requires the spirit of understanding to be *poured forth* – an essentially *prophetic* expression. Thus 39.6 (cf. 50.27):

> If the great Lord is willing,
>   he will be filled with the spirit of understanding:
> he will pour forth words of wisdom of his own
>   and give thanks to the Lord in prayer.

Thus we see how in the figure of Ben Sira prophecy has become the preserve of the scribe. This is a particular example of a general trend. With the decline of prophecy as understood in the biblical period, the same impulse was in the course of time channelled in two directions. A new form of prophecy arose among apocalyptic writers, expressed in practical terms by groups like the Essenes and the Zealots. On the other hand, Ben Sira's example leads to the institutionalizing of exegesis – a process taken to its ultimate form by the rabbinic movement in Judaism. It might be agued that Christianity borrowed elements from both possibilities, with the latter eventually dominating. For in the end, as the post exilic community and the restructured Judaism of the second century AD also discovered, free prophecy is a threat to authority, and no institution can live with that sort of reality. Prophecy didn't die. It was the victim of involuntary euthanasia!

The Temple cult in Sirach

On the whole the wisdom writers in the Hebrew Scriptures are somewhat distanced from the cult. Proverbs and Qoheleth scarcely mention it; Job does so somewhat obliquely, and is really more concerned to establish a personal encounter with God. It is the more striking, then, that Sirach not only describes the cult in detail, but associates wisdom very closely with it. He displays also, again in contrast with traditional wisdom writers, a strong concern for the integrity of Israel as a nation. What emerges is a nationalistic/apologetic programme: wisdom and rationality – characteristic of the competing Greek philosophies (especially stoicism[12]) – are shown to be (a) identified with God in his creation of the world and humankind (24.1–7; 1.15), (b) identified with the particular people of God, the nation of Israel (24.8–12), and with its special forms of worship, and (c) very specially identified with the sacred scripture of

---

12 See further, the next section.

the cult of that particular people (24.23), which thus has an importance for all peoples as the source of that universal principle of reason which is the wisdom of Yahweh.

This being so, Ben Sira's unusually strong interest in the cult is understandable: it forms the core of his argument from the specifics of Israelite life and worship to the generality of the relationship of God to all humanity. The former provides the basis (perhaps surprisingly) for a general principle: Torah, because it can be identified with wisdom (Hebrew *hokhmah*, Greek *sophia*), constitutes a universal mode of understanding of the one creator and judge of the *whole* world. In order to clarify this theme we shall look at a number of relevant passages.

1 Chapter 7.8–10 and 34.21–31

The first passage begins with the kind of criticism of cultic observance that was typical of Amos, Hosea, Isaiah and Micah – a critique which is amplified in chapter 34. While this is consonant with the older prophetic judgment against a corrupt priestly order, and expresses vividly the veniality of the hypocritical separation between religious observance and daily life, Ben Sira, as we shall see, in no sense denounces the cult as such. Indeed, both passages conclude with observations that reinforce the validity of the cult:

> Do not grow weary when you pray;
>   do not neglect to give alms.   (7.10)

> So if someone fasts for his sins,
>   and goes again and does the same things,
> who will listen to his prayer?
>   And what has he gained by humbling himself?   (34.31)

The first of these is a direct affirmation of the validity of religious duties, while the second quite clearly attacks not the propriety of fasting and prayer but their futility if sincerity is lacking.

2 Chapter 7.29–31

> With all your soul fear the Lord,
>   and revere his priests.
> With all your might love your Maker,
>   and do not neglect his ministers.
> Fear the Lord and honour the priest,
>   and give him his portion, as you have been commanded:
> the first fruits, the guilt offering, the gift of the shoulders,
>   the sacrifice of sanctification and the first fruits of the holy things.

There are two points of particular interest in these verses, which are strikingly different from anything in the other wisdom literature: Ben Sira's enthusiastic insistence that the priests and ministers should be revered and honoured (a dimension, I believe, entirely lacking from other wisdom and prophetic material), and his treatment of tithes. The first of these coheres with the emphasis given to various priestly figures such as Aaron, Phineas and Simeon in the Praise of the Fathers. As regards the second, Ben Sira reveals a detailed knowledge of the system of tithes. Even if this is to some extent culled from his scriptural sources, the fact that he spells it out is surely of some significance. Given that we know that Pharisaic tithing as recorded in Mishnah is significantly different from the Levitical and biblical regulations, it may be that Sirach is an important primary witness to the varieties of practice in pre-rabbinic Judaism.

3 Chapter 24.8–17

The fact that this poem is central to the whole book, and that it contains Ben Sira's fundamentally original contribution to the theology of wisdom in Israel, should alert us to the likelihood that references of a cultic nature here are far from accidental or incidental. Wisdom has already been exalted to a position of near-equality with God (24.3–7; see the detailed discussion in Chapter 10). She is now, as an eternal quality, portrayed as 'ministering' to God in his holy tabernacle in Zion (v. 10). The list of terms of cultic significance in vv. 8–12 is striking:

v. 8   'my tent', 'dwelling in Jacob', 'in Israel receive your inheritance'
v. 10 'In the holy tabernacle I ministered before him', 'established in Zion'
v. 11 'the beloved city', 'in Jerusalem was my dominion' (cf. Ps. 132.13f)
v. 12 'an honoured people', 'the portion of the Lord, who is their inheritance'.

A different set of metaphors is deployed in vv. 13–17, where wisdom is praised in lavish terms. The theme of incense and 'odours of sanctity' is an important part of the writer's thought. This is especially true of v. 15:

Like *cassia* and camel's thorn I gave forth perfume,
    and like choice *myrrh* I spread my fragrance,
like *galbanum*, *onycha*, and *stacte*,
    and like the odour of incense in the tent.

Cassia and myrrh are two of the ingredients of the sacred oil used to anoint the priests and the furniture of the Temple (Ex. 30.23–25); galbanum, onycha and stacte are constituent parts of the incense used in the Temple (Ex. 30.34–38). These parallels identify wisdom metaphorically as being like the anointing oils and the incense whose smell pervaded the Temple.

Finally we turn to v. 17:

Like the vine I bud forth delights,
    and my blossoms become glorious and abundant fruit.[13]

The use here of the image of the fruitful vine, taps an important cultic and nationalist source in Jewish piety (cf. Isa. 5.1–7, the parable of the vineyard; Ps. 80.8–19, the extended description of Israel as 'a vine out of Egypt'; and Ps. 128.3 which described the ideal Israelite wife as being 'like a fruitful vine'). Taken together these allusions and quotations show the depth of Ben Sira's commitment to the cult of the Temple and his conviction that what defines wisdom in Israel far transcends intellectual or ethical considerations.

4 Chapter 35.1–13

In this passage, where a number of ethical virtues are referred to, several are of a clearly cultic nature: offerings of various kinds (well-being or peace, flour, thanksgiving, first fruits, tithes) are listed, atonement is mentioned (v. 5) and the odour of the altar is described (v. 8). But these are combined with the idea that the righteous, the ethically upright man, is the one whose sacrifice is good and acceptable (vv. 5, 8–9). What Ben Sira does here is to enhance the cult by making it the proper expression of virtues elsewhere spoken of in terms either of purely secular wisdom.

5 The fear of the Lord

The generalized idea of the 'fear of Yahweh' was noted in previous chapters, particularly in relation to the theme of Proverbs 1—9 and the meditation on wisdom in Job 28. In Sirach the fear of Yahweh becomes a major expression throughout the book, and is described at length in 1.11—2.18. I will discuss this passage further in Chapter 10, where a detailed listing of the theme of fear in Sirach will be found. In the meantime, I note that

---

13 It is hard to resist the idea that this verse forms an intertext with the butler's dream in Gen. 40.9–10: 'In my dream there was a vine before me, and on the vine there were three branches. As soon as it budded, its blossoms came out and the clusters ripened into grapes.' It is the butler's dream, of course, that leads to reinstatement.

there are 18 instances in these two chapters. Of particular relevance to the present discussion is the fact that in 1.26–27 a significant connection is made between wisdom, the law, and the fear of Yahweh:

> If you desire wisdom, keep the commandments,
>   and the Lord will lavish her upon you.
> For the fear of the Lord is wisdom and discipline,
>   fidelity and humility are his delight.

Here the fear of the Lord is brought specifically into the sphere of Torah (and hence cult). In Proverbs the fear of the Lord is said to be the beginning of wisdom, so that ethical observance is merely a wise, a prudent thing. Now, in Sirach, wisdom is made equal to Torah, and so a cultic connection is made which results in the idea of ethical observance as a cultic matter. 35.1–11 is an expression of this, and is therefore fundamentally distinct from the rhetoric of the eighth-century prophets. In this context we should note also the importance of 2.15–17, which identifies fear with obedience to the Law (and hence to the cult):

> Those who fear the Lord do not disobey his words,
>   and those who love him keep his ways.
> Those who fear the Lord seek to please him,
>   and those who love him are filled with his law.
> Those who fear the Lord prepare their hearts,
>   and humble themselves before him.

Ben Sira and the philosophers

The principal philosophical schools of Ben Sira's time were forms of Platonism, Epicureanism and Stoicism. It is of course uncertain whether he would have studied any of these directly; that is perhaps unlikely. But as a participant in intellectual discourse in a city where Hellenism was fashionable, it is probable that he would at least have encountered them at second hand, and may have been familiar with popular texts. On his travels, too, he may have come across alternatives to his own Jewish wisdom philosophy.

Platonism was a wide-ranging philosophy which changed significantly over time. Originally derived from Plato's teaching about the ideal and his method of dialectical interrogation of philosophical claims, it later acquired dualistic tendencies which set the physical and the ideal in direct contrast and opened the way to a quasi-religious doctrine of *daimons* and supernatural intermediaries, with the concept of the *logos* functioning in some ways as the sole mode of recognition of God by human beings – perhaps indeed as a kind of intermediary. There are some signs, particularly in 24.3 where wisdom is presented as having come from 'the mouth of the Most High', that Ben Sira may have been influenced in this direction in his interpretation of wisdom.

Epicureanism offered a kind of humanist alternative to religious explanations of cause and effect, in which all events resulted from the movement of atoms. Piety should be addressed, not to the gods or to worship, but to the independence and imperturbability of the wise man (sic), and was made real in forms of happiness and friendship. There is little evidence that thinking of this kind influenced Ben Sira.

Stoicism was founded by Zeno[14] of Cittium (late fourth to early third centuries BC). The name of the philosophical school comes from his habit of teaching in the *stoa* (see above on 'The City'). From the start Stoicism was cosmopolitan and pantheistic, understanding local gods in universal terms. For Stoics, the *logos* and the *cosmos* are unified (in other, though perhaps misleading terms, 'god and the universe are one', a formulation which has affinities with Hindu philosophy). In its teaching Stoicism made much use of allegory. It seems likely that aspects of Ben Sira's thinking were influenced by this kind of philosophy.

In Sirach 24 we encounter a fascinating and provocative investigation of the nature and role of wisdom in Israel. The background to the chapter is surely the presence in thoughtful society of that persuasive, rationalist, Hellenized philosophy which offers a total apprehension of the created universe on the basis of a principle of divine order: Stoicism. Beside this, the petulant, vengeful, bloodthirsty, capricious, wonder-working, overly anthropomorphized deity of Jewish narrative and liturgy might be too readily dismissed. All right for the unthinking, unreflective masses, maybe; but a travesty to those of a rational outlook. It was Ben Sira's great accomplishment to have taken these various and seemingly irreconcilable forces and forged them into one potent hymn at the centre of which is neither Yahweh, nor law – not even cult or nation – but wisdom. We move through the mythic language of creation (vv. 3–5) and wisdom accompanies us. We remember the great narratives of the formation of Israel as God's special and holy people, and we find wisdom at the heart of them (vv. 6–12). She is the very incense of the sacred altar (vv. 13–17) at the centre of Israel's cult; and she is praised in the language of wisdom (vv. 19–22). But finally, and sealing all, she is revealed to be the personification of the 'book of the covenant of the Most High God'.

The significance of this is that Ben Sira is using wisdom to validate Torah, not the other way round – a remarkable reversal of what would seem to be the priorities at the heart of Jewish values from the time of

---

14 Not to be confused with the early fifth-century mathematician from Elea famous for Zeno's paradox.

the Great Synagogue.[15] At the heart of chapter 24 it is wisdom, not Torah that speaks: Torah is the junior partner. This, of course, indicates that wisdom was held in high esteem among those for whom Ben Sira wrote. We can, I think, see in this Ben Sira's master-stroke in his defence of 'the faith of the fathers' in the face of the Hellenistic challenge, for he has stolen a march on the Stoics. They set wisdom equal to *logos*, the principle of order in the universe. He sets wisdom equal to Torah, Yahweh's principle of order in the universe; wisdom and law have become one. There is a double benefit from this identification: on the one hand, the rather abstract principle of *logos* has been replaced with something much more powerful, persuasive and personal – the Torah of Yahweh (there are echoes here of earlier wisdom with its slogan, 'The fear of Yahweh is the beginning of wisdom'); and on the other hand the wild and unpredictable religion of the Hebrews has been – dare I say it? – tamed and rationalized. 'In this way', says Martin Hengel, 'the many-layered conception of cosmic wisdom . . . was indissolubly associated with the history of Israel and, conversely, the law which was attacked in Jerusalem at the time of Ben Sira was given a supra-historical and at the same time a rational basis.'[16]

Sirach: a possible theodicy[17]

In Chapter 6 I introduced the study of Job with a brief discussion of theodicy, and in the course of our examination of Qoheleth I had occasion to note that his views on the meaning of life are constrained by a fairly explicit rejection of any doctrine of the afterlife. Ben Sira too seems to adhere to that older tradition, despite the evidence (which we noted in Chapter 8) from Daniel of a growing interest in the idea of a day of judgement. Thus the book of Sirach takes a realistic, if not fatalistic, view of humankind's ultimate fate: we come from the earth, and return to it, and nothing further can be hoped for. In this the book echoes (or anticipates) Qoheleth, and reflects a significant strand in Genesis; thus:

> All living beings become old like a garment,
>> for the decree from of old is, 'You must die!'   (14.17)

---

15 The assembly reported in Nehemiah 8 when the people confirmed their covenant with God under the aegis of the Torah.

16 Martin Hengel, *Judaism and Hellenism* (SCM Press, 1974), Vol. I, Ch. III, p. 160 (*passim* 131–53, 157–62).

17 The material in this section is based on an article by James L. Crenshaw, 'The Problem of Theodicy in Sirach' in *Journal of Biblical Literature* 94 (1975), pp. 49–64.

> The Lord created human beings out of the earth,
>   and makes them return to it again.   (17.1)

In a longer passage (40.1–11) which is bracketed (vv.1, 10–11) by clear references to Genesis 1—11, Ben Sira muses on the fact that life is burdensome and full of grief for all, prince and pauper alike (vv. 3–5a):

> From the one who sits on a splendid throne
>   to the one who grovels in dust and ashes,
> from the one who wears purple and a crown
>   to the one who is clothed in sackcloth,
> there is anger and envy and trouble and unrest.

Whatever happens in life, however, is constrained by the inevitability of our return to the place from which we came:

> . . . from the day they come forth from their mother's womb
>   until the day they return to the mother of all the living. (v. 1b)
> All that is of the earth returns to the earth,
>   and what is from above returns above. (v. 11)

The last verse is slightly opaque, but can be compared with Qoheleth 3.21 ('Who knows whether the human spirit goes upwards and the spirit of the animals goes downward to the earth?') and 12.7 ('and the dust returns to the earth as it was, and the breath returns to God who gave it') – a comparison which might suggest that Ben Sira, too, is thinking of the return of the spirit or breath to God, not as an identifiable individual soul, but as a life-giving quality which belongs solely to God.

Thus Ben Sira, like Qoheleth, faces a challenge: to resist the new theology, and to defend the coherence of the old. Crenshaw suggests that Ben Sira addresses this issue primarily in three didactic poems (16.24–17.14; 39.12–35; 42.15—43.33) which relate organically to his untypical use of the formula 'Do not say' which is frequent in Egyptian wisdom literature, but only rarely found in Qoheleth and Proverbs. It occurs in 5.1, 3, 4, 6; 11.23, 24; 15.11, 12; and 16.17. The last three are in the context of the first poem, and there is a refrain in the second which is similar: 'No one can say, "What is this? Why is that?"' (39.17, 21, cf. 34).

The first poem, which we will discuss in more detail in Chapter 10, answers (in the affirmative!) the question, 'Does God observe sin?', providing a basis for that answer in the supreme harmony of God's creation. The second poem deals with natural catastrophes; thus Crenshaw:

> God sees everything and his power is unlimited. In infinite wisdom he created good things for the virtuous and evil things for sinners. But even good things are perverted by wicked men and become occasions of stumbling. Thus Sirach claims that evil is attitudinal; faith and obedi-

ence are presuppositions for understanding God's ways, and much that goes under the name of evil only appears that way. *In its time* everything will be revealed for what it is, and evil will function punitively in behalf of its creator. Consequently, no man can say one thing is absolutely superior to another. [Author's emphasis].[18]

The key to this approach is *complementarity* (see especially 33.7–15). God's works *appear* ambivalent, but in time their coherence will be revealed:

> Why is one day more important than another,
>   when all the daylight in the year is from the sun?
> By the Lord's wisdom they were distinquished,
>   and he appointed the different seasons and festivals.
> Some days he exalted and hallowed,
>   and some he made ordinary days.
> All human beings come from the ground,
>   and humankind was created out of the dust.
> In the fullness of his knowledge the Lord distinguished them
>   and appointed their different ways.
>
>   . . .
>
> Good is the opposite of evil,
>   and life the opposite of death;
> so the sinner is the opposite of the godly.
> Look at all the works of the Most High;
>   they come in pairs, one the opposite of the other.
>
>   (33.7–11, 14–15)

The third poem is more praise than polemic, as if Ben Sira has now (in his own mind) reached a kind of contentment or calm, and sees the ultimate duty of humanity as that of praising God (a theme, of course, which is adumbrated in the first poem).

Ben Sira, as we know, was well aware of the thinking of earlier writers in the wisdom tradition (see pp. 192–3 above). Thus Job and Qoheleth, who also struggled with theodicy, are part of his inheritance. Yet in his own day he confronts both the rival philosophies of the Hellenistic world, which lay claim to cosmic explanations of ultimate coherence which have little to do with the idea of a personal deity, and the attractions of apocalyptic and eschatological Jewish literature. Hence his determination to show that Wisdom/Torah is that same principle of coherence that the Greeks argue for, but rooted in the personal nature of Yahweh. On the other hand, the question of justice has to be defined and answered in the

---

18 Crenshaw, 'The Problem of Theodicy in Sirach', p. 55.

context of death as the ultimate problem. It is perhaps too strong to suggest that Ben Sira has an answer to these dilemmas; but there are indications that he favoured a kind of psychological/spiritual resolution of the problem. This is most clearly articulated in the combination of 11.28 and 40.7–9, where it is claimed, first, that happiness cannot be defined before death, and secondly, that the sinner will suffer sevenfold. The second verse is in a passage (40.1–11) which deals with humanity's suffering, fear of death, and final end:

> Call no one happy before his death;
>> by how he ends, a person becomes known.
>
>   · · ·
>
> At the moment he reaches safety he wakes up,
>> astonished that his fears were groundless.
> To all creatures, human and animal,
>> but to sinners seven times more,
> come death and bloodshed and strife and sword,
>> calamities and famine and ruin and plague.

This idea is accompanied by another one which suggests that the idea of *the appropriate time* was of importance to Sirach (1.13; 3.26; 9.11; 11.21, 26, 28; 51.30). That is to say that our understanding is fatally flawed by our inability to see the whole picture. Only when the end comes is the pattern fully clear. Thus, in the end, Sirach's theodicy comes down to *resignation* to the fact that we cannot know the meaning of 'it all' combined with *trust* in God to have our best interests at heart. This should issue accordingly in the twin disciplines of *praise* and *obedience*.

Some points to think about

Test the claim that Sirach displays considerable intertextuality by examining the following parallels:

2.18 (cf. 2 Sam 24.14)	24.23–28 (references to Eden)
25.24 (reference to Eve)	33.10; 40.1 (references to Adam)
34.17–20 (Psalm 121)	17.1–6 (the creation account)

Read James Crenshaw's article for yourself and evaluate its contribution to the discussion of theodicy. It can be found in his *Urgent Advice and Probing Questions: collected writings on Old Testament wisdom* (Macon, GA, Mercer University Press, 1995), pp. 155–74.

Does the material in 25.16—26.18 deserve to be denounced for its misogyny and sexism, and if so how might this affect our reading of Ben Sira's work more generally?

10

The Wisdom of the Book of Sirach

While we have had occasion in Chapter 9 to refer to a range of passages in Sirach, we have not yet examined any in significant detail. In this chapter I shall look more closely at a very select range of passages. Clearly this cannot be representative of the book as a whole, and a more diagnostic overview has been provided in the previous chapter. Indeed, since two of the passages I shall consider could be regarded as potentially not from Ben Sira himself, there may appear to be something lacking in the selection. Inevitably, in a volume of this kind which seeks to provide a review of wisdom as a whole, we can only dip into a book as long as Sirach. The commentaries and other books listed at the end of this chapter are available to provide further reading which might compensate for the inevitable lacunae here present. The passages that I will examine are, in the order in which they will be treated: The first hymn: 'In praise of wisdom' (1.1–30); 'Eden revisited' (16.26—17.24); 'The "goddess" and her acolyte' (24.1–34); 'A life in teaching' (51.13–30) and the grandson's prologue.

Note on the text of Sirach

Sirach was preserved and transmitted in a variety of forms. The principal form it took in Christian canons was the Greek of the Septuagint, translated into the Latin Vulgate.

The original Hebrew, for long thought to have been lost, has now surfaced in various places, both from the genizah of the Cairo Synagogue and from the Dead Sea Scrolls.

As a result, there is confusion as to what might constitute the 'best' text. The version used in this book is that of the NRSV, which attempts to restore what a scholarly tradition regards as probably authentic.

As a result, the verse numbering often jumps, moving (as in Chapter 1) from v. 6 directly to v. 8, because v. 7 is regarded as relatively inauthentic. A number of passages in the NRSV version are printed in italics, thus 26.19–27, and the additional hymn placed after 51.12. Individual verses which have been rejected are given in footnotes.

The first hymn: 'In praise of wisdom' (1.1–30)

1 General remarks

The opening poem of Sirach is in two parts: the first ten verses celebrate the creation of wisdom – we may compare 24.1–7 and Proverbs 8.22–36, and also Wisdom of Solomon 7 and Baruch 3.9—4.4 – while the rest of the chapter constitutes a meditation on 'The fear of the Lord'. Both, of course, are major topics in earlier wisdom texts, as we have seen in our earlier discussion of Proverbs 1—9 and Job. But, as we shall see, Ben Sira has his own particular interpretation to offer.

Some have argued that the kind of encomium found in vv. 1–10 is related to (or in Sirach's case perhaps, indebted to) those first person eulogies to the Hellenistic goddess Isis which are classed as *aretalogies* (from the Greek *areté* meaning virtue). While it is almost impossible to prove or disprove such claims, it might seem reasonable to suppose that an educated and literate scholar in Hellenistic Jerusalem would at the very least be familiar with such material. Eclecticism and syncretism are common features of religions as they borrow and adapt material from each other. An example of one of these follows: you might be interested to compare it with the Hebrew passages in praise of Wisdom which have just been listed.

An Isis Aretalogy
(trans. Frederick C. Grant)

I am Isis, the mistress of every land, and I was taught by Hermes and with Hermes I devised letters, both the sacred (hieroglyphs) and the demotic, that all things might not be written with the same (letters).

I gave and ordained laws for men, which no one is able to change.
I am eldest daughter of Kronos.
I am wife and sister of King Osiris.
I am she who findeth fruit for men.
I am mother of King Horus.
I am she that riseth in the Dog Star.
I am she that is called goddess by women.
For me was the city of Bubastis built.
I divided the earth from the heaven.
I showed the paths of the stars.
I ordered the course of the sun and the moon.
I devised business in the sea.
I made strong the right.

I brought together woman and man.
I appointed to women to bring their infants to birth in the tenth month.
I ordained that parents should be loved by children.
I laid punishment on those disposed without natural affection toward
    their parents.
I made with my brother Osiris an end to the eating of men.
I revealed mysteries unto men.
I taught (men) to honor images of the gods.
I consecrated the precincts of the gods.
I broke down the governments of tyrants.
I made an end to murders.
I compelled women to be loved by men.
I made the right to be stronger than gold and silver.
I ordained that the true should be thought good.
I devised marriage contracts.
I assigned to Greeks and barbarians their languages.
I made the beautiful and the shameful to be distinguished by nature.
I ordained that nothing should be more feared than an oath.
I have delivered the plotter of evil against other men into the hands of
    the one he plotted against.
I established penalties for those who practice injustice.
I decreed mercy to suppliants.
I protect (or: honour) righteous guards.
With me the right prevails.
I am the Queen of rivers and winds and sea.
No one is held in honor without my knowing it.
I am the Queen of war.
I am the Queen of the thunderbolt.
I stir up the sea and I calm it.
I am in the rays of the sun.
I inspect the courses of the sun.
Whatever I please, this too shall come to an end.
With me everything is reasonable.
I set free those in bonds.
I am the Queen of seamanship.
I make the navigable unnavigable when it pleases me.
I created walls of cities.
I am called the Lawgiver (Thesmophoros).
I brought up islands out of the depths into the light.
I am Lord of rainstorms.
I overcome Fate.
Fate hearkens to me.
Hail, O Egypt, that nourished me!

Two textual points should be noted. In v. 19a there is a phrase ('He saw her and took her measure') which should perhaps be deleted since it is out of place, and repeats v. 9b (the NRSV relegates this line to a footnote). And second, DiLella argues that the words of v. 21, which most versions put in a footnote, should be retained as part of the main text. If these points are accepted, the second half of the poem has exactly 22 bicola. This implies an alphabetical basis – such patterns are in fact quite common in both wisdom and poetic literature – and further constitutes a link with the concluding poem in the book (51.13–30) which, in its Hebrew form (found in the Dead Sea Psalms Scroll 11QPsa), is a 23-line alphabetical acrostic. Together these two passages form an *inclusio* (a technical 'bracketing' device found frequently in Hebrew writing). The fact that Proverbs concludes, in 31.10–31, with an alphabetical acrostic which forms a parallel with the themes of 1—9 is another interesting case in point.

A further consequence of the emendations we have suggested is that the second part of the poem itself divides into two eleven-verse sections (11–21, 22–30), with a rather neat change at the end of v. 21.[1] Read as a whole, the second part of the poem has two purposes: to identify Wisdom with the *fear of the Lord* (vv. 11, 12, 13, 14, 16, 18, 20, 21, 27, 28, 30) and in particular to identify her with *Torah obedience* (25, 26, 27).

Fear in Sirach

There are three Greek words used in the majority of cases: *phobos* (fear), *phobein* (to fear) and *phoberos* (an adjective describing something which is to be feared). They occur respectively 31, 29 and 3 times in the Greek text of Sirach. Of this total of 63 occurrences, all but 13 refer to the standard biblical idea of 'the fear of Yahweh'. The greatest density of usage is in the first two chapters (18 instances); thereafter they are spread fairly evenly through chapters 4—40.[2]

The Hebrew root is *yare'*, and the main bulk of Septuagint passages translate it using the *phobos* group. There is, however, one other convention which might be worth mentioning: a sense of 'fearful' which is better rendered in English by words like 'marvellous' or 'wonderful'.

---

1 Skehan and DiLella point out that v. 22 in Greek begins with the negative *ou* which in Hebrew would be *lo'*, thus ensuring that the second set of eleven verses commences (appropriately) with the twelfth letter (*lamedh*) of the Hebrew alphabet. Unfortunately the original Hebrew is not extant, and there do not appear to be any signs of a full alphabetical acrostic here.

2 6.16, 17; 7.31; 9.16; 10.19, 20, 22, 24; 15.1, 13, 19; 16.2; 19.20; 21.6, 11; 23.27; 25.6, 10, 11; 26.3; 27.3; 32.14, 16; 33.1; 34.14, 16, 17; 40.26, 27; 43.29; 45.23.

There are a handful of instances of this in Sirach[3] (the Greek is *thaumastos*), but they do not significantly alter the general point, which is that Ben Sira has quite clearly and deliberately extended and elaborated the older tradition from Proverbs and elsewhere.

2 Specific comments (1.1–10)

The theme of vv. 1–10 is that all wisdom is from God (v. 1) and is a gift to those who love the Lord (vv. 9–10):

> It is he who created her;
>   he saw her and took her measure;
>   he poured her out upon all his works,
> upon all the living according to his gift;
>   he lavished her upon those who loved him.

This is strong language, which, as we shall shortly see, echoes certain equally powerful ideas elsewhere in the Old Testament. Attentive readers will recall that the idea that Wisdom as a gift is relatively rare in the main canon, where the emphasis is much more on the individual's acquiring of wisdom through study, piety and obedience (see Chapter 1), so that Ben Sira's introduction of this motif right at the start of his book takes on added significance. The same can be said of a second important theme, in v. 4: the prior existence of wisdom. This is not entirely new – it features in Proverbs 8.22 – but the specific statement that 'prudent understanding [was created] from all eternity' reinforces the notion that somehow wisdom exists prior to and outside the creation. We shall return to this point below, in connection with our comments on v. 26.

In v. 6 the traditional idea of the secrecy and impenetrability of wisdom is described in terms very similar to Proverbs 1.5f – where, however, the wise man can *acquire* the necessary skills. This theme is also to be found in Job 28 and Qoheleth 8.17; 5.2. The Stoics used an allegory based on Homer's account of how Penelope fended off her suitors, even though her handmaidens succumbed to their blandishments. Penelope embodies true wisdom (*sophia*) while her handmaidens represent the preliminaries to true wisdom which all could master (the encyclicals). All of this suggests a common-sense view that there was something remote, esoteric and inaccessible about wisdom, in both Greek and Hebrew learning.

The use of rhetorical questions in v. 6 (as also in vv. 2–3) is similar to its deployment in Isaiah 40.12–14 and Job 42.1–6. This is a device which

---

3 11.4; 16.11; 39.20; 43.2, 8, 29.

is often used when the writer wishes to emphasize the superiority of God – hence the predictable answer in the next verse (v. 8). In this verse the image of God enthroned is one of *power* and also of *threat* – compare Psalms 2.4; 9.4; 47.8; and Isaiah 6.1. Compare also the exchange between the rich ruler and Jesus in Mark 10.17f, where Jesus' answer ('No one is good but God alone') bears comparison with Ben Sira's 'There is but one who is wise'.

Verse 10 makes an important point: wisdom is present in *all* humans, but is *lavished* on 'those who love him'. It may not be out of order to suggest a link with Exodus 20.6, where God's steadfast love is promised to a thousand generations of 'those who love [him] and keep [his] commandments'. Once again, wisdom is bound up with Torah: it is those who obey Torah who will most truly know wisdom.

3 Specific comments (1.11–30)

We have already observed that the subject matter of vv. 11–30 is an exploration of the familiar concept of 'the fear of the Lord'. The nature of this 'fear' is spelled out right at the start, in vv. 11–12, where it is clear that this is a complex and affirmative quality:

> The fear of the Lord is glory and exultation,
>   and gladness and a crown of rejoicing.
> The fear of the Lord delights the heart,
>   and gives gladness and joy and long life.

The word translated 'gladness' is in Greek *euphrosune* – which means, according to Skehan and DiLella, 'a good mental and moral state, a sense of serenity and happiness, resulting from an upright and virtuous life'. We should not, however, lose sight of its classical meanings of 'mirth' 'celebration in happy circumstances'. It occurs rather frequently in Sirach (1.12b, 13b; 2.9b; 6.28b; 9.10d; 15.6a; 30.16b, 22a; 31.27d, 28d, 31b; 35.11b; 37.4a), and its range of meanings bears some relationship to the complex of signification built into the Hebrew terms 'peace' (*shalom*) and 'righteousness' (*tsedaqah*), which convey the sense of well-being and prosperity (*shalom*) which comes from a good relationship (*tsedaqah*) with God. Another example of what this means is to be found in v. 18:

> The fear of the Lord is the crown of wisdom,
>   making peace and perfect health to flourish.

The combination of peace and health sums up rather nicely what shalom is about.

Verse 13, with its references to 'a happy end' and 'on the day of his death he will be blessed', belongs to the theodicy which seems to have characterized Ben Sira's efforts to make sense of life, and which we discussed more fully at the end of Chapter 9.

There are a number of echoes of Proverbs in the next verses (14–20): the idea that to fear the Lord is the *beginning* of wisdom (where in both Greek and Hebrew this can mean any or all of 'starting point', 'most important' or 'best'); Wisdom's commitment to dwelling among human beings (cf. Proverbs 8.31 'rejoicing in his inhabited world and delighting in the human race'); the idea that Wisdom is intoxicating (Prov. 5.20); and her role as the bringer of worldly prosperity (Prov. 3.16–18, 8.20); and the promise she offers of peace, health and long life (compare Prov. 3.16, 'Long life is in her right hand'). But there are two new ideas: the suggestion that wisdom 'heightened the glory of those who held her fast' (v. 19), and the concept of the 'root of wisdom' (see also v. 6). The former seems to impinge upon a quality usually reserved for the deity, and is reminiscent of the similar sentiment in Psalm 8.5. This somewhat exalted image may be part of an identifiable trend in Sirach towards a certain blurring of the boundaries between human and divine which will reappear in chapter 24, and in Ben Sira's clearly exalted sense of his own significance. It may be that some echoes of middle Platonism can be found here, similar to Philo's concept of the power of human minds at their best to reach towards the mediatory realm of the Logos.

The metaphor of the root of wisdom, an image not directly attested in the Old Testament proper, may have some connection with the portrait of the righteous in Psalm 1.2–3, whose

> delight is in the law of the LORD,
>   and on his law they meditate day and night.
> They are like trees
>   planted by streams of water,
> which yield their fruit in its season,
>   and their leaves do not wither.
> In all that they do, they prosper.

We should note also the representation of Wisdom in Proverbs 3.18:

> She is a tree of life to those who lay hold of her;
>   those who hold her fast are called happy.

We can surely trace a lineage from these representations to the 'root and branch' delineation of Sirach 1.20:

> To fear the Lord is the root of wisdom,
>   and her branches are long life.

The same idea recurs in 24.12, where wisdom declares:

> I took root in an honoured people,
>   in the portion of the Lord, his heritage.

The second part of this poem on the fear of the Lord is marked by the bridge between vv. 21 and 22. I have already indicated that there are good reasons to retain the former verse, despite its being relegated to the footnotes of most editions. Its language ('The fear of the Lord drives away sins; / and where it abides, it will turn away all anger') affords a neat bridge between parts one and two of the second hymn, in that the motif of 'turning away anger' leads immediately into a condemnation of 'unjust anger' – a nice example of the literary device known as *stichwort* ('linking word').

As we shall see in our study of Sirach 24, the link between Wisdom and Torah is a key to understanding Ben Sira's theology. A similar connection is found in Baruch 4.1, which might have been composed around the same time as, or a little later than Sirach. It may be, therefore, that this was an idea 'whose time had come'. In the present composition it occurs in vv. 26–27 as a kind of equation (and see also 15.1; 21.11; 24.23; and 34.8):

> fear of the Lord = wisdom = gift of the Lord = discipline = keeping the commandments

> If you desire *wisdom, keep the commandments,*
>   and the *Lord will lavish her upon you.*
> For the *fear of the Lord* is *wisdom* and *discipline,*
>   fidelity and humility are his delight.

A further element of this 'equation of holiness', the love of God, is missing here but forms part of the equation in v. 10 and in 2.15–16:

> Those who fear the Lord do not disobey his words,
>   and those who love him keep his ways.
> Those who fear the Lord seek to please him,
>   and those who love him are filled with his law.

The concept of the pre-existence of Wisdom which we commented on in relation to v. 4, above, takes on another significance when we mark this identification of Wisdom with Torah. There is on the one hand the parallel Christian teaching of the pre-existence of Christ/the Logos. Here John's theology is of particular importance; in particular the prologue. We may suspect that Ben Sira, and later Philo's reading of Plato, may have been of significance for the Johannine interpretation of the meaning of Jesus' life and death. On the other hand there is a rabbinic tradition of the pre-existence of Torah; Skehan and DiLella cite in this regard a saying from *Midrash Bereshith Rabba* 8 which reads:

> According to R Simeon ben Laqish the Torah was in existence 2000 years before the creation of the world.

The poem concludes with a passage on the dangers of hypocrisy, of a 'divided mind' (*kardia dissé*). The literal meaning is 'a double heart': a similar phrase occurs in Psalm 12.2 (Hebrew *lev valev*). In both Greek and Hebrew 'heart' signifies 'mind' or 'will' – internal actions – while 'tongue' (v. 29) represents the external expression of these virtues. Skehan and DiLella observe that 'The heart is the root of choice and the tongue is the expression of choice.' Hence 'heart' and 'tongue' are intimately connected. A similar phrase, 'double tongue' (*diglossos*) is used in 5.9, 14 and 6.1 (which in turn is reminiscent of James 1.8 and 4.8). Finally, though the hypocritical may think that their secrets are safe, they will (in Ben Sira's view) inevitably be 'outed'. The wrongdoer's secrets are surely ironically related to the hidden mysteries of v. 6, and the passage as a whole could well be a reflection on Proverbs 5.12–14. Ben Sira valued 'the assembly' – it is referred to a number of times, in 4.7; 7.7; 23.24; 41.18 and 42.11. Perhaps, as a leading scholar, he had a part to play in its deliberations, and knew something of the seamier side of life from cases he had heard? Mere speculation – but interesting!

Excursus on intertextuality

In the previous chapter I pointed out that Sirach is representative of a process (intertextuality), highly developed in this case, whereby scriptural writing depends on the appropriation in various ways of earlier sacred material with a view to extending or expanding upon its meaning. In what we have already said about Sirach 1 it will be clear that this is an important aspect of the work. In this excursus I want to examine more closely how intertextuality functions and how it can be recognized in the work of Ben Sira.

There are particular problems with this book which are perhaps not to be found in other Old Testament texts, and these are associated with both the language that we presume Ben Sira to have written in and the language of his sources. If he wrote in Hebrew in Jerusalem (the predominant assumption) then he would have consulted Hebrew Scriptures. But then we have the difficulty of identifying intertexts between the Greek text of Sirach and its Hebrew forerunners. Some parts of Sirach have survived in Hebrew, but unfortunately of the sections which I shall examine only chapter 51 is extant, and we have already noted that as problematic in relation to the bulk of the book. Rather than engage upon a complex textual critical exercise involving back-formation of the ur-Hebrew of Sirach, I propose to illustrate its intertextuality by looking at some examples from 1.1–10 where the Greek of Sirach can be matched with key Septuagint terms used to translate specific Hebrew words or phrases, and thus gain access to the likely Old Testament sources for some of the book's development. I hope that the few examples here cited will serve to illustrate, if not demonstrate, the importance of this theme in discussion of Sirach.

The first point to make is that there is a general indebtedness to Proverbs 8.22–31 which comes out at a number of particular points as well as in the general tone of the two passages, both of which deal with the origins of wisdom before creation, go on to describe aspects of creation, and conclude with the beneficial relationship between wisdom and the world. Turning to the particular, I observe the following:

1 The language in v. 2 – 'the sand of the sea', 'the drops of rain', 'who can count them' – can be found in a number of Old Testament passages. Thus Genesis 32.12, 'I will make your offspring as the sand of the sea, which cannot be counted because of their number', an image taken up in Hosea 1.10. Psalm 139.17–18 is closer to the idea of the immeasurability of wisdom:

> How weighty to me are your thoughts, O God!
>   How vast is the sum of them!
> I try to count them – they are more than the sand;
>   I come to the end – I am still with you

and Solomon's wisdom is said to be 'as vast as the sand on the seashore' (1 Kings 4.29). Finally, there is a description of God's attributes in Job 36.27–30 which touches on several of the linguistic bases in these verses from Sirach:

> For he draws up the *drops of water*;
>   he distils his mist in rain,
> which the skies pour down
>   and *drop upon mortals abundantly*.
> *Can anyone understand* the spreading of the clouds,
>   the thunderings of his pavilion?
> See, he scatters his lightning around him
>   and covers the *roots* of the sea.

2 While individual terms in v. 3 are found in a number of places, there are two passages in Job which provide more detailed connections.

One is found within God's first speech to Job, in 38.16, 18:

Have you entered into the springs of the sea,
  or walked in the recesses of the deep?

. . .

Have you comprehended the expanse of the earth?
  Declare, if you know all this.

Three of the terms in v. 3 are reflected here: the deep, the expanse of earth, and the rhetorical question about human capabilities. The other passage is the famous poem on the place of wisdom in Job 28. The question, 'who can search them out?' is of course a dominant motif of the Job passage, given particular expression in vv. 12–13, 14, and 20–22. Other terms from v. 3 are picked up from vv.14 and 23–24:

The deep says, 'It is not in me',
  and the sea says, 'It is not with me.'

. . .

God understands the way to it,
  and he knows its place.
For he looks to the ends of the earth,
  and sees everything under the heavens.

3 Verse 4 (and its echo in 9a) clearly have in mind Proverbs 8.22–23, though the paralleling of wisdom and prudent understanding may also owe something to Proverbs 3.19, if it not merely a stock pairing of terms regularly taken together.

4 In v. 6 'her subtleties' takes us into the realm of a Hebrew root of some interest. It first appears in Genesis 3.1 as a description of the serpent who 'was more crafty than any other wild animal that the Lord God had made'. There is a possible pun in this instance, since the word for 'crafty' or 'subtle' is almost identical to the word for 'naked'. The more direct parallels are to be found in Proverbs: in 1.4 where 'shrewdness' is one of the virtues to be learned as part of wisdom (compare 8.5, 'O simple ones, learn prudence'); and in 8.12 where the direct association with wisdom is affirmed: 'I, wisdom, live with prudence.' The term is ethically neutral, and sometimes negative in that it is used for those who might best be described as 'cunning'. The possible reference to Genesis is interesting because, as we shall see, Ben Sira makes more use of the creation stories in other places, and by no means sees these as negative accounts of a fall. It is possible that the craftiness of the serpent was not, for Ben Sira, a bad thing!

5 In v. 8 there is a forward reference which is hard to avoid, to Luke 18.18–19, where the exchange between the ruler and Jesus elicits the latter's comment that 'No one is good but God alone'. Within the Old Testament the more obvious reference is to the awesome God enthroned in the prophet's Temple vision in Isaiah 6.1–5.

6 Turning finally to vv. 9 and 10, we have already effectively dealt with the cross references in the first two phrases of v. 9, and have suggested that the idea of God's lavishing wisdom 'upon all the living' constitutes one more of the strands connecting Sirach to Proverbs 8 – in particular 8.31: 'rejoicing in his inhabited world and delighting in the human race'. The remaining concept, of the pouring out of wisdom, has a prophetic resonance, most obviously with Joel 2.28–9:

> Then afterwards
>   I will pour out my spirit on all flesh;
> your sons and your daughters shall prophesy,
>   your old men shall dream dreams,
>   and your young men shall see visions.
> Even on the male and female slaves,
>   in those days I will pour out my spirit.

Eden revisited (16.26—17.24)

1 General remarks

This poem is prefaced, in 16.17, by a question that uses a formal rhetorical device from the setting of a 'debate with an antagonist' which I discussed in Chapter 9 (p. 201) and which uses the question-form 'Do not say . . .'. It is mostly used in the context of discussions about justice – and it is precisely that concern which informs its use in 16.17. The sinner is warned not to imagine that God is ignorant of or blind to his sin. Ben Sira first responds with a passage in which God's advent is anticipated (vv. 18–23), accompanied by the usual theophanic phenomena. He then gives an extended account of the close involvement of Yahweh in every aspect of his creation (the poem under discussion), and concludes (17.15–20) by answering, with a decided affirmative, the unspoken question: 'Does God observe sin?'

The form 'Do not say . . .', though rare in the Old Testament, occurs nine times in Sirach – a frequency large enough to merit some comment. In the run-up to the present context it is found three times (15.11, 12; 16.17), each time putting forward an example of the kind of excuse or defence the wicked might attempt. In fact the other six uses are also in the general context of theodicy, the relationship between right living and prosperity, wrong-doing and suffering. Thus:

5.1   Don't boast of your prosperity.
5.3   Don't imagine you are beyond the reach of authority.
5.4   Don't say that you have sinned and expect there to be no consequences.
5.6   Don't rely on God's mercy to forgive a multitude of sins.
11.23 Don't take pride in the sufficiency of your possessions.
11.24 Don't assume that you are immune to catastrophe.

In addition to these examples, there is a repeated motif in the didactic poem in 39.12–35 (see vv. 16b, 17b, 31c, 33b, 34b) whose theme is that, ultimately, God has a time and a purpose for everything (cf. Qoheleth 3.1–9) – and that includes justice for the righteous and judgement for the riotous. So there is no need to repeat (vv. 17, 21, 34) 'What is this? Why is that? This is worse than that!'

The poem under consideration here can be structured in different ways. Alonso-Schökel[4] sees in the poem several asymmetric groups with some internal tension. Thus we find the two traditional planes of creation – heaven and earth – in each of which there are created orders: the stars and heavenly bodies on the one hand, humankind and the living creatures on the other. Humanity is balanced between the two, sharing some things with the stars and some with the beasts, but having a special place of their own. Thus Alonso-Schökel:

> As all living things on the earth are to die, so must man, because he is of the earth. As the celestial beings have a dominion, a function, a mandate and companions, so does man have a dominion, function, law and companions.

But human beings have further distinctions, which we will note in due course, relating to their vocation for praise and their having been endowed with the law of life. Alonso-Schökel breaks the poem into three strophes corresponding to these observations:

A   Creation (16.26—17.4)
B   Praise (17.6–10)
C   Torah (17.11–14).

It is possible to identify a different kind of order in the poem not unlike that which is to be found also in chapter 24: a progression from the widest to the narrowest spheres of wisdom's influence, which in the end blossoms out again to embrace the whole world. Thus we begin with the creation of the heavens and the stars and planets (16.26–28); we then come (literally) down to earth in the creation of the world and its creatures (16.29–30), and humankind (17.1–10); the scope then narrows (by clear implication) to the special people of Israel and the law which is God's gift to them (17.11–14). Finally, just as chapter 24 issues out in an application to the whole world of Israel's special place, so too we find in 17.17,[5] 15, 19 an account of God's interrogation of the whole world. The works of all human beings are known to him, while Israel has a special position ('He appointed a ruler for every nation, but Israel is the Lord's own portion', v. 17). This suggests a characteristic (if slightly distorted!) 'hour-glass' structure – from general to particular to general.

A: 16.26–28   All Creation
   B: 16.29–30   Earth in general
      C: 17.1–10   Humankind
         D: 17.11–14   Israel
      E: 17.17, 15, 19   All people

2 Specific comments (16.26–28)

The Greek of v. 26 has 'judged', but this is a simple misreading of the word for 'created' (in Greek they are similar: *krisei* and *ktisei*). There is a conscious reference to Genesis 1, where also the ordered creation of the world precedes the creation of humankind. The next verse states that 'He arranged his works in an eternal order'. There may be links with the Stoic concept of *nomos* as a world principle (interestingly, there is a typically Stoic addition in 17.5, which is placed in the footnotes of the NRSV); but connections with Genesis are much more significant. Thus, we find in this verse associations with Genesis 1.14–19, especially v. 16 ('God made the two great lights – the greater light to rule the day and the lesser light to rule the night – and the stars'). The rule (Sirach: 'dominion') of the heavenly bodies determines times and seasons:

He arranged his works in an eternal order,
    and their dominion for all generations.

---

5 The re-ordering of v. 17 requires some explanation. There are no textual grounds for this; however it is undeniable that the last part of the poem makes better sense in this order – the reference to Israel's special position among the nations forming a neat bridge between D and E in the 'hourglass' structure.

They neither hunger nor grow weary,
  and they do not abandon their tasks. (Sirach 16.27)

That they 'neither hunger nor grow weary' is reminiscent in different ways of Psalm 121.4 ('He who keeps Israel will neither slumber nor sleep') and 1 Kings 18.27, where Elijah mocks the prophets of Baal for worshipping a God who requires regular sleep.

3 Specific comments (16.29—17.4)

The reference to 'good things' in 16.29 is a concretization of the somewhat metaphysical refrain in Genesis: 'God saw that it was very good.' Ben Sira makes a specific connection: what is good is literally the abundance of plants and animals which God has created to cover the earth (v. 30). Note also two other Genesis phrases in v. 30: 'covered its surface', which refers to the potent waters covering the earth and which is found in both of the Genesis creation accounts (1.2; 2.6), and the idea of 'return' which we shall return to in our discussion of 17.1.

It is noteworthy that the order in 7.1–4 (*mortality, dominion, image of God*) is the reverse of that in Genesis. Moreover, Ben Sira takes humanity's mortality to be natural, a consequence of the creation, not any kind of fall (a concept which is entirely absent from Sirach, and is indeed scarcely appealed to in Jewish tradition generally). The thought of the inevitable mortality of humanity is repeated in 40.1–11 and 48.3–4, where the appropriate response to this natural condition is resignation. The passage as a whole belongs to the same kind of reflection on creation that we find in Psalm 8; it appears that the material of the creation myths was by this time widely available for theological speculation. Ben Sira does not confine himself to the opening chapters of Genesis, for his concept of the fear which the beasts have of human beings derives from Genesis 9.2. It is instructive to see how Ben Sira blends the two Genesis accounts in his survey. Thus 17.1 begins with Genesis 1.27 ('the Lord created human beings', cf. 'So God created humankind'), then moves to 2.7 ('out of earth', cf. 'from the dust of the ground') and 3.19 ('and makes them return to it again', cf. 'until you return to the ground'), and at the end of 17.2 returns to Genesis 1.28 ('granted them authority over everything on earth', cf. 'have dominion over . . . every living thing'). In between, he speaks of humanity's fixed span of life – something which is not referred to in the creation stories, but may reflect Genesis 6.3 or Psalm 90.10.

The phrase in v. 3, 'he endowed ['clothed' is the literal meaning of the Greek] them with strength' may be an allegorization of Genesis 3.21, though the only other place where this combination of terms occurs is, interestingly, to be found in the portrait of the powerful woman in Proverbs 31.25, 'Strength and dignity are her clothing'. Other writers use

the image of being clothed with such qualities as righteousness or justice
(Job 29.14; Ps. 132.9; Wisd. 5.18; Sirach 27.8), honour or majesty (Pss
93.1; 104.1) or salvation (Ps. 132.16). Ben Sira in one place speaks of the
pursuer of wisdom as wearing her 'like a glorious robe' (6.31).

At the end of v. 3 Ben Sira returns to Genesis 1.26–27 ('made them in
his own image') – though he does not refer to the 'male and female' aspect
of humanity's likeness to God. Finally, in this series of explicit allusions
to Genesis, in v. 4 there is a repetition of the theme of domination over
all creatures combined with a reference ('He put the fear of them in all
living beings') which does not appear in Genesis until after the Flood,
in 9.2 where fear is first mentioned as an instrument of human rule over
creation.

4 Specific comments (17.6–19)

So far Ben Sira has used Scripture straightforwardly, without introducing wisdom material. As we move into the next verses, however, we encounter his development of the traditions of Scripture in wisdom terms.
Humankind as a creation is different from the animals and the heavenly
bodies in a very particular way: that they have the capacity to understand, evaluate and praise (see the list of gifts of an intellectual nature in
vv. 6, 8: tongue, eyes, ears, mind, heart). In this aspect of their destiny
human beings exceed the stars which, though they have (unlike humanity) a kind of permanence (16.27), have no knowledge and cannot praise
the Creator. The thought here is very similar to Psalm 8 whose refrain
('O Lord our Sovereign, how majestic is your name in all the earth') should
be understood as the willing confession of God's highest creatures.

In our discussion of 17.1–3 we noted a shift from the point of view in
Genesis, in that Ben Sira understands human mortality to be natural.
Another important shift occurs in v. 7, for here it is plain that the knowledge of good and evil is a positive thing. Indeed, coming as it does in this
later part of the passage it is a key to the whole. MacKenzie[6] sees Sirach's
interpretation as being in fact a proper reading of Genesis:

> Verse 7 is important: it pictures God as already imparting the great gift
> of wisdom to the first humans and, in parallel with that, showing them
> good and evil. This is a noteworthy and probably correct interpreta-
> tion of the 'tree of knowledge' of Genesis 2.9, 17; 3.5, 22.

Since Adam is elsewhere praised (see 49.16: 'Shem and Seth and Enosh
were honoured, but above every other created living being was Adam') it
seems that, far from identifying him as the rebellious founding father of

---

6 R. A. F. MacKenzie, *Sirach* (Gill and Macmillan, 1983).

sin demonized in the Augustinian doctrine of the fall, Ben Sira regards him as the sage *par excellence.*

In keeping with the progression from the widest compass of all to increasingly more specific orientation, the next verses introduce an Israelite theme which is nevertheless closely linked with what has gone before. Thus, on the 'living beings' he has created (16.30) God bestows the 'law of life' (17.11). The full purpose of the gift of 'eyes and ears' (17.6) is now made plain (17.13 'Their eyes saw his glorious majesty, and their ears heard the glory of his voice'). And 'knowledge' is now linked not just with the perception of good and evil (17.7) – an attribute of all humanity – but with the special gift of the law (17.11). That Ben Sira intends this law of life to be the same as the Torah of Moses is spelled out very clearly in 45.5, describing Moses:

> He allowed him to hear his voice,
>   and led him into the dark cloud,
> and gave him the commandments face to face,
>   the law of life and knowledge,
> so that he might teach Jacob the covenant,
>   and Israel his decrees.

Verses 11–14 are replete with the language of Torah; thus, for example, the parallel in v. 12 between *covenant* and *decrees*, and the phrases 'glorious majesty' and 'glory of his voice' in v. 13 which recall the Pentateuchal understanding of the presence of God. The deity may not be seen, and the manifestation which is open to human beings is God's glory (Hebrew *kabod*). This language is particularly appropriate to the Decalogue theophany (Ex. 16.7; 24.16; 29.43; 40.34f; Deut. 5.24) in which the revelation takes the form of God's speaking to the people. Thus v. 13 provides a recognizable preface which implies that what follows immediately will be Torah. In v. 14 Ben Sira succeeds in summing up the content of the Decalogue at the same time with great succinctness and admirable comprehensiveness, in a fashion not unlike more modern accounts, which see the laws as falling into two categories: commandments concerning God ('beware of all evil') and commandments concerning one's neighbour.

I have made the assumption that the final verses should be in the order 17–15–19. Whether or not this change can be defended, what the concluding passage indicates is the eternally vigilant eye of God on the works of all of his creatures – a somewhat frightening prospect, no doubt; but in view of the framework within which this poem is set (an argument from theodicy regarding the sinner's claim that he or she will escape the consequences of their wrong-doing) it is entirely appropriate. The idea of God's having appointed a ruler for every nation might allude to Deuteronomy 32.8:

When the Most High apportioned the nations,
   when he divided humankind,
he fixed the boundaries of the peoples
   according to the number of the gods

– a passage which has been interpreted as a reference to the belief in tutelary deities for each nation. Just as Sirach 17.17 goes on to make it clear that Israel is God's own choice, so does the next verse in Deuteronomy:

the LORD's own portion was his people,
   Jacob his allotted share.

And so the sequence ends, in vv. 20–24, with a promise of judgement, but also a chance to repent. 'Do not say, "It does not matter what I do"'; indeed it does matter, as this lesson from creation amply demonstrates.

The 'goddess' and her acolyte (24.1–34)

1 General Remarks

At the heart of this chapter there is an identification – already alluded to more than once – which marks something of a breakthrough in the development of pre-rabbinic Jewish thought. The chapter is introduced by a couple of verses which announce Wisdom's intention to glorify herself, and which set the chapter firmly in the same genre as Proverbs 8.

Wisdom announces herself	
Proverbs 8.1–3	**Sirach 24.1–2**
Does not wisdom call, and does not understanding raise her voice? On the heights, beside the way, at the crossroads she takes her stand; beside the gates in front of the town, at the entrance of the portals she cries out.	Wisdom praises herself and tells of her glory in the midst of her people. In the assembly of the Most High she opens her mouth, and in the presence of his hosts she tells of her glory.

As we have seen, Ben Sira made deliberate and extensive use of Scripture to express the distillation of a lifetime's meditation on the nature and purpose of wisdom, but he never used it slavishly. Thus chapter 24, unlike Proverbs 8, moves immediately to the key dramatic moment: Wisdom as the firstborn of creation (a topic delayed until v. 22 of Proverbs 8). What Sirach omits is Proverbs' listing of Wisdom's secular virtues, though the reference in Proverbs to Wisdom's dwelling in 'prudence, knowledge and discretion' (8.12) may inform Ben Sira's dramatic picture of Wisdom dwelling in the midst of the chosen people and its worship. Wisdom in both writers begins as a cosmic, international principle, and is quite radically personified. But the later writer introduces a whole range of ideas specific to Israel which Proverbs never even hints at. It is these that mark off this passage as different, as a creative step forward, an advance on anything we find in the Scriptures before it.

Structurally, we can shape this chapter using the same 'hour-glass' principle which we applied to the material in the previous section. Wisdom begins her account in the most general of terms (vv. 3–6), then describes her choice of Israel for a dwelling (vv. 7–9), and still more specifically, the Temple in Jerusalem (vv. 10–12). In a truly bold move, Ben Sira then identifies her with the sacred oil and the sweet incense which symbolize the presence of God in the holiest place of all (vv. 13–22). The climax is in v. 23, where Wisdom is identified with Torah; the theme concludes (vv. 25–29) with a tremendous flooding of this newly baptized Israelite Torah/Wisdom out into the whole world, represented by the language of the four rivers of Eden (Pishon, Tigris, Euphrates and Gihon) and the two which represent Israel's redemption through water (the Jordan and the Nile). We can set this structure out as follows:

Prologue 24.1–2		Wisdom introduces herself
A: 24.3–6		Wisdom the firstborn
B: 24.7–9		Wisdom in Israel
C: 24.10–12		Wisdom in Jerusalem
D: 24.13–22		Wisdom in the Sanctuary
E: 24.23		Wisdom is Torah
F: 24.25–29		Wisdom/Torah for all humankind
Epilogue 24.30–34		Ben Sira takes on Wisdom's mantle

2 Specific comments (24.1–22)

In the prologue Wisdom is introduced in terms which already indicate the special character given to her by Ben Sira. In v. 1 she is already referring to 'her people', anticipating vv. 8–12, while in v. 2 she stands in the 'assembly of the Most High' and in 'the presence of his hosts' – language which belongs to the long tradition of the divine court of Yahweh and which places Wisdom firmly among the supernatural beings who surround him (see Ps. 29.1–2; 82.1; 1 Kings 22.19; Job 1.6; 2.1). This is of course an ambiguous placing in terms of the Old Testament (is Wisdom to be compared with the Satan of Job or the rebellious gods of Psalm 82?); the fact that Wisdom is everywhere presented as a wholly positive figure should perhaps give us reason to reconsider our traditional view of the metaphor of the assembly of the gods in the presence of Yahweh.

The hymn itself opens (v. 3a) with a striking image: Wisdom is a word 'from the mouth of the Most High'. This is an important idea, which is prefigured in certain places in the Old Testament: Isaiah 45.23 ('from my mouth has gone forth in righteousness / a word that shall not return); 55.11 ('so shall my word be that goes out from my mouth; / it shall not return to me empty'); and the curiously embodied 'word' which appears to Elijah in the cave on Horeb in 1 Kings 19.9 ('Then the word of the Lord came to him, saying'). That this last appearance is a kind of personified being is made clear when 'he' (the word) speaks again in v. 11: 'He said, "Go out and stand on the mountain before the Lord . . .".' The 'word' here speaks, and refers separately to Yahweh. With Ben Sira's equating of Wisdom with Word (*sophia* with *logos*, *hokhmah* with *davar*) we are close to the theological world of Philo and John.

What follows in vv. 3b–6 represents a highly concentrated series of allusions to well-known motifs in both the Pentateuch and the wider Scripture.[7] Together they add up to a daringly radical proposal. To begin with, the phrase 'covered the earth like a mist' – which needs both Genesis 1.2 *and* 2.6 to provide the elements of *covering,* and *mist* (the Greek also means *cloudy darkness*) – places Wisdom in the role of the Spirit of God at the very beginning of creation. We then find, in v. 4, a series of references to the wilderness traditions.

'I dwelt in the highest heavens.'

A better verb would be 'I encamped', since the Greek verb used here is also used in the Septuagint to refer to the *shekinah*, the dwelling place of God's glory in the wilderness tabernacle, and a term, incidentally, which becomes significant later in Kabbalistic Judaism. Wisdom is here being associated very closely with the formative historical and cultic events of the story of Israel's origins in the wilderness.

'My throne was in a pillar of cloud.'

The enthronement of wisdom in a pillar of cloud binds together the theo-

---

7 Some of the discussion that follows is based on Shephard's ground-breaking study of intertextuality, *Wisdom as a Hermeneutical Construct* (Berlin, de Gruyter, 1980) pp. 19–71.

phanic symbolism of the divine throne with the characteristic emblem of divine presence in the wilderness traditions. The total effect of 'dwelling', 'throne' and 'pillar of cloud' is to suggest very strongly that wisdom, if not divine, is – *within her allotted sphere* – virtually indistinguishable from God.

Verses 5 and 6 take us into different territory. Not Torah now, but wisdom and prophetic literature. Wisdom is never described as 'alone' in the Old Testament, but Isaiah 44.24 and Job 9.8 refer to God in this way; further echoes (again referring to God's traversing of the uttermost boundaries of the world) are to be found in Job 22.14; 38.16; Proverbs 8.27–29; and Isaiah 40.22. The strong impression is given that Ben Sira was very familiar with the creation/wisdom theology of the post exilic period, as represented in Deutero-Isaiah, Proverbs and Job – and of course, Genesis 1—9. Moreover, his use of it is bold and original, taking the concept of wisdom much closer to hypostatization.[8] Most of the features which characterize Wisdom in vv. 4–5 properly belong to God in the source traditions; thus Wisdom is effectively filling a role formerly reserved for God alone.

Verse 7 affords a bridge into the next theme while at the same time returning to the language of the wilderness, in particular to the Deuteronomistic langage of *search, rest,* and *inheritance.* According to Snaith: 'Ben Sira is here in marked contrast to other writers: for in other books of the time wisdom seeks for a place on earth, but does not find any and returns to heaven.'[9] The key ideas of rest and inheritance recur throughout chapter 24 (vv. 7, 11, 12, 20, 23); elsewhere in the Old Testament this pairing of terms is only commonly found in Deuteronomy (3.18–20; 12.1–11; 25.19; cf. Josh. 11.13–15), and the phrase 'to seek a resting place' (or inheritance) is used in the Old Testament exclusively of the tribes of Israel in pursuit of their allocation of territory within the promised land (Num. 10.33; Deut. 1.33; Judg. 18.1). The first two of these references also speak of the pillar of cloud. The use of these close pentateuchal biblical associations means that the thought of vv. 8–12 comes as no surprise. To anyone steeped in the language of the Scriptures wisdom has already (though not yet explicitly) been defined in Israelite terms. It remains only to spell out this definition, and this is done in the very explicit Israelite Temple cult language of vv. 8–12, followed by the equally pointed metaphors of the vine, the ingredients of the anointing oil and other images from nature which are developed in vv. 13–17. A detailed exposition of this material has already been given in the previous chapter (pp. 196–7 above) to which the reader is directed at this point.

8 A form of personification of abstract qualities which assumes them into a quasi-divine status.

9 *Ecclesiastes* (1974), p. 121.

The final verses before the climactic v. 23 present Wisdom's delights. The picture of wisdom as something which is very appetizing is a common one in the Old Testament, while the language of v. 21 cannot fail to remind us of passages in John's Gospel, especially 4.14 ('those who drink of the water that I will give them will never be thirsty'). It is interesting, however, that the two writers use the same imagery to make opposite points: for Sirach wisdom is so delightful that her admirers will want to have more and more of her; for John, Jesus provides a kind of spiritual food which will quench all other appetites – though in the end the two are, in their different ways, expressing a similar thought. For other examples of food imagery see Psalms 19.10 and 119.103.

3 Specific comments (24.23–34)

Having described wisdom lavishly and at considerable length, Ben Sira now makes explicit the identification which is perhaps inevitable given the source of his imagery. He says that everything which he has been speaking of is 'the book of the covenant of the Most High God'. In other words, all the time he has been speaking of Wisdom, the reality to which she points is the Torah of the people of Israel. One of the implications of this equation is the idea of the pre-existent Torah – a belief found in rabbinic circles (see the comments above on Sirach 1.4, 26–27). In this way Sirach and later Judaism do for wisdom and Torah what Christianity did for Jesus and the Logos.

Having gradually narrowed the terms of his discussion of wisdom until it is finally particularized in that essence of Judaism, the Torah, Ben Sira now takes this newly understood principle of wisdom and gives it a completely universal reference. His language is graphic: as farmers depend on the rivers for a successful crop, so do men and women depend on the law for life. And now, of course, having made the link in v. 23, Sirach can speak of the Torah which gives wisdom. The metaphor of the rivers serves a double purpose, for it also speaks of the world-wide extent of the law's influence: the four rivers of Eden (Pishon, Gihon, Tigris and Euphrates) together with the Jordan and the Nile. But not only does the Law have the widest possible geographical reference, it extends equally throughout time. The use of terms drawn from the Eden myth provides an entree into v. 28 – which contrasts the first and the last man – and to v. 29 in which a cosmic dimension is given to law/wisdom (compare also Sirach 1.2–3). The reference to the first and last man has echoes both in Paul's theology of the second Adam, and in the Kabbalistic concept of Adam Kadmon – the primeval man who is the first emanation from God, and who also represents the possibility of repair (*tikkun*). In Sirach, however, a relatively simple idea is presented: neither the first nor the last man can fathom wisdom. And so we return, after a long journey, to that central rock of the wisdom school's teaching: only God, after all is said and done, holds the key to wisdom.

Sirach 24.30–34 brings this fascinating chapter to a close with what may be the boldest step of all, in which Ben Sira describes himself and his own calling in words which compel the conclusion that *he himself* is the embodiment of this law, this wisdom, and that *his* teaching is for the whole world. He does not even (as modesty might demand) describe himself as a channel for wisdom, for these verses clearly imply that *he* is what fills the channel. It is worth quoting his words directly, so powerful are they:

> As for me, I was like a canal from a river,
>   like a water channel into a garden.
> I said, 'I will water my garden
>   and drench my flower-beds.'
> And lo, my canal became a river,
>   and my river a sea.
> I will again make instruction shine forth like the dawn,
>   and I will make it clear from far away.
> I will again pour out teaching like prophecy,
>   and leave it to all future generations.

All this indicates strongly that Ben Sira held the highest possible opinion of what he was doing, that he did indeed regard himself as standing in the same tradition as that of the prophets and sages whose teaching he so graphically interprets. As Nickelsburg[10] says:

> The place of prophecy has been taken by the scribe's study and interpretation of the ancient writings, especially the Torah. This produces a deposit of teaching which Ben Sira considers to be authoritative, to judge from his claim to prophecy (24.33) and perhaps his use of prophetic forms.

A life in teaching (51.13–30)

Sirach concludes with an autobiographical review of the writer's life's work which falls neatly into two parts: vv. 13–22, 'The teacher's quest for wisdom' and vv. 23–30, 'The teacher's offer of wisdom'. Several themes are present:

---

10 G. W. E. Nickelsburg, *Jewish Literature between the Bible and the Mishnah* (SCM Press, 1981), pp. 55–69.

Wisdom as the object of a lover's quest;
The integration of intellect and cult;
The unending nature of the search for knowledge;
The benefits of wisdom;
The scholar as professional teacher.

As we have already noted, there are some doubts about the authenticity of this as a personal account by Ben Sira himself. We shall, nevertheless, construe the poem as good evidence for a type of intellectual who, if not Ben Sira himself, is remarkably consonant with what we know of him from elsewhere in the book.

In a form of the Hebrew text found at Qumran this passage seems to be the adaptation of a love song in the form of an alphabetical poem. Little of this remains in the Greek version, though there are some hints of the metaphor of the lover in vv. 15 and 21:

From the first blossom to the ripening grape
   my heart delighted in her.

     . . .

My heart was stirred to seek her;
   therefore I have gained a prize possession.

A similar meditation in 14.20–27 recalls the persistent lover laying siege to the object of his devotion, though by v. 26 the metaphor has become rather mixed, and the presentation of Wisdom as the object of, in effect, an exercise in stalking might not go down to well in a contemporary context ('pursuing her like a hunter, and lying in wait on her paths; [peering] through her windows and [listening] at her doors' vv. 22–3). In Wisdom 8.2–18 there is a passage in which the motif of the lover is more explicit (especially vv. 2, 9, 16), and where the importance of a youthful start to the quest for wisdom is also stressed.

I loved her and sought her from my youth
   I desired to take her for my bride
and became enamoured of her beauty.
 	
        (Wisdom 8.2)
	While I was still young,
	before I went on my travels,
	   I sought wisdom
	   openly in my prayer
	     (Sirach 51.13)

An associated image – that of friendship and companionship – is also found in the Wisdom passage (vv. 17–18), and may be a better way to understand the Sirach material:

When I considered these things inwardly,
   and pondered in my heart

that in kinship with wisdom there is immortality,
   and in friendship with her, pure delight,
and in the labours of her hands unfailing wealth,
   and in the experience of her company, understanding,
and renown in sharing her words,
   I went about seeking how to get her for myself.

1 *The teacher's quest for wisdom (51.13–22)*

The first part of this poem can readily be understood as establishing Ben
Sira's credentials for setting up, in the second part, as a purveyor of that
which is of far greater value than gold or silver. His quest for wisdom has
been relentless: from youth (13a) to old age (14b) Ben Sira has pursued
her through the avenue of worship (vv. 13b, 14a) and with the intensity
of a lover (v. 15). These themes are then elaborated. The pursuit of wisdom is both an intellectual and ethical struggle (vv. 16–18), and a spiritual odyssey (vv. 19–20a); but it is one that is guaranteed success. The
commitment of mind and spirit forges a powerful and living relationship
which can never be broken (vv. 20b–21).

   The end result is a reward – and it is interesting to note that it is not the
usual reward of wealth and prosperity. He is given a tongue with which
to praise God ('The Lord gave me a tongue as a reward, and I will praise
him with it', v. 22). We surely cannot escape the associations with 24.3
where wisdom is described as a word from the mouth of God, and with
17.10 (the ability to praise as the one characteristic of man not shared
by either the animals or the heavenly bodies). Of course, alongside these
theologically significant interpretations of the gift we must note an important practical one: the tongue is the tool of Ben Sira's trade, the instrument without which he cannot effectively pursue his profession. Thus,
v. 22 not only sums up the account of Ben Sira's personal quest: it leads
us into and provides an effective link with the second part of the passage:
the teacher's calling.

   A few particular comments will suffice to round off this section. Note
in v. 13 the reference to 'my travels' (cf. 39.4 where it is a characteristic of
the scholar that 'he travels in foreign lands and learns what is good and
evil in the human lot') – a human touch: Ben Sira seems to have been very
proud of his reputation as a seasoned traveller! On a more serious note,
the same verse makes reference to the fact that he sought wisdom in his
prayers. Though there is an obvious model for this in the life of Solomon
(1 Kings 3.3–14) it is not an example found in earlier wisdom books.
Moreover, when Ben Sira stresses the connections between wisdom and
religious observance it is quite clearly a matter of conviction for him, and
no mere convention. The next verse, 14, continues this motif ('Before the
temple I asked for her, and I will search for her until the end'), and may

refer to the actual place where he received some of his education as a youngster (cf. Jesus and the scribes in the Temple, in Luke 2.41–52). Verse 15a further suggests his youthfulness when he began to study: 'From the first blossom to the ripening grape' – a highly sexually loaded metaphor which also points to the language of Israel as vine while describing his own journey from youth to maturity. Finally, v. 17 constitutes a tribute to his own teachers, and perhaps a hint in turn of the respect which he looked for from his own pupils ('I made progress in her; to him who gives wisdom I will give glory').

2 The teacher's offer of wisdom (51.23–30)

Here some of the ideas from vv. 13–22 are picked up, with of course a reversal of roles: Ben Sira now represents that wisdom which is available to his students. He addresses potential undergraduates who are at present in the same state of ignorance that he once was (v. 24, cf. 19b). And just as his ignorance was a curable disease, so they can remedy their ailment if they accept his offer and enrol in his academy (v. 23, cf. 17). But a certain struggle is required (v. 26a, cf. 16–20a), though it is interesting that in contrast with the elaborate account of his travails in the first part, Sirach rather minimizes them here – perhaps so as not to discourage the faint- hearted from engaging in the noble pursuit of wisdom (v. 27 'See with your own eyes that I have laboured but little and found for myself much serenity)! Certainly in the end there will be a reward for those who seek wisdom, just as Ben Sira was rewarded (vv. 29–30, cf. 22). Now, of course, there is not the same theological significance to the reward, for it is expressed in general terms appropriate to all. Not everyone, after all, could follow Sirach and become a teacher. It is given in the form of a benediction, which includes the key idea of praising God (v. 29), and an assurance that in due course, in God's good time, suitable rewards will be forthcoming (v. 30b).

There may be a 'Prospectus' concealed in this passage: (1) 'the house of instruction' (Hebrew *beth hammidrash*) in v. 23 contains the first recorded use of this Hebrew term; (2) free education – a traditional rabbinic principle (v. 25 'Acquire wisdom for yourself without money'); but (3) there is an indication that Ben Sira looked for some financial reward for his labours (v. 28, footnote 'Get instruction with a large sum of silver, and you will gain by it much gold'); (4) a possible reading of v. 29a in Hebrew is 'my *yeshiba*' – the term used for the school for the study of Talmud.

To conclude: was Ben Sira a kind of proto-rabbi, who had his own income, and who therefore taught and studied as a religious duty? If he did not charge the students in his school was he, like Paul and the rabbis and the Pharisees, a man with a 'day job' which gave him the wherewithal to live? On his own account this seems unlikely; the best explanation is probably that there was no formal fee, but students (or their parents) were expected to give a decent honorarium. Whatever the truth, it remains clear that we meet in the pages of Sirach a man whose work repays detailed study.

The prologue

The foreword to Sirach, written by the author's grandson, has already been 'mined' for information in connection with themes we discussed in Chapter 9: the dating and provenance of Sirach; the authorship of Sirach; the shape of the canon in the second century BC; and Sirach as a writer of Scripture. There is no need to repeat here what has already been covered. There is, however, one other theme of importance which emerges from the grandson's words: techniques and limitations of translation. His modesty in dealing with this matter is striking, and it is worth setting out the whole of the second paragraph in which his thoughts are given expression:

> You are invited therefore to read it with goodwill and attention, and to be indulgent in cases where, despite our diligent labour in translating, we may seem to have rendered some phrases imperfectly. For what was originally expressed in Hebrew does not have exactly the same sense when translated into another language. Not only this book, but even the Law itself, the Prophecies, and the rest of the books differ not a little when read in the original.

The points made here may at first sight appear to be obvious, but they are more controversial when understood in the context of biblical translation. For example, he asks for our patience and understanding where his work falls short of perfection – a reality which those who invest too much literal significance in contemporary English translations might do well to bear in mind. Interestingly, the translators of the Authorized Version of King James make similar points, neither pretending to be doing the job for the first time, nor claiming that theirs will be the last word.[11]

He notes the real difficulty in translating from Hebrew to Greek because

---

11 Their exact words are: 'Truly (good Christian Reader) we never thought from the beginning that we should need to make a new translation, nor yet to make of a bad one a good one . . ., but to make a good one better, or out of many good ones one principal good one' in Robert Carroll and Stephen Prickett (eds), *The Bible with Apocrypha* (World's Classics; Oxford, Oxford University Press, 1997) p. lxv. Note the clear implication that still better translations would follow in due course.

of the differences between the languages – and when we recall that we are reading this comment in English, perhaps we should allow for another level of possible confusion! The truth of this is well known to those who have worked with the Septuagint and seen how often the Greek struggles to make clear sense of the Hebrew, or misunderstands it. In particular he acknowledges that existing translations of the Law, the Prophets and the Writings are similarly, and should not be thought to provide a perfect interpretation of the originals. When we recall the legend of the creation of the Septuagint – in which 72 elders from Jerusalem are shut away in 72 cells on the island of Pharos to work independently, all producing (but for a few minor variants) identical translations of Torah – we realize just how radical are Ben Sira's grandson's few remarks on the subject of translation. There may even be an element of polemic in his brief reflection on the subject, for the document which is the source of the legend just cited – the Letter of Aristeas – was actually produced in the time of Ben Sira's grandson and not a century earlier, as its author pretends.[12]

Some points to think about

Does the exclusion of Sirach from the canon seem more or less understandable in the light of the discussion of the various excerpts provided in this chapter?

Review the relevance of Sirach to the New Testament writers by exploring cross references and allusions between the two with the help of a suitable edition of the Bible (the NRSV cross-reference edition is useful for this kind of exercise).

By examining the references in the Hymn to the Ancestors (44–49) can you put together a picture of Ben Sira's knowledge of and bias in respect of the Scriptures which he clearly had available for study?

Using the exegeses in this chapter as a model, write your own analysis of the pursuit of wisdom in Sirach 14.20—15.10.

Further reading

Blenkinsopp, J. (1983) *Wisdom and Law in the Old Testament*, Oxford, Oxford University Press, esp. chapters 1–3, 6

Calduch-Benages, N. and J. Vermeylen (eds) (1999) *Treasures of wisdom: studies in Ben Sira and the Book of Wisdom*, Leuven University Press

---

12 Ostemsibly dated to the reign of Ptolemy II (286–242), it is now widely recognized to be a forgery, datable to some time in the second century BC.

Coggins, R. J. (1998) *Sirach*, Sheffield, Sheffield Academic Press

Coley, Jeremy (2001) *Ben Sira's Teaching on Friendship*, Brown Judaic Studies

Crenshaw, J. L. (1975) 'The Problem of Theodicy in Sirach' in *JBL* 94, p. 47

DiLella, A. A. (1966) 'Conservative and Progressive Theology' in *CBQ* 18, p. 141

Gammie, John G. (ed.) (1978) *Israelite Wisdom: theological and literary essays in honor of Samuel Terrien*, Scholar's Press

Harrington, Daniel J. (1999) *Jesus Ben Sira of Jerusalem: a biblical guide to living wisely*, Liturgical Press

Liesen Jan (2000) *Full of Praise: an exegetical study of Sir 39, 12–35*, Leiden, Brill

Mack, Burton L. (1985) *Wisdom and the Hebrew Epic: Ben Sira's hymn in praise of the fathers*, University of Chicago Press

MacKenzie, R. A. F. (1983) *Sirach*, Gill & Macmillan

Martin, J. (1986) 'Ben Sira – a Child of His Time' in James D. Martin and Philip R. Davies (eds), *A Word in Season*, Sheffield, Sheffield Academic Press, pp. 141–61

Martin, J. (1986) 'Ben Sira's Hymn to the Fathers. A Messianic Perspective' in *OTS* XXIV, pp. 107–23

McKeating, H. (1973–4) 'Jesus ben Sira's Attitude to Women' in *ET* 85, pp. 85–7

Sanders, J. T. (1984) *Ben Sira and Demotic Wisdom*, Scholars Press

Schnabel, E. J. (1985) *Law and Wisdom from Ben Sira to Paul*, Tübingen, Mohr, pp. 8–92

Sheppard, Gerald T. (1980) *Wisdom as a Hermeneutical Construct: a study in the sapientializing of the Old Testament*, BZAW 151; Berlin, Walter de Gruyter.

Skehan, P. and A. A. DiLella (1987) *The Wisdom of Ben Sira*, New York, Doubleday

Snaith, J. G. (1974) *Ecclesiasticus*, Cambridge, Cambridge University Press

Snaith, J. G. (1963–4) 'The Importance of Ecclesiasticus' in *ET* 15, pp. 66–9

Snaith, J. G. (1975) 'Ben Sira's Supposed Love of Liturgy' in *VT* 25, p. 167

PART 3

Folk-tales and Fairy tales

11

Folk-tales, Myths and Legends: Biblical wisdom in its anthropological setting

A theoretical overview

The modern discussion of folk-tales within the pages of the Bible really began with Hermann Gunkel (1921 [1987]). Gunkel's original approach to Genesis had been to class much of it as *saga*; but later – influenced by Wilhelm Wundt – he came to hold the position that all other forms of popular oral narrative are derived from the folk-tale as the fundamental type. All such studies were, of course, influenced by the groundbreaking work of the brothers Grimm,[1] and were hugely controversial when they first appeared. Despite the fact that the historicity of the biblical materials had been under considerable attack since early in the nineteenth century, it seemed somehow more shocking (and perhaps still does) to describe the stories in Genesis and elsewhere as 'fairy tales'.[2] It is perhaps of some significance that the first English translation of Gunkel's study appeared in 1987.

Theoretical studies of folk-tales considerably predate the use of such theory in biblical scholarship (a pattern repeated throughout the twentieth century as studies of the Bible catch up belatedly with successive fashions in literary theory – new criticism, structuralism, deconstruction and the like). While this may constitute a comment on the isolation of biblical studies (or its practitioners!), it has not been an entirely bad thing, since it enabled the appropriation of new theories to be done some time after their more egregious faults had been identified (if not cured). This has not prevented a certain naivety in biblical applications; but it would at least be fair to say that there has never been any lack of a contrary voice to rein

---

1 One of the most accessible modern editions is the selection by David Luke (1982) in the Penguin Classics series.

2 The commonest translation of the German word *Märchen*. Of course not all folk-tales feature fairies; and fairies are in any case rarely the prettified creatures of Edwardian childhood stories.

in that unconstrained speculation which attends the discovery of what seems to be a new hermeneutical key.

The importance of the study of folk-tale is twofold. On the one hand it allows us to investigate shared traditions between biblical and other human story-telling (a famous example is the discovery of a story from ancient Egypt which bears many similarities with the tale of Joseph's unjust condemnation for his supposed assault on Potiphar's wife[3]). And on the other it serves to remind us that humanity's own mythic powers of explanation are universal and important: this is, if you like, a humanistic lesson. Those who prefer to emphasize the primacy of revelation may need to introduce a divinity who is happy to use the human imagination as a means of communication: this does not appear to be either unreasonable or especially irreligious.

With these preliminary remarks, we turn now to some of the theoretical approaches to folklore studies with a view to the possibility of their application to biblical examples. The names of Axel Olrik and Claude Lévi-Strauss are those we shall deal with;[4] those who have sought to apply them include Susan Niditch, John Van Seters and Edmund Leach. Neither list is exclusive.

Olrik's laws

Axel Olrik (1864–1917) is the earliest of the theoreticians whose work has influenced biblical studies. Right at the beginning it is necessary to sound a note of caution: the very use of the word 'law' is bound to encourage the wrong sort of certainty. Nothing which proceeds from the varied imaginations of human women and men can be constrained by law in its usual sense, any more than a language can be bounded by the grammars we derived from it at a certain time and place. That said, and perhaps with a tacit replacement of 'laws' with something like 'principles', we can still find use for Olrik's ideas.

The thirteen principles have in many cases a certain inherent plausibility – they reflect what we know from our own reading (or perhaps, what we should have known had we stopped to think about it!). But whether they reflect any deeper structure is another matter entirely. When such frameworks are proposed they can have a validity *post factum*; that is, they *describe* more or less efficiently what is to be expected when we read

---

3 'The Two Brothers' (written down at the end of the nineteenth dynasty, c. 1225 BC) See Hallo, *The Context of Scripture* (Vol. 1) (Brill, 2003), pp. 85–9.

4 The other major figure whose work should be addressed is Vladimir Propp. His approach was peculiarly formal and complex, and is arguably too difficult to be included in the kind of introductory overview here offered. Pamela Milne has made a study of his work in relation to Old Testament material.

a folk-tale. Some uses of such theories as Olrik's, however, go further and confer a certain a priori quality to them; that is, the principles are deemed to be *prescriptive* – anything we call a folk-tale must display a significant subset of these principles. The case for the latter position (and it applies to all the theories we shall present) is attractive. In so far as we have a shared humanity, with brains and minds which work in a similar fashion, surely the stories and concepts we produce must in some way be rooted in the materiality of that which allows us to think. This module will not take a position on these metaphysical matters. In so far as the theories allow us some insight into the material we study, we may deem them to be useful. Whether they open a window into the soul, as it were, we must leave to the philosophers.

OL1 Law[5] *of opening and law of closing*

Folk-tales neither begin nor end *in medias res*. There is always an introduction to set the scene and a conclusion to bring us back to rest (hence the familiar 'Once upon a time' opening, and 'they all lived happily ever after' closure). A survey of any serious collection of folk-tales will demonstrate the broad truth of this principle. A simple, but significant, consequence of this law is that each folk-tale is essentially self-contained (whatever its broader cultural context in the society in which it is told).

OL2 Law of repetition

In folk-tales it is common for events and episodes to be repeated.

OL3 Law of three

These two are very similar, for – as Olrik himself observes – repetition is often threefold. But it is nevertheless important to signal the special significance of threefold repetitions. The repeating of actions scarcely needs to be exemplified – hardly anyone ever does anything only once in the world of the folk-tale (think of the parallel in the structure of the joke, where suspense is built up by the repetition of the same or a similar sequence of actions or phrases; and as for three, need we look further than 'There was a Scotsman, an Englishman and an Irishman'?). The mystical meaning of 'three' is a familiar religious theme; that it recurs in folk-tales will not be surprising. One example will suffice, from the story of Rumplestiltskin (Luke, 1982, pp. 53–5). When the mysterious little man spins the straw into gold, we read 'whirr, whirr, whirr, round it went

---

5 Though we have entered reservations about the use of the word 'law', the term is retained out of respect for Olrik's own preference.

three times and the bobbin was full'. This phrase is repeated; and the scene in which the little man turns up at night is repeated on *three* successive nights, at the end of which the miller's daughter marries the king. When the little man turns up a year later to claim his reward, he gives her *three* days to guess his name. Her guesses list two sets of three names[6] (Caspar, Melchior, Balthazar; and Twizzlebotham, Hirpletonthwaite, Screwthorpe) and the third recital provides two wrong names (Bert and Sid) before the correct name is given in third place.

OL4 Law of two to a scene

Given that most folk-tales are fairly simple, and do not feature a large number of characters, this may not at first sight seem to be a law of much importance. However, it does have the effect of focusing both the action and the hearer's attention. The general absence of scenes in which three or more people are in conversation gives these stories a directness which is absent from literary conventions. Conversely, when novels provide scenes in which two people feature alone, these scenes can often be the most effective. Think, for example, of Elizabeth Bennet's confrontation with Lady Catherine de Burgh in *Pride and Prejudice* or the interrogation of the suspect by the hero-detective (or spy-hunter) in modern detective or spy fiction.

OL5 Law of contrast

The phenomenon of contrast is peculiarly important in the folk-tale. The same scene can be repeated with quite different outcomes (the brothers who scorn the old woman contrasted with the brother who helps her), and characters are polar opposites (the good fairy who neutralizes the curse imposed by the wicked fairy).

OL6 Law of twins

While literal twins are a not uncommon feature of folk-tales, this law of course refers to a broader phenomenon in which two characters – who might be siblings, but who could well be unrelated – perform similar roles. Perhaps the classic non-sibling twinning is that of the king with the marriageable daughter who has some deterrent problem (such as being unable to smile!). The hero who accepts the challenge to win the daughter at the same time effectively sets out to win the king(dom). Clearly this twinning effect applies also to rivals – and so in a sense even polarized

---

6 These are the names provided by Luke in his translation. Presumably similarly improbable names are to be found in the German original.

characters can also be thought of as twinned. Cinderella and her sisters as rivals to marry the prince, for example, constitute such a formal twinning.

OL7 Law of initial and final position

The character who is last in sequence wins in the end. Thus, for example, it is the youngest brother or the last and least likely suitor or the true daughter despised by her step-sisters who has our sympathy and wins the prince or princess. This can apply also to episodes within the story: it is the very last guest at the princess's birthday celebration who neutralizes the curse (Sleeping Beauty). Shakespeare uses this convention in *King Lear* where Cordelia, the youngest sister, is the noble and tragic figure.

OL8 Law of the single strand

In literary fiction there is often a wide difference between the story *as it is told* and the order of events *as they would have happened in real time*. Techniques like flashback (and forward) and the re-telling of the same events by different characters serve to heighten the dramatic effect of the narrative and to introduce mystery and uncertainty. In the language of Russian formalism two technical terms describe these two aspects of narration: *sujet* (the presentational process) and *fabula* (the order of events in 'real time'). In folk-tales the *sujet* follows the *fabula*: the story is presented as a single, linear strand, with events presented as they happen, by an omniscient narrator. This explains the somewhat childlike or naive character often associated with folk-tales.

OL9 Law of patterning

Some of Olrik's laws are to a certain extent vague or repetitive. Thus laws (2)–(6) seem to be specific cases of (9), while (10) does not seem to be particularly characteristic of the folk-tale. All forms of writing make use of stock scenes which can be populated by the characters of the particular narrative.

OL10 Use of tableaux scenes

There is a strong visual dimension to many set-piece scenes.

OL11 The logic of the sage

There is a 'grammar' of the folk-tale which enables certain events, how-ever implausible, to take place. Thus we are not surprised (as we would be in naturalistic fiction[7]) to encounter talking birds, magic rings and the like; indeed, we *expect* such devices to figure – this is part of what defines the genre.

OL12 Unity of plot

Everything in the narrative contributes to the eventual outcome: there are no sub-plots or side-stories.

OL13 Concentration on a leading character

In folk-tale narrative, everything signifies – whether on the level of plot or character. No one is redundant, no one is included only for colour or incidental effect, and nothing happens which does not concern the movement of the story towards its resolution. In the story of the Sleeping Beauty, for example, the king's attempts to hide all needles and sharp objects so that his daughter will not prick her finger is the direct cause of that precise event: for when she finds an old spinning wheel she does not know that it contains a sharp point, and pricks her finger. In other stories, the old woman whom the hero meets at the start of his quest is not incidental: his willingness to help her provides him with the key which will eventually enable him to fulfill his quest. Unity of plot is reinforced in turn by the tendency to focus on a single leading character – we rarely if ever follow the adventures of minor characters.

Lévi-Strauss and structural anthropology

Lévi-Strauss, born in 1908, produced the major work which constitutes his theories of structural anthropology in a series of publications between 1955 and 1971. Peter Munz (*When the Golden Bough Breaks*, pp. 5–6) summarized his work in the form of four basic principles:

1 'Myths think themselves in men [*sic*].'

---

7 There is a genre in modern fiction – 'magical realism' – often associated with Latin American writing, in which curious and unbelievable phenomena appear as if in a naturalistic narrative. The most famous example is Gabriel Garcia Marquez's *One Hundred Years of Solitude*; Louis de Bernières is also influenced by this style of writing – in particular in his novel *The War of Don Emmanuel's Nether Parts*.

2 They must be interpreted serially – broken into constituent episodes which form a series. Each episode makes the same point.

3 Episodes alternately overrate and underrate something.

4 This alternation effects a resolution of conflict, tension or incompatibility between two situations or phenomena.

Lévi-Strauss uses the notion of 'mythemes' – equivalent to the phonemes of structural linguistics – to show how these are subject to structures which control the way they can be combined. More important, for Lévi-Strauss, is the theory that different versions of a myth (and we might well ask what he meant by 'a myth' – a reified essence or a hypothetical original form?), despite seeming totally different, may be systemically related.

Behind this formal system lies a belief that human beings attempt, in the course of history, to make sense of their world by imposing (mythic) structures on it. These are, of course, always incomplete and unsatisfactory – not least because the world itself is in constant flux. In closed, isolated societies little modification is required ('cold' societies); others, open to external contact and internal variation, are termed 'hot': in them the mythic transformations can themselves affect the cultural environment and prompt further change. Most societies are somewhere between these two extremes.

The difficulty with either summarizing or applying this methodology is that it has a kind of all-or-nothing character which makes it very difficult to evaluate. For example, before deciding on the meaning or function of a particular society's myths we need to carry out the kind of close study of *all* of them which Lévi-Strauss advocates, paying particular attention to polar oppositions and to the way that a variety of categories of language have a bearing on kinship relationships. This is clearly a daunting task, made worse by, first of all, the problems of defining the boundaries of any given society, and second, the possibility (explicitly endorsed by Lévi-Strauss) that myths can be appealed to universally in dialogue with each other. As Edmund Leach has pointed out (*Lévi-Strauss*, p. 61), this brings us perilously close to Frazer's *Golden Bough* and its forlorn attempt to find a single explanatory system for all the world's myths. It is interesting that George Eliot presented her character Casaubon in *Middlemarch* as a failed mythologist of the Frazer kind some 20 years before the publication of *The Golden Bough*. It is intriguing to speculate on how much she knew of Frazer's enterprise in the making, and whether her satirical portrait has proleptic effect.

There are two ways in which the work of Lévi-Strauss has been and can be applied to biblical materials. First, his interest in kinship systems and the way these symbolize humankind's relationship to the natural world has echoes in the Bible, where arguably such themes pervade both the families of the patriarchs and the relationship of God to Israel. Indeed, the doctrine of the Trinity sets up an intra-divine father–son link which is explicitly designed to resolve the twin dilemmas of creation's relation to the Creator and humankind's simultaneous need for and yet failure to achieve wholeness. One of the most interesting writers in this area is the anthropologist Seth Kunin whose books, *The Logic of Incest: a structuralist analysis of Hebrew mythology* (1995) and *We Think What We Eat* (2004) explore the implications of kinship in the Old Testament for a structuralist interpretation and understanding of what the biblical myths and legends have to offer.

The second approach, for those who are attracted by quasi-algebraic analyses, involves the use of such equivalences as $I : II : : III : IV$ (where I and II are mythically presented oppositions of one kind, and III and IV similarly but of another kind). This has proved to be attractive to a certain type of mind, but may prove to be mystifyingly reductionist to others. Kunin makes extensive use of such formulae; one of the most useful introductions to this form of structuralism remains Robert Polzin's *Biblical Structuralism* (1977).

Excursus on structure

Many readers instinctively shy away from the kind of methodologies outlined in this section. There is a natural resistance to what seems to represent a loss of meaning, of drama, of emotion, of literary subtlety in those forms of analysis which emphasize structure. Surely a folk-tale is more than a series of stock motifs? Surely literary art cannot be confined to a set of technical laws? Surely the stories of the Bible are misrepresented when we reduce them to mythemes in a process of interpretation, or – even worse – when we encapsulate them in sterile formulae.

I want to urge the reader to resist such judgements and to allow that, as *part* of the heremeneutical task of making sense of myth, we accept the proper role of structural analysis in its broad sense. I mean that we should be open to the argument that just as all language is structured (through grammar, phonetics, etc.) so the things we make out of language are also formally shaped. Moreover, just as the grammatical underpinning of our native tongues is for the most part hidden, so is our instinctive patterning of stories, narratives, poems and dialogue. It makes perfect sense, therefore, to study these aspects of 'literary product' both as unconscious structuring devices but also – where the use of language is knowingly artful – as evidence of quite deliberate shaping of material. More than a century ago the form-critical movement began this approach to biblical texts, observing that certain formulae regularly accompany certain kinds of writing. 'Once upon a time' opens a fairy tale; 'Dear John' a letter, and (in the modern world) 'Hi' a text message or email. Given that we regularly use our awareness of literary conventions to decode and interpret what we hear and read, is it not equally probable that other conventions of a less familiar type might be at work in forms of human oral and written tradition? It is on the basis of such assumptions as these that structuralism is founded.

I will endeavour to provide as many illustrations as possible; but space is limited here, and you are urged to go to the supporting bibiliography to explore individual topics in greater depth – and at greater length.

Defining terms

In this short section we shall offer working definitions for the various literary genres which are assumed to be of relevance to the wisdom literature of the Old Testament. Not all are necessarily represented within its pages in any straightforward way, but all are or have been discussed within the terms of the debate about how best to classify the literature of the Old Testament. The broader context for all such terminology is that of folklore studies, which attempts in various ways to investigate the whole range of popular story-telling, music, art and performance in an essentially oral context. As regards biblical studies, the following brief account is helpful:

> . . . two generally accepted aspects of folklore have been particularly significant [for biblical studies]. On the one hand, folklore is the investigation of popular customs and customary behaviour, and their meaning for the society in which they are at home. On the other hand, it studies the popular, verbal expressions of such a society, by classifying them into various categories, such as myths, legends, folk-tales, riddles and proverbs, with a special interest in the origin and development of the material in oral tradition.[8]

1 Folk-tale (Märchen)[9]

A useful starting point is the suggestion that folk-tales are '. . . straightforwardly fictional traditional tales recounted for the purpose of enter-

---

8 J. R. Porter in R. Coggins and J. L. Houlden (eds.), *A Dictionary of Biblical Interpretation* (SCM Press, 1990), p. 238.

9 The German term Märchen, which Gunkel used in his study of the folk-tale, is sometimes used in the literature. Since this module seeks to distinguish *fairy tales* as a sub-genre of *folk-tales*, it is best to reserve the German term as a collective for *all* such stories. (Note that Märchen is grammatically singular.)

tainment or illustrating a moral point . . .'.[10] The purest forms of folk-tales lack all historical, geographical or biographical specificity: setting, dates and names are resolutely anonymous; indeed, personal names (even invented) are rarely provided, and when they are they often have a meaning drawn from the story itself ('Cinderella' = 'Ashiepattle') or from the needs of the plot (the name Rumpelstiltskin). They frequently involve magic,[11] either in the form of a token of some kind (Ashiepattle's twigs which grow into a tree which attracts the gift-giving doves) or the person of a witch or wise woman. Animals and plants feature as important plot elements, with the former regularly given voice.

The question of morality deserves a particular comment. Many folk-tales are quite unashamedly bloodthirsty – the fate of both good and bad characters not infrequently involves the loss of body parts and a variety of imaginative and unpleasant deaths; and revenge is not stinted. The mean step-sisters in Ashiepattle have their eyes pecked out by the same doves that previously helped the heroine, and the story concludes – with chilling morality – 'And thus, for their malice and deceitfulness, they were punished with blindness for the rest of their days.'[12] In biblical materials a similar ruthlessness is sometimes found: Samuel's 'hewing' of Agag in pieces (1 Sam. 15.33), Elisha's cursing of the boys who called him names, which leads to 42 of them being mauled by two she-bears (2 Kings 2.23–25), or the divine slaughter of Ananias and Sapphira for not handing over the correct money to the church (Acts 5.1–11). More generally, there is a certain air of amorality about such stories: the principal purpose is that the hero/heroine should succeed, and the means are not subject to moral scrutiny.

It is universally assumed that folk-tales originated as *performed* stories in an oral context. Furthermore, they are international in character (Luke in his introduction offers a number of examples of stories and motifs which are found in a wide diversity of cultures). Unfortunately, for the most part orality has been lost in its European contexts. We encounter these tales almost exclusively in written form; and there is considerable doubt as to how close such written versions are to any presumed oral form. We have already referred to the fact that the materials collected by the Grimms had often had a prior literary life before reaching them.

---

10 William Hansen, *Ariadne's Thread* (Ithaca: Cornell University Press, 2002) p. 25, fn 2.

11 In biblical instances, as we shall see, the place of magic is often taken by the involvement of the deity as a character in the story. This is to be distinguished from 'God' as the subject of reflection and the object of worship. The striking difference in tone between the prologue to Job (chapters 1 and 2) and the sequence of dialogues which form the bulk of the book, is an instructive example.

12 Luke, 1982, p. 231. All specific references to folk-tales are to versions found in Luke.

It is further the case that collectors of 'folk-tales' often modify them in the process of recording them, partly as an inevitable consequence of the transcription process, and partly out of a need to make them 'tidier' and more acceptable to a *reading* public. We shall return to the question of oral versus written later in this chapter.

2 Fairy-tale

The fairy tale is not, of course, a story about fairies – at least, not in the sense that we see them represented in European children's literature. A better way to understand them is to say that they deal with 'the realm of the Fairy', or Faërie – the deliberate use of a somewhat pretentious spelling serves to alert the reader to the fact that something more adult is intended. Tolkien, who employed this concept to good effect in *The Lord of the Rings*, was clear about the distinction; his 'fairies' are capable of both war and love, and are very far from the kind of emasculated and prettified beings perched on toadstools that we associate with the Flower Fairies of Cicely Mary Barker and the illustrations to Enid Blyton's children's books. (An example of the former is reproduced below.)

It may seem unlikely that there are fairy tales to be found in the Bible. Motifs relevant to the genre can certainly be found – the strange being encountered by Jacob at the Jabbok (Gen. 32.22–32) might hint at a lost fairy story, and the tale of Tobias and the Angel in the Apocrypha – and magic items are noted from time to time, such as Moses' staff or Elijah's cloak, which could perhaps be an invisibility charm, thus explaining his sudden appearances and disappearances (1 Kings 18.7,12; 2 Kings 2.9–12). But on the whole this kind of tale is absent.

Fairy tales share many features with folk-tales (they are, in fact, a sub-genre of that wider category). We shall note here a few specific characteristics which help to define the genre, in particular as it was studied by Vladimir Propp:

the presence of magic;
a transformation, either a physical transformation (the beast turns into a handsome prince) or a character transformation (the ugly duckling turns out to have been a swan all along);
a task involving both risk and reward, and which is carried out by –
the hero, who benefits from the encounter with someone or something from the Faërie realm.

Like folk-tales, fairy tales are presumed to have had oral origins; but most people are likely to encounter them today in the form either of a literary work (perhaps based on an oral tradition) or – as children – in an oral recital from an adult's memory or read from a book. Another interesting mode of communication of fairy tales is to be found in the tradition of the pantomime, which in turn includes a range of its own customary motifs and formulae which have entered the oral realm.

3 Legend

The word is derived from a Latin expression, *legenda*, which means 'that which is read aloud'. Originally it was used to denote readings that were given in enclosed orders during meal times, when the residents were expected to focus their minds on higher things, rather than indulge in idle chatter or think too much about the quality of the food!

Such readings could have been from the Bible but were more often drawn from the lives of the saints, whose devotion and marvellous deeds and experiences were presented as a model of behaviour and belief to inspire those who heard them. In time the term 'legend' changed from being a technical word describing a mode of performance to a term describing *that which was performed*. And since the content of the lives of the saints – certainly in the medieval period – was replete with miraculous events and (to a modern ear) unbelievable wonders, the term has come in modern times to mean 'something unbelievable because of its incredible content' even though it seems to refer to real people, places and times.

The last point is important: legends are *not* to be considered a sub-

genre of folk-tales. They belong to the historical and biographical, whatever we may think of their believability, and the question of historicity
is not irrelevant to them, as it is for folk-tales. If a succinct definition is
sought, it would be along the following lines:

> A *legend* is a story of a broadly edifying nature which has as a primary
> focus the involvement of a divine being in the lives of its characters.
> Such stories are located in time and place, and the people they deal
> with are (at least from the perspective of the legend) historical. They
> typically show how the 'hero' triumphs in circumstances of extreme
> danger, assisted by supernatural forces.

Because of their superficially historical appearance, when legends appear
in biblical sources many readers have difficulty in evaluating them. The
perceived status of the Bible, combined with a clear context in place and
time, foregrounds the question of historicity. As an example of the crucial nature of the problems they raise, consider the status of the stories of
Jesus' birth and infancy in Matthew 1.18—2.23 and Luke 1.5—2.52. In
literary terms they are surely legends; how then are they to be regarded in
respect of the life of Jesus?[13]

The term *legend* is sometimes extended to stories which are concerned
with giving an account of the origins of certain cultic institutions. The
complex of stories in 1 Samuel 4—6 together with 2 Samuel 6 is an example of this type. In such legends (which may be compared with birth
legends of the hero) the 'hero' is the institution or cult object, which has
to survive various threats before becoming established as a part of the
culture's formal religious insitutions.

4 Myth

The use of the term *myth* in the same breath as 'Bible' provokes more instinctive opposition than almost any other single term. It is not so many
years ago that a volume of essays, *The Myth of God Incarnate*[14] caused a
storm by its frank recognition of a mythic dimension to the key Christian
doctrine of the nature of Jesus. Perhaps there was an intention to rattle
cages – but it is certainly undeniable that the *form* in which many theologically intense biblical narratives are presented is closer to myth than to
history on the one hand or systematic theology on the other.

The word, of course, suffers from the same problem of popular usage
that affects 'legend': it is widely held to mean 'something untrue which

---

13 There are also Old Testament legends surrounding the birth of heroes –
Moses in Ex. 1—2 and Samuel in 1 Sam. 1–3.

14 Edited by John Hick (SCM Press, 1977).

is used – as though it were true – to mislead deliberately' (as for example if the *Guardian* were to condemn the 'myth', put about by the tabloid press, that Britain is being swamped by illegal immigrants or false asylum seekers). It is unnecessary to point out that this bears no resemblance to its literary use; but the uninformed reader can be forgiven for being confused.

The commonest definition of *myth* in literary terms is 'a story about the gods' – a definition which reflects the origins of the term in the study of classical Greek folklore. As a consequence, it is often held that there cannot, by definition, be *myths* in the Old Testament; but many scholars have argued that the essential characteristics of the myth as a literary form persist even where some kind of monotheism is in place; for purposes of literary analysis, it is sufficient that there be at least one god present. The following is a suggested list of defining characteristics of myth as a literary form:

> a concern with origins;
> remoteness in time;
> the location is often otherworldly, or located at the very beginning of this world;
> universal questions are addressed;
> a god or god(s) is/are involved in the action.

Some of these are similar to features of folk-tales, but with key differences. While folk-tales do not specify time or place, they nevertheless indicate *human* time and place, whereas myths take us in many instances either to the very beginning of things or even to the timeless realm of the gods. This is related to the general truth that the matters addressed by myths (which have a seriousness not found in folk-tales) are of universal concern and belong to the origins of life. Finally, when the gods appear in a myth they are there on their own account, not as a means of assistance to the hero. Indeed, the hero is conspicuous by his or her absence from the realm of myth, which does not typically deal with the kind of quest and rescue which is the hallmark of the fairy tale.[15]

---

15 Two examples only will be given here: Prometheus' theft of fire on behalf of humankind, and Pandora and the origins of both plague and hope. A ready supply of myths can be found amongst the traditions of the Greeks – Robert Graves' two-volume *Greek Myths* (Penguin) is a convenient source; though reservations have been expressed about the reliability of Graves' work. An alternative, perhaps more scholarly resource is Timothy Gantz's *Early Greek Myth* (2 vols; Johns Hopkins University Press, 1993).

A structuralist approach to the definition of myth

Seth Kunin, in *We Think What We Eat*, pp. 20–22, addresses the problem of defining myth from the standpoint not of the contents of narratives, but of their structures. In direct contrast to the common distinction between 'myth' and 'history', he points out that these are only two terms for a similar urge among human collectives to seek ways to 'model self and the world', and so are 'functionally identical'.

> The difference is one of content: myth uses events that may or may not be fictional (it can use historical events), history uses events understood to be factual. This difference in content suggests that the two forms are based on cultural choices: our society chooses to privilege fact, and therefore we construct our significant narratives out of factual/objective (self-defined) data. Thus science as a model of causality uses 'objective' data to create its understanding of reality and history uses analogous information. In other societies that do not have the same emphasis on 'objective' reality other material may be privileged. On this basis myth, history and science can only be distinguished on the basis of an ethnographic privileging of our model of understanding. From a structuralist perspective they are identical.

Note that this does not claim that nothing is objective, or that science is in the same category as fiction. What it argues is, first, that 'myth' means something like 'the way we choose to structure and explain reality', second, that we are as generally unconscious of this process as any society which uses non-objective building blocks to construct its reality, and third, that we can therefore investigate both types of society on the basis of the same *structural* principles. The 'histories' we write and recount are subject to the same rules of transmission and transformation as are the 'myths' of others.

5 Saga

In the early days of folk-tale study and the Bible it was commonly claimed that the patriarchal narratives could best be understood as *sagas*. A group of Scandinavian scholars promoted this thesis, based on parallels between Icelandic sagas and biblical materials. While there is little support now for this approach, it is instructive to set out – in the form of a comparison of *saga* with *history* – some of the reasons why it appealed:

Saga	*compared with*	*History*
oral		written
family		political
tradition		witnesses

Saga	compared with	History
imagination		records
marvels		commonplaces
poetic		prosaic

The most obvious difficulties in making this comparison are that the Genesis materials are not strictly speaking poetic in form, and do not really form a single extended tale. They represent rather a collection of somewhat disparate material linked together by political and theological positions – a form of writing not at all characteristic of the sagas of northern Europe.

6 Novella

One final genre merits mention in our survey of wisdom literature: that of the short story, or *novella*. As with legend, stories in the Bible come with a burden of historical association which makes the genre attribution suspect for many. The key aspects of novellas are (1) that they conform to the demands of a clear plot which structures the whole piece – unlike history, which is much more messy, and fails to deliver the kind of closure which is common to short stories[16] – and (2) that they display considerable literary artifice and rhetorical skill.

Within the Old Testament and the Apocrypha there are a number of books (or parts of books) which might be categorized as novellas:[17] Genesis 37, 39ff (the story of Joseph), Ruth, Esther, Daniel 1–6, Tobit, Judith, Susanna, Bel and the Dragon, and the Additions to Esther. One interesting feature of this group is that (with the exception of Ruth and Joseph) they are all located in the exilic period.[18] They represent, arguably, the development of a genre which is first placed in the service of Jewish religious tradition at this time. They are characterized by the use they make of legends, but with a more sophisticated literary presentation. Indeed, they must be assumed to have arisen from a literate community. Whatever oral tales may lie behind them, they are essentially texts, not oral traditions, and so it is appropriate to read them in that light. That is, the

---

16 The description given here might not apply to the literary short story form as it developed from the early twentieth century; but when we consider ancient materials, the demands of a coherent plot and narrative are dominant features.

17 Some of these might equally qualify as legends or folk-tales – to some extent the judgement hangs on the degree to which the written form has been worked over as a literary piece displaying authorial skills.

18 It is likely that Ruth was composed then too – it is indicative that the book is not included with the former prophets section of the Hebrew Bible, but with the writings.

vocabulary they use and the structures and patterns they contain are a key element of their form rather than an accident of repeated telling.

Thus when we find that certain key expressions in the story of Joseph are found only there and in the book of Daniel, a natural question arises about their interconnection. When we realize further that the themes of the two narratives are remarkably similar – a devout Jewish boy is taken into exile where (after imprisonment) he succeeds in becoming the king's adviser through his prowess in interpreting dreams and visions – the links become more suggestive. And when we discover that at least one expert Egyptologist (Donald Redford[19]) finds the Egyptian details in the story of Joseph to be more appropriate to the sixth century than the thirteenth, the serious possibility emerges that the *written* story of Joseph, like that of Daniel, is the product of the exilic period.

Folk-tales in the Old Testament

I propose to take Olrik's laws as a basis for the identification of two recognizable folk-tale types which seem to lie behind a number of the stories in Genesis. These are, first, the *folk-tale proper*, and, second, *the trickster tale*. In general these seem to conform to Olrik's laws 1, 4, 5, 6, 8, 11, 12 and 13; of these I want to focus on four themes:

A   Linear narrative (8)
B   Economy of plot and character (12)
C   Intervention from outside (11)
C* Successful deception and disguise, or 'trick' (11)
D   Twinning (Abram = Pharaoh; Sarai = Hagar) (6)

and to add a fifth, which Olrik does not explicitly deal with, but which we have already noted as a characteristic of folk-tales:

E   Amorality

In the case of the *folk-tale proper*, the narrative line moves from a perceived problem through its resolution, which in turn creates another problem, and so on until an outside intervention (miraculous, magic or divine) puts an end to what seemed potentially to be an open-ended sequence, at the same time rewarding the lead character. *Trickster tales* are somewhat different,[20] in that the narrative line begins with a desired object which is destined for one character but will be diverted, by means of a trick, to

---

19 *A Study of the Biblical Story of Joseph* (Supplements to Vetus Testamentum, 20, Leiden, Brill, 1970).

20 See, for example, Susan Niditch, *Underdogs and tricksters: a prelude to biblical folklore* (Harper & Row, 1987).

that character's twin. The trickster is not necessarily the character who benefits from the trick, and there is usually an element of compensation for the character who is deceived.

The narrative context of most of the stories in the Old Testament precludes any strict identification of them as pure folk-tales, for strictly speaking the genre does not provide historical names, identifiable places and dating information. Thus, at the outset, we need to admit that what we are dealing with is at best a folk-tale *form* which has been appropriated to a quasi-historical discourse. That said, it is nonetheless plausible to categorize numbers of the Genesis traditions as being sufficiently similar to folk-tales to merit consideration under that heading. Abram's trip to Egypt during the famine, recorded first in chapter 12, with variants in chapters 20 and 26 (involving Isaac) is a good example, as are the various stories of barren wives, rivalry between brothers, and contests to win wives which feature largely in Genesis. I have chosen four of these to illustrate the two types I have identified: Abram in Egypt, the barrenness of Sarai, Jacob's theft of Isaac's blessing, and the contest to win Rachel as his wife. In what follows I have set out the structural framework of these stories; a closer examination will reveal evidence of other features of Olrik's Laws to be found in the stories.

Examples of the folk-tale proper and the trickster tale

The analysis of the stories is set out in the tables which follow. Clearly there is a certain simplification of the narratives in order to represent the underlying structure, which is by no means intended to be a full interpretation of these tales. However, I do claim that the distinctive differences between the two types of story are well represented by this structural account. In particular, the role of the trickster tale in biblical traditions is important, since the trickster as a religious and mythic figure is widespread in folk-tales. A number of relevant discussions are to be found in the bibliography; the concept has also found its way into fictional stories – most strikingly, perhaps, in the American tales of Brer Rabbit, and more recently in Richard Adams's *Watership Down*. The figure of the trickster may have some remote connections with the figure of the jester in European court traditions: the permitted voice of dissent which gives the appearance of opposition to authority without substantively challenging it. The trickster too is an apparently anarchic character who is paradoxically necessary to the advancement of the primary narrative and the assuring of the correct outcome for the mythic story.

1 Genesis 12.10–20

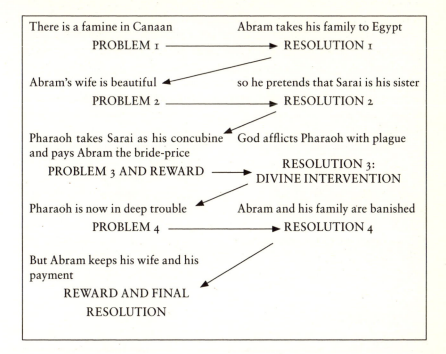

2 Genesis 16

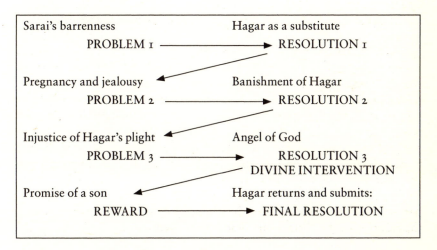

In both of these there is a continuous sequence from the opening problem to the final resolution.

3 Genesis 27.1–40

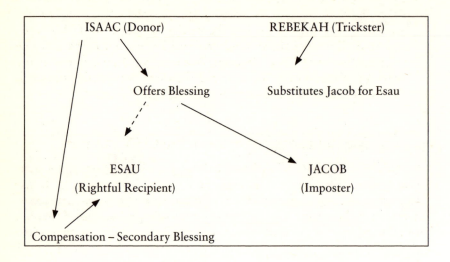

4 Genesis 29

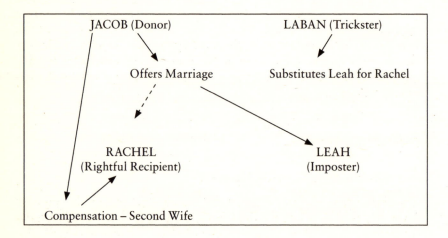

Notes

1 The dotted arrow signifies the intended narrative line, which is diverted by the trickster's act of deception.

2 The two tricksters – Laban and Rebekah – are brother and sister.

3 In each case the beneficiary of the successful trick becomes the principal ancestor in the line of succession (Jacob is the father of Judah, the ancestor of David, and Leah is the mother of Judah). In fact it is the case that all four of the stories here outlined are concerned with the safeguarding of the line of descent, the ancestry of Israel; indeed, many years ago Klaus Koch characterized the three 'wife-sister' stories in Genesis as stories of the ancestress of Israel endangered.[21]

Structuralism and myths in the Old Testament

Structuralist approaches have adopted two broad strategies: (a) the analysis of underlying formal structures, and (b) the teasing out of the transformation of myths through their involvement in repeated structures. The first of these has something in common with the canons of Russian formalism, in that the work of the structuralist, as such, in done when the structure itself is disclosed. What implications for meaning it might have belong to another level of interpretation. The second, by contrast, *uses* the structure to elucidate ways in which a culture or society's myths evolve in a continuing attempt to explain/understand questions which experience poses. This is the process – generally understood as *structural anthropology* – developed by Claude Lévi-Strauss. In making this distinction, it should perhaps be made clear that *both* approaches refrain from developing any detailed exegesis of the 'surface script'. Structure is always at a deeper level than the incidentals which constitute the particular set of words, phrases, idioms and metaphors in which a specific narrative is presented. I shall illustrate each approach briefly in the following sections.

Formal structuralism

1 Structures in Genesis 1.1—2.3

The structure of Genesis 1 is rather complex; for, despite the imposed seven-day framework of the final form, there are four separate underlying patterns, none of which coincides with that of the original week. The completion of creation at the end of the sixth day is followed by the announcement of the Sabbath, a day quite unlike the others, whose significance is presented in the form of a pun (the Hebrew *shabbath* is similar to the verb 'to rest'). There is, in fact, little *formal* relationship between this

---

21 Klaus Koch, *The Growth of the Biblical Tradition* (London: A. & C. Black, 1969), p. 111.

conclusion and the structure of chapter 1 – it is as though this has been added on artificially, the result being a transformation of the material from a patterned account of the process of creation into a liturgical piece celebrating (or perhaps inaugurating) the Sabbath. The overt structures of the first creation narrative may be summarized as follows:

An eightfold repetition of the enabling statement, 'And God said';
A sevenfold repetition of the concluding phrase, 'And it was so';
Seven examples of the evaluation, 'God saw that it was [very] good';
Six examples of the formula, 'And there was evening, and there was morning, the nth day'.

These represent a structural problem, for it would seem that logically all four should be found together to provide the framework for each episode in the narrative. But this is not so, as is clear from the table below, in which these various formulae are set out according to their positions in Genesis 1.1—2.3. There are in fact only four instances where all of them come together; what this means is not immediately clear, but it might sound a warning that, coherent as they seem in a group, they did not ever form a basic defining structure.

In addition to those already identified, two other structures should be noted: first, a series of subdivisions within the various created orders:

Day and night (vv. 4–5)
   Waters above and below the firmament (vv. 6–7)
      Earth and sea (vv. 9–10)
         Plants and trees (vv. 11–12)
         Lights in heaven, greater and lesser lights (vv. 14–18)
      Fish and birds (vv. 20–21)
   Cattle, creeping things, wild animals (vv. 24–25)
Male and female (vv. 27)

And second, an overarching division ('the heavens and the earth) which is not part of the creation, but is presupposed. Together with an opening phrase ('In the beginning . . .') and a closing one ('. . . were finished') these form an *inclusio* which embraces the whole narrative. Incidentally, by *excluding* the description of the seventh day, this inclusio strengthens the likelihood that (as we remarked above) this represents an afterthought, not part of the basic creation account.

The following table sets out these various structures in a formulaic way intended to show the essential 'bones' of the matter.

'God said' ×8		3a	6	9a	11a	14–15a	20	24a	26	
'And it was so' ×7		3b	7b	9b	11b	15b	*	24b	30b	
End of day ×6		5b	8b		13	19	23		31b	
'It was good' ×7		4a	*	10b	12b	18b	21b	25b	31a	
Divisions of creation ×8		4–5	6–7	9–10	11–12	14–18	20–21	24–25	27	
Inclusio	1.1									2.1

Several observations may be made on the basis of this reduction of Genesis 1 to its structural bones, in addition to the general remark that there is no single, simple pattern to be discerned.

(a) Surprisingly, the pattern of the seven-day week which is universally taken to be at the heart of the first creation story turns out, structurally, to be far from original. It is clear that the two sevenfold structures in the chapter are problematic. Both appear to be defective rather than defining – a point emphasized by the fact that commentators have regularly noted that the relevant phrases are 'missing' from the two cells marked *. The most natural explanation of this – assuming that the 'missing' phrases were never there and were not accidentally omitted – is that they represent a later stage of development. I would go so far as to suggest that the pattern of seven is the last element to be added, since it depends upon the Sabbath aetiology which is appended in 2.2–3.

(b) The *inclusio* between 1.1 and 2.1 is a very strong one. The two verses, which are almost identical in length, display a chiastic parallelism which would not be out of place in two linked verses in Hebrew poetry. I have set them out in such a way as to preserve the original Hebrew word order:

In the beginning (a)   created (b)   God (c)   the-heavens-and-the-earth (d)
They were finished (a+b)   the-heavens-and-the-earth (d)   and all-their-hosts (c)

By way of explanation, the phrase 'They were finished' is in Hebrew a single verb form which expresses both action and completion, and thus combines the ideas in the first two phrases in 1.1; and the pairing of 'God' and 'All their hosts' is based on the title 'Lord of Hosts' frequently allocated to the deity in Hebrew, which uses the same word as in 2.1.

Unless these parallels are accidental – which does not seem likely – we have here a strong defining structure with which to interpret the chapter,[22] and which further supports the proposal that an earlier structure had no reference to 'seven' and concluded with 2.1.

(c)   There are two pronounced eightfold structures which link God's command to create with the detail of what was created. These appear to be fundamental, since they ignore both of the diurnal structures, whether of six or seven days. In this connection it is just possible that the sevenfold 'and it was so' and 'it was good' were originally eight in number, and were reduced at the final stage to fit the sacred week. The table below shows the structure which remains when the sevens are stripped out, and I shall comment now on that reduced form.

'God said' × 8		3a	6	9a	11a	14–15a	20	24a	26	
End of day × 6		5b	8b		13	19	23		31b	
Divisions of creation × 8		4–5	6–7	9–10	11–12	14–18	20–21	24–25	27	
Inclusio	1.1									2.1
		1st Day	2nd Day		3rd Day	4th Day	5th Day		6th Day	

(d) The six-day structure, while at odds with the preceding, has at least been carefully worked into it by attributing two aspects of creation to each of the third and sixth days. This is perhaps the most surprising pattern, since it seems to suggest a point in time when a six-day week might have been natural (at least to the writers). This possibility has been effectively lost within the later Sabbath structure and the universal acceptance of the seven-day week as a natural unit in human society.[23]

---

22 Incidentally, the next few verses exhibit further organizing structures which go beyond the example developed here, but which make it very clear that conscious organizing of this material was carried out more than once. Thus, the association of creation with Sabbath is found elsewhere in Torah – most explicitly in the Exodus version of the Ten Commandments (Exodus 20.8–11) but not in the parallel passage in Deuteronomy 5.12–15. The opening section of 2.4 ('These are the generations of the heavens and the earth') is a structural introduction repeatedly found in Genesis (e.g. 5.1; 6.9; 10.1; 11.27). And the opening of the second creation story in 2.4b ('In the day that the Lord God made the earth and the heavens') is expressly modelled on 1.1.

23 The origins of the week are notoriously difficult to ascertain. Many scholars attribute the seven-day structure to Hebrew circles, perhaps building upon

(e) A closer study of the details of each of the eight stages of creation reveals a pairing which further strengthens what now seems clearly to be the 'original' shape of the narrative of creation in Genesis 1:

Day 1	Night and day	Day 4	Sun, moon and stars
Day 2	Separation of waters	Day 5	Birds above, fish below
Day 3a	Dry land fashioned	Day 6a	Three classes of animal created
Day 3b	Vegetation appears	Day 6b	Humans created; given plants to eat

Our examination of this familiar passage has, I hope, shown that there is more to structuralism as an interpretative technique than the mere listing of symbolic markers. I have deliberately expanded upon this example because I believe that it shows just how much can be deduced from what at first sight might appear to be a somewhat formalistic or even arid process.

Lévi-Strauss and kinship myths

There can be no doubting the centrality of kinship as a motivating factor both for individuals within the Old Testament narratives and for the narrative itself. Rivalry between brothers, with the regular triumph of the younger over the older; the paradox of the barren mother; rivalry between wives; hints of incest; and rivalry between fathers and sons – all of these are to be found, most of them more than once. It follows that if structural anthropology as a discipline has something to offer the study of myths and folk-tales, surely it has a role in the study of the oral roots of the Old Testament within a typical near eastern society of the late second to early first millennium BC.

What I propose to do here is to summarize some of the work carried out by Seth Kunin in this field by way of an example of what can be done. Those who would like to look more deeply into the subject should read more of Kunin, look at Edmund Leach's study of Genesis and (for the very enthusiasic) take up Lévi-Strauss himself. A thoughtful critique of structural anthropology is to be found in Peter Munz's *When the Golden Bough Breaks*.

Babylonian precedents. There is no evidence (outside the text of Genesis 1) for a six-day pattern, though such a scheme was briefly deployed in Soviet Russia, and the French Revolutionary Government notoriously introduced a short-lived ten-day week. According to an article to be found at www.biblestudy.org/godsrest/sevencyc.html the ancient Egyptians used a ten-day week, the Mayans weeks of thirteen and twenty days, and the Lithuanians (prior to accepting Christianity) a nine-day week. Finally, lovers of the idiosyncratic might test the site www.dbeat.com/28/ which advocates a six-day week of twenty-eight hours in every day. While this fits nicely into the seven-day framework, and adds eight hours to the weekend, it seems designed to wreak havoc with the circadian rhythm!

Among the many kinship strands which run through the stories of Genesis those involving fathers and sons on the one hand, and rival brothers on the other, are particularly strongly represented. Tensions between the various parties involved are a commonplace, and the resolution of these tensions often involves acts (or intended acts) of violence. Kunin looks at a number of these; for purposes of this brief survey I will refer to two: the notorious account of Abraham's plan to sacrifice Isaac in Genesis 22, and the story of Joseph and his brothers in 37. The analysis which follows is expressly *not* ethical or moral. Questions of this kind, which are undoubtedly legitimate, are to be addressed in other forums; but it may be useful to point out that structural anthropology of its nature sets to one side all questions of historicity and factuality, and as a consequence asks us to look at factors other than those raised by the assumption of verisimilitude.

1 Genesis 22

We begin by listing the characters in the story, and we immediately see that there is evidence of doubling (a common feature both of biblical stories and of the folk-tale genre as a whole). Thus God is paired with Abraham and Isaac with the ram which is ultimately sacrificed in his place. The young men who accompany Abraham and Isaac are in an ambivalent position, since for the most part they seem to play a quite passive role.

The way that the characters are related is significant: Abraham (God) – A – is both *father* and *sacrificer*; Isaac – B – is both *son* and *victim* (as also is the ram). The young men – C – cannot be defined in a relationship at this point; however, in keeping with Lévi-Strauss's thesis that mythic structures are transformed in frequent re-telling, it will become apparent from a later form of this myth what their role is.

To clarify the key features of his analysis, Kunin uses a diagram:

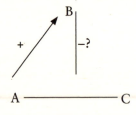

Figure 1

The relationship between Abraham and Isaac, despite the intended sacrifice, is in mythic terms positive because it is divinely ordained. It is also presented in the narrative as a physically upward journey (to the mountain top). The relationship between Isaac and the young men cannot be said at this stage to be either positive or negative, though their passive non-involvement might hint at a negative rather than a positive connection. The mythic theme of the story is that of symbolic death and rebirth, a process which confirms the dominant role of Isaac in the succession of the patriarchs – and which incidentally and implicitly invalidates the claims which might be made by another aspiring descendants.

2 *Genesis 37*

The story of Joseph and his brothers – or that part of it which is found in Genesis 37 – is in essence another story involving symbolic death and rebirth. As we shall see it forms a precise inversion of the structure we identified in Genesis 22. The characters here are Jacob – A – the *father*, Joseph – B – the *son*, and Reuben *et al.* – C – the *brothers*. We notice at once that if this is one in a sequence of transformed myths, it offers an interpretation of the mysterious 'young men' in the previous story: might the young men be Isaac's brothers – Ishmael and Eliezer of Damascus (Gen. 15.2)? The brothers of Joseph also bring out another important point: that the rivals constituted by C represent *tribes* or *nations* (see, for example, Esau who stands for Edom in relation to Jacob/Israel); of course Ishmael represents the Arabs and Eliezer the Aramaeans.

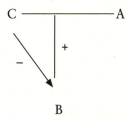

Figure 2

In this diagram the roles of the previous diagram (Figure 1 opposite) have been reversed (the combined situation is presented in the diagram on p. 262). Thus it is the brothers who bring Joseph down (literally) to death – and since this intended sacrifice is not sanctioned by God it forms a purely negative relational bond. But the other bond is also explicit – that between Joseph and his father is strongly positive.

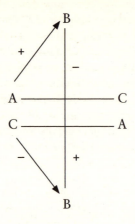

Figure 3

When we combine Figures 1 and 2 we see clearly both the inversions and the way that the structure of the second story clarifies the missing element of the first. In both the myth is of a real transformation through a symbolic death. The son (B) is in each case confirmed as the real heir; the rival sons (C) are displaced, but also made to accept their roles as representatives of other nations or tribes. There is also, incidentally a negative relationship between C and A explicitly in Genesis 37 and so implied in Genesis 22.

Conclusion

Undoubtedly much of the material in the foregoing sections is complex, and presents a daunting prospect to the novice reader. Some may be tempted to give up, reckoning that it ought not to be that difficult to make sense of the Bible, or at least, of the use the Bible makes of the story form. Some may disparage these theoretical systems as being needlessly complicated, an artificial attempt to lend scholarly respectability to what is in reality plain sailing. Others again may fear that irrelevant disciplines from the wider field of the humanities have been brought to bear where they do not belong.

However natural they may appear, such responses are misplaced. If we are willing to devote immense intellectual resources to understanding the nature of matter and the way that its fundamental particles relate, surely language and its consequences, which arguably define us as human and without which we would have none of the benefits (as well as the curses) of civilization, merit equal attention. And if the structures of matter turn out to be infinitely more complex and more paradoxical than is apparent

to our naive examination, what is so surprising if we discover an analogous – and equally surprising – complexity to language in *all* its forms.
The stunning intricacy of that marvellous organ, the brain, is commonly
accepted. Small wonder then that language – whatever its precise relationship to the workings of the brain – should be innately intricate too.
The least we can do is to recognize that fact and to allow it to feature in
our efforts to understand what we (and our ancestors) are about when
we tell a story.

An oral tradition?

There is an obvious and insurmountable difficulty in pursuing the oral
origins – however probable it is that they existed – of societies like those
of Ancient Israel and Judah: we have no witnesses left to give account of
the phenomenon we want to describe. Worse, such evidence as we have
is either written – in the form of ostraca, parchment or papyrus scrolls,[24]
clay tablets or monumental inscriptions – or mute, in the form of non-
literary archaeological remains. Some of these – such as the supposed
writing benches and inkwells found at Qumran – point to literary activity; others – such as standardized symbolic or pictorial representations of
deities or of episodes from familiar myths and stories[25] – might suggest
a largely oral society. An analogous phenomenon might be the extensive
use of illustrations on the walls and windows of churches in medieval
Europe, which presumably served to inform largely illiterate congrega-
tions and to remind them of the history and teachings of Christianity.
That example will serve to make another point which is of the utmost
importance: there can be no doubt that writing and limited forms of
literacy emerged early on in the history of Egypt and the city states of
Mesopotamia, so that the reality we might try to reconstruct is not that
of 'purely oral' societies which became 'largely literate', but rather societies in which widespread illiteracy to a greater or lesser extent accompanied the specialized use of writing in elite circles. The populations of
Egypt, Sumer, Assyria, Babylon and the rest almost certainly knew what
writing was, but had no use for it in most circumstances, and certainly
no opportunity to master what was probably a difficult and esoteric skill.
That this bears on our understanding of the development, communication and preservation of the traditions of Israel and Judah hardly needs

---

24 The book or *codex* as it was termed, did not appear until the Christian era;
indeed the invention of the book may well be attributed to the Church. Until then
writing was confined either to single (or double-sided) surfaces of a rigid kind
(clay tablets, inscribed stone or the Roman re-usable wax surfaces contained in
a wooden box), or to scrolls.

25 See Othmar Keel, *The Symbolism of the Biblical World* (SPCK, 1978).

to be spelled out; just *how* the interplay of oral and written worked out in fact is a far more difficult question.

I shall not attempt to give any detailed answer here. What I propose to do in this final section is to introduce some of the theories which have been developed both to explain how (largely) oral societies operate and to identify evidence to support these theories. Those who are interested in exploring the oral/literary interface should read Susan Niditch's comprehensive and helpful study of just these questions in her *Oral World and Written Word: orality and literacy in Ancient Israel* (1996). Alan Dundes's *Holy Writ as Oral Lit* (1999) is also interesting, written as it is from the perspective of a scholar whose interest in the Old Testament is secondary to his professional expertise in folk literature.

Problems of orality in biblical studies

Theories as to how orality functions range from the claim at one extreme (ironically most often found among those with a strong desire to protect the verbal accuracy of *written* Scriptures) that pre-literate societies were capable of prodigious feats of precise memorizing of large quantities of material, to a considerable scepticism that oral tradition can preserve more than the most dramatic (and therefore least probable) elements of past history.

Modern forms of oral communication

Most people are familiar with the game of *Chinese Whispers* in which a message is whispered in the ear of the first of a chain of people, and the last in the chain is asked to repeat what he or she heard, with predictably confused results.

Monty Python's *Life of Brian* contains a good example, which may well conceal a truth beneath its satire. Our heroes are parked at the edge of the crowd listening to the Sermon on the Mount. To their consternation they hear the phrases 'Blessed are the Greeks' and 'Blessed are the cheese-makers' and are understandably puzzled as to why Jesus should single these categories of people out for special blessing.

Another familiar form of contemporary orality is the *urban myth* by means of which stories, held to be factual, circulate authoritatively but without supporting evidence. Perhaps the most famous of these is the claim that someone, somewhere once fried a poodle in a microwave oven when trying to dry its fur.

The discussion of orality in the context of the Bible is somewhat fraught, since it raises questions of authority, accuracy and authenticity in a particularly acute form, and adds to the already mounting evidence[26] against the belief that there existed at some time an *ur-text* for individual books or for the Old Testament and the New Testament as a whole from which our available versions descend. Part of the fundamentalist argument was that, even if the Bible as we now have it contains apparent errors, these are absent from the text 'as originally given' – an argument which now seems to be decidedly founded in sand. Here is the problem, set out in simplistic form:

> The oldest events reported in the Old Testament are probably to be dated in the mid to late second millennium BC (i.e. 1500–1000 BC).
>
> No one imagines that the pre-monarchic Israelites (whoever they were) had any structure capable of written traditions.
>
> The earliest that even the most conservative scholar dates the production of written 'histories' or 'sagas' is the reign of Solomon (?950 BC).
>
> Many (see Niditch, Jamieson-Drake) now regard this early dating as highly unlikely, and argue that the archaeological evidence points to no earlier than the seventh century BC for the emergence of effective scribal literacy based on centralized government.
>
> Note that this does *not* imply or depend upon any claim that the majority of the population was literate.
>
> At the radical end of the scholarly spectrum are those who see the bulk of the scriptures as the result of an intensive period of productivity around or after 400 BC (thus, for example, Philip Davies).
>
> It is clear, therefore, that what eventually became the written Scriptures must be rooted in a substantial oral tradition, stretching for at least five hundred years, and possibly as much as a millennium.

Given this context, it is not surprising that the evaluation of orality in respect of ancient Israel (not to mention Christian circles in the first century AD) can be delicate. Do those who argue for a hyper-reliable oral tradition based on superb feats of memory do so on the basis of anthropological parallels, rose-tinted memories of the schooling of a former era, or the wish that it be so? A complicating factor is the post-literate phenomenon

---

26 Specifically, the fact that the oldest documents we have for biblical books come from Qumran, and they certainly display *more* rather than *less* variation from whatever we like to think of as the norm. In other words, it seems that the further back in time we go the less reliable is the scriptural tradition.

of individuals who memorize the Qur'an or the Hindu vedas. While such feats are impressive, they are not true parallels for two reasons: the existence of the written control document protects against the normal variation that takes place in oral systems; and the motivation is to enhance a religious position already based on a precious and perfect written text (especially in the case of the Qur'an).

Many years ago M. I. Finley pointed out that genealogies in Greek myth and legend rise very rapidly to a divine or heroic founding figure and that this fits the reality that, with the possible exception of powerful ruling dynasties, genealogical information is confined to the few ancestors who are roughly speaking within living memory.[27] Others have challenged this somewhat reductive claim, but it might well explain the fact that all of the genealogies in both the Old Testament and the New Testament are unreliable and inconsistent. No doubt familiar events, personalities and tales were handed down without benefit of texts, but the evidence of European traditions since the fifth century suggests that considerable variation, licence and imagination is to be expected in the telling and re-telling of stories that later became absorbed in the first attempts at serious history. At least one recent writer, for example, assesses the entire Arthur legend as being wholly devoid of historic factuality[28] – a disappointing result for Glastonbury, Tintagel and the English and Welsh tourist boards, no doubt. In the remaining paragraphs I shall briefly outline the kind of mechanisms that might serve to explain how the sort of documents which now constitute the Old Testament might have, as least in part, been transmitted orally.

The epic model

This approach is best suited to those longer narrative sections which might bear some comparison with the family sagas associated with

---

27 'Myth, Memory and History' in *History and Theory*, 4 (1964–65) pp. 296f.: 'Wherever tradition can be studied among living people, the evidence is not only that it does not exist apart from a connection with a practice or belief, but also that other kinds of memory, irrelevant memories, so to speak, are short-lived, going back to the third generation, to the grandfather's generation, and, with the rarest of exceptions, no further. This is true even of genealogies, unless they are recorded in writing; it may be taken as a rule that orally transmitted genealogies, unless some very powerful interest intervenes (such as charismatic kingship), are usually fictitious beyond the fourth generation, and often even beyond the third. There is a nice Greek illustration: the Homeric heroes recite their genealogies frequently and in detail, and without exception a few steps take them from human ancestors to gods or goddesses.'

28 N. J. Higham, *King Arthur: Mythmaking and History* (Routledge, 2002).

Icelandic traditions. Specifically, it is claimed that large stretches of material were preserved more or less accurately for a long period of time until they were committed to writing – perhaps in the crisis circumstances of the exile, when the destruction of Jerusalem and the loss of the homeland threatened the loss of the religious and historical traditions of the people. This thesis goes back to the Swedish scholar H. S. Nyberg (1935), was elaborated by H. Birkeland (1938), who drew comparisons with such feats of memory in the Muslim world as the word-perfect memorization of the Qur'an, and became a characteristic feature of the Scandinavian school after the Second World War, represented by Engnell, Kapelrud and Nielsen. The assumptions behind this form of the oral tradition hypothesis are, first, that in a pre- or marginally-literate society human memory is much more efficient than in our own highly literate world; second, that the preservation of long passages of material is normal; and third, that the process is essentially conservative – that is, that changes to the tradition are consciously avoided. The first of these assumptions may well be justified; but the other two are very dubious. Epic poems *may* have been memorized by professional bards (though this is hardly relevant to the material in the Pentateuch), but the Islamic comparison is misplaced – as we have already noted – because it exemplifies the memorization of a written text, not the remembering of an oral tradition. And the conservative nature of the process is a quite unfounded assumption; indeed, the evidence suggests rather that variability and transformation are the normal marks of orally communicated material.

The difficulty with this model is the identification of a mechanism within which it might work. Romantic conceits involving campfires and pre-monarchic clans gathered round to listen to the stories of their ancestors are charming but improbable – and would certainly not be likely to lead to the kind of centrally agreed main narrative which the saga model requires. The work of Parry and Lord, in particular Lord's *Singer of Tales*, is more apposite, in that it offers a context, a mechanism, and a body of material which derives from just such a set of circumstances – verified, moreover, through extensive field studies. Without going into extensive detail, the so-called Parry-Lord Hypothesis can be summarized as follows:

The Homeric epics display extensive regularity of rhythm, metre, and use of standard epithets. They also display lack of enjambment (that is, there are very few cases of semantic run-on from one line into the start of the next).

Tradition has it that Homer was a blind poet, a performer rather than a writer.

Taking these together, Parry proposed that there was, in effect, a bardic language which consisted of several elements:

- Well-known plot lines, sub-plots, themes and motifs;
- Familiar characters;
- A ready-made metrical system accompanied by a simple musical instrument;
- A stock of phrases of standard lengths suitable for use as 'fillers' during the on-going process of performance/composition;
- A guild of skilled singers who could use these features just as ordinary speakers use a language, without conscious effort of thought, in order to reproduce well-known epics.

The testing of the hypothesis took the form of many years of study of oral traditions in the Slav territories where there existed, at the beginning of the twentieth century, a living oral performance genre. Lord (Parry having died in an accident) succeeded in showing that the hypothesis devised to explain the Homeric epics matched remarkably closely what he observed on the ground. Moreover, what became clear was (a) that different singers performed the same epic in different ways, (b) that the same singer introduced changes in repeated performances separated by long intervals, and (c) that these epics were often anachronistic, in that they introduced material familiar to the hearers, whether or not it was relevant to the supposed historical context.

Attempts to apply this theory to biblical materials have not met with much success. Robert Culley analysed the Psalms in his 1967 study, *Oral Formulaic Language in the Biblical Psalms*, but did not find much to support the possibility that they had been created in the way suggested by Parry and Lord. The Genesis material is very far from the kind of regular metrical writing that characterizes the Homeric epics, though it is undoubtedly shot through with characteristic repeated phrases. It must be concluded, unfortunately, that there is little evidence of anything like an epic tradition in Israel.

The sanctuary model

Another trend has been to see the development of texts as partly oral. Traditions which circulated in spoken form for many generations were at length recorded (often in a variety of forms – compare Gen. 12.10–20 and 20.1–18, for example, and Alan Dundes's *Holy Writ as Oral Lit* in which a plethora of examples will be found). This approach is broadly known as *tradition history*, and was evoked at length by Martin Noth in his analyses of the Pentateuchal texts. His particular preference was to attach tales to sites of the burial of notable figures; a more frequently proposed locus for such stories is that of the sanctuary. It has been suggested that different cycles of stories were preserved at different religious centres in ancient Israel, such as Shechem, Bethel, Dan, Gilgal and so on. Then, as the different clans and tribes began to coalesce into a confederacy and finally a political state, the stories were shared, becoming eventually the common property of the whole people. Eventually they were recorded for use in religious, cultural and political circles. An obvious problem for this hypothesis is that – as we have seen – the process of writing down is not likely to have taken place until long after such sanctuaries were merged into the centralized, Jerusalem-based cult of the seventh century and later. It is hard to see how cycles of the kind envisaged might have persisted through this time gap.

The professional poet/composer

As an alternative to the Parry-Lord hypothesis, Ruth Finegan and others have studied a wide range of oral societies (or oral traditions within semi-literate societies) and have shown that there is no single 'one-fits-all' the-ory available. Some traditional materials are indeed memorized in some detail. Where there is sufficient cause, such as the reliable performance of detailed religious rituals, trained professionals can have command of quite detailed information. This might have relevance to the exist-ence in Judaism of a strong tradition of oral preservation of the extensive halakhic material which eventually came to make up the Mishnah. It is not impossible to conceive of a body of Pharisees, and later, rabbis, who devoted their minds to the safeguarding of such traditions. However, even within rabbinic texts there is significant variation and considerable disagreement, which suggests something more like the folk-tale process than a precise feat of memory.

Some performers compose their work in written form, then memorize it and proceed to perform it orally. It is difficult to assess the implications of this for subsequent transmission. Obviously, if the written form sur-vives, we are not talking so much of oral provenance as of oral perform-ance and written preservation. If, however, the original text is lost (or destroyed by its author) there could be a subsequent oral descent based (presumably) on repeated performances heard and handed down. Some of the skilled poems in a book like Amos could conceivably testify to a process of that kind. The oracles against the nations in the first two chap-ters, for example, or the 'Do two walk together?' piece in 3.2–8, might have been spoken more than once, and impressed earlier listeners just as they impress modern readers.

The folklore model

The essence of folklore, according to Dundes, is that it displays 'multiple existence and variation' (*Holy Writ as Oral Lit*, p. 2). The reason for this is perfectly simple: people do not in fact remember things precisely. Most orally communicated matter is approximate, and varies both according to the speaker and according to the time of speaking. Given that most Israelites and Judeans were non-literate for most of the period during which the Bible was shaped, it is perfectly natural that what went into the Bible took various forms, and was often recorded at different points. Dundes is clear that this is as true of the New Testament Gospels as it is of the stories of Genesis, and his little book is largely a succession of examples in support of his case.

The advantage of this model is that it removes the need for professional performers or for rather contrived centres of shared traditions, and leaves the process much more open to the vicissitudes of common human experience. Thus, when these stories, beliefs, myths and legends came to be recorded, the scribes or authors tapped into a popular *and* skilled body of information to put together their books.

Some points to think about

While this chapter provides definitions of various terms appropriate to their use in literary theory, many of them have more popular uses. Look up the following terms in a dictionary and try to assess the gap between the two fields, and what problems that might create: folk-tale, fairy tale, legend, myth, saga, novella.

Is the claim that the stories of Elijah, Elisha and Daniel are good examples of legends justified? Evaluate it by looking at one of them closely.

Assess the proposition that myth is an appropriate way to describe much of the material in Genesis 1—11.

Bearing in mind what was said in Chapter 2 about literacy in ancient Israel, and the comments in this chapter on orality, do these combine to force a rather late date for the emergence of the Bible, or can some combination of tradition and formal records be used to argue for an earlier provenance?

Further reading

Coats, G. W. (1985) *Saga, Legend, Tale, Novella, Fable*, Sheffield, JSOT Press

Culley, R. C. (1967) *Oral Formulaic Language in the Biblical Psalms*, Toronto.

Culley, R. (ed.) (1976) *Oral Tradition and OT Studies (Semeia Vol 5)*, Missoula, Montana, SBL

Dundes, Alan, (1999) *Holy Writ as Oral Lit: the Bible as folklore*, Lanham, MD; Oxford, Rowman & Littlefield

Finnegan, R. and M. Orbell (eds) (1996) *South Pacific Oral Traditions*, Indiana UP, 1996.

Foley, J. M. (1995), *The Singer of Tales in Performance*, Indiana University Press

Graham, William A. (1988) *Beyond the Written Word*, Cambridge, Cambridge University Press

Grimm, Jacob and Wilhelm, *Selected Tales* (1982) translated with introduction and notes by David Luke, Harmondsworth, Penguin Classics

Gunkel, H. (1987 [1921]) *The Folktale in the Old Testament*, Sheffield, Almond Press

Harrison, A. (1989) *The Irish Trickster*, Sheffield, Sheffield Academic Press

Kirkpatrick, P. G. (1987) *The Old Testament and Folklore Study*, Sheffield, JSOT Press

Kunin, Seth D. (1995) *The Logic of Incest: a structuralist analysis of Hebrew mythology*, Sheffield, Sheffield Academic Press

Kunin, Seth D. (2004) *We Think What We Eat: structural analysis of Israelite food rules and other mythological domains*, Edinburgh, T. & T. Clark

Leach, Edmund R. (1969) *Genesis As Myth and other essays*, London, Cape

Leach, Edmund R. (1974) *Lévi-Strauss*, Fontana Modern Masters, Collins

Lord, A. (1988 [1960]) *The Singer of Tales*, Harvard University Press

Luke, David, *see*: Grimm, Jacob and Wilhelm

Milne, P. J. (1988) *Vladimir Propp and the Study of Structure in Hebrew Biblical Narrative*, Sheffield, Sheffield Academic Press

Munz, Peter (1973) *When the Golden Bough Breaks: structuralism or typology?*, London, Routledge & Kegan Paul

Niditch, S. (1987) *Underdogs and Tricksters: a prelude to biblical folklore*, San Francisco, London, Harper & Row

Niditch, S. (1993) *Folklore and the Hebrew Bible*, Minneapolis, Fortress Press, 1993.

Niditch, S. (1997), *Oral World and Written Word*, London, SPCK

Olrik, Axel (1992) *Principles for Oral Narrative Research*, Indiana University Press

Propp, V. (1968 [1928]) *Morphology of the Folktale*, L. A. Wagner (ed.), second revised edn, University of Texas Press

Index of Names and Subjects

Driver, S. R. 6
Dundes, Alan 264, 268, 270–1
Duquoc, C. 145
dust ('aphar) 77, 143, 163, 165–8,
    172, 201–2, 208

Eaton, J. H. 145
Ecclesiastes: see Qoheleth
Ecclesiasticus: see Sirach
Eden 23, 203–4, 215, 222, 225
Edinburgh, University of 10
editing: Proverbs 69–73, 98,
    Job 132–5
Edom 42, 261
Egypt 3–4, 10–11, 13, 15, 22,
    27–8, 30–1, 35–6, 42, 47–51,
    53–5, 57, 60–1, 77, 84, 97, 99,
    101–2, 180–4, 186–7, 197, 201,
    206, 236, 251–3, 259, 263
El 99, 102
Elephantine 61, 102
Eliezer of Damascus 261
Elihu 16, 19, 120, 125, 131–4,
    137, 139, 141–4
Elijah 142, 192, 218, 223, 246,
    270
Eliphaz 117–18, 120–3, 125–6,
    128, 131–3
Elisha 244, 270
Elliot, George: Middlemarch 241
Endor 12, 31
Enoch 192–3
Enosh 219
Epic 266–8
Epicureanism 160, 198–9
Esau 261
Essenes 194
Esther 154–5, 189, 250
etymology 10
Eve 24, 111, 166
Ezekiel 34–5, 77, 100
evil 108
Ezra 30, 38–40, 155, 182, 190,
    192–3

fables 32, 35, 60–1, 77–8
fabula 239
fairy tales 235, 238, 242–3,
    245–6, 248, 270
fall, doctrine of 110, 220
Farber, J. Joel 61
father 15–16, 22, 52–4, 76, 88,
    99, 183, 186, 191, 200
Fathers, Praise of 192–3, 196
fear of the Lord (see wisdom)
Finegan, Ruth 269, 271
Finley, M. I. 266
Flood, the 111
Foley, J. M. 271
folk-tale, folklore (Märchen): as a
    genre 3, 24, 29, 235–7, 242–8,
    260, 270, in the Bible 24, 134,
    235, 250–2, amorality 244,
    251
folly 81–3, 103–7
Fontaine, Carole R. 107
foreign (nokri, nokriyah) 92–4,
    96–8
Fox, Michael V. 89, 175
Frazer, James 241
friends (Job's): see Job
Frydrych, Tomas 175
Fyall, Robert S. 145

Gammie, John G. 232
Gantz, Timothy 248
Genesis 69, 164–70, 214, 218–
    19, 224, 235, 250, 252, 255–62,
    268
Gilgamesh 24
Glasgow, University of 10
Glatzer, N. H. 145
Goddess (see wisdom)
good and evil 219–20
Gomer 91
Gordis, R. 145, 175
Gospels 33, 40, 62, 270
Grabbe, Lester L. 27, 46, 180
Graham, William A. 271

Index of Bible References

Old Testament

Genesis

I	53, 165	4.2	156	40.9–10	197
1.2	218, 223	5.1	258	41.9	10
1.14–19	217	6.3	218	41.33	10
1.26–27	219	6.5–9	111	41.39–40	10
1.27	165, 218	6.6	165	43.16	106
1.28	218	6.9	258		
1.28–30	165	6.13	165	*Exodus*	
1.1–2.3	256–9	6.17	167	1–2	247
2–3	30, 94	7.15	167	1.10	14
2.4	258	7.22	167	2.5	106
2.6	218, 223	8.21–22	165	7.11	10
2.7	165–7, 218	9.2	218, 219	16.7	230
		10.1	258	20.6	209
2.9	219	10.9	79	20.8–11	258
2.15–16	165	11.1–9	25	22.18	12, 31
2.17	165, 219	11.27	258	23.23–30	112
2.18–19	165f	12.10–20	252–3, 268	24.16	220
2.23	168			28.2–4	9
3.1	168, 214	14.19	103	29.43	220
3.3–4	165	14.22	103	30.23–25	197
3.5	165, 219	16	253	30.34–38	197
3.7	168	18.16–33	111	31.3–6	9
3.14–19	111, 165	19.24–25	111	35	9
3.19–24	165	20.1–18	268	36.1–8	9
3.19	165–7, 218	22	91, 260–2	40.34–35	220
3.20	168	25.10	103	*Numbers*	
3.21	218	27.1–40	254	10.33	224
3.22	165, 219	29	254	12.8	34
4.1–16	168–70	32.12	213	22.22	131
4.1	103	32.22–32	245	22.32	131
		37	260–2	23.7–24.23	78

New Testament

DATE DUE

DATE DUE		
DEC 2 3 2009		
JUL 2 2 2013		
GAYLORD		PRINTED IN U.S.A.